Beyond Burnout

Beyond Burnout

Helping Teachers,
Nurses, Therapists,
and Lawyers
Recover from Stress
and Disillusionment

Cary Cherniss

Routledge
New York and London

Published in 1995 by
Routledge
29 West 35th Street
New York, NY 10001

Published in Great Britain by
Routledge
11 New Fetter Lane
London EC4P 4EE

Printed in the United States of America on acid-free paper.

Library of Congress Cataloging-in-Publication Data

Cherniss, Cary.
    Beyond burnout : helping teachers, nurses, therapists, and lawyers recover from stress and disillusionment / by Cary Cherniss.
        p.   cm.
    Includes bibliographical references (p.   ) and index.
    ISBN 0-415-91205-9. — ISBN 0-415-91206-7 (pbk.)
    1. Burn out (Psychology)   2. Job stress.   3. Stress management.
    4. Stress management—case studies.   5. Stress (Psychology)   I. Title.
BF481C45   1995
158.7—dc20
                                                                95-3601
                                                                CIP

To Deborah,
who has taught me—and many others—
so much about caring and compassion.

And to all the professional caregivers
who struggle valiantly
to keep their idealism.

Contents

Preface   ix
Acknowledgments   xiii

Part One: Setting the Stage

1. Introduction   3
2. The First Year: "Thought I'd Died and Gone to Hell"   17
3. From Stress to Burnout   37

Part Two: The Next Decade

4. The Flight from Public Service   51
5. More Compassion—For Those Who Deserve It   63
6. More Open to Change—On Their Terms   77
7. Why Work? Shifting Priorities   83
8. Fulfillment and Regret   97

Part Three: How Some Overcame Burnout

9. Five Who Prevailed   107
10. Antidotes to Burnout: Finding Meaningful Work   121
11. Antidotes to Burnout:
    Finding Greater Professional Autonomy and Support   135
12. Antidotes to Burnout:
    What the Individual Brings to the Work   151
13. Some Implications for Policy and Practice   169
14. What's Missing? The Quest for Meaning   181

Appendix: Research Methods   191
Notes   197
References   213
Index   221

Preface

This book is about a group of people who became human service professionals. They were poverty lawyers, public health nurses, high school teachers, social workers, and psychologists. They wanted to serve others, and they began their careers with enthusiasm and commitment, caring and compassion.

I originally studied these professionals during their first year of practice. Using in-depth interviews, I learned about the stresses they experienced as their idealism collided with the realities of public schools, legal aid clinics, and mental health centers. I witnessed how, in response to these stresses, they lost much of their idealism and commitment. The study became an examination of early career burnout.

Ten years later I decided to track down all of those professionals to see what had become of them. Had any of them regained their idealism? Had they remained in public service? What effect had a growing social conservatism in the country had on their outlooks and actions? This book is about these two studies.

In the first chapter, I set the stage by relating how I became interested in the plight of human service professionals. I also describe how I did both studies. (A more detailed description of the research methodology is presented in the appendix.) Chapters 2 and 3 summarize what I learned in the initial study and indicate what the professionals were like when I left them at the end of their first year of practice.

Part 2 of the book describes how the professionals changed during the next decade. In chapter 4 I examine how their careers evolved. Some had remained in public service while others had gone into private practice; some continued to work as helping professionals while others had made radical career changes. I describe the different career paths that they took.

The next four chapters explore how the professionals' attitudes and values changed. In chapter 5 I focus on their attitudes toward their clients—the fate of caring and compassion. Chapter 6 deals with another set of attitudes important for practice: flexibility and openness to change. Chapter 7 examines how the professionals' attitudes toward work and career changed over time—how their values and priorities shifted in response to their experiences at work, their family lives, and the changes that were occurring in the larger society. Chapter 8 concludes Part 2 of the book with a look at how the professionals felt about their lives as they moved into the second decade of their careers.

Part 3 shifts the focus as I address the question of why some of the professionals were able to overcome or avoid early career burnout. I begin to look at *differences* in experience and outcome rather than commonalities. Chapter 9 describes five professionals who initially were among the most stressed and burned out, but who managed to recover. By the time of the follow-up study, they were among the most committed, compassionate, and satisfied.

Chapter 10 takes up one set of factors that helped professionals recover from burnout: the nature of the work itself. Not all professional work is intrinsically rewarding. In this chapter I explore what makes work fulfilling for professionals and the importance of doing fulfilling work for sustained commitment and caring. Chapter 11 presents another important factor in the recovery from burnout: the work setting. Professionals who recovered from burnout—or avoided it from the beginning—worked in settings that provided both support and autonomy. Chapter 12 switches the focus to the individual, noting the personal characteristics that helped some to sustain commitment and caring for a decade or more.

Chapter 13 is the most practical in the book. I identify seven implications for public policy and practice that come out of the preceding chapters. I suggest how professional caring and commitment can be enhanced through changes in selection and training of professionals and management of human service programs.

The final chapter is somewhat more speculative, addressing a factor that *didn't* come up in the interviews: the quest for meaning. Even the most committed and satisfied professionals seemed to have lost something they had when they began their careers: they no longer expected their work to be meaningful. I explore what it is about modern life and professional helping that makes it so difficult for professionals even to strive for more meaningful work. In the end even the most successful ones settle for less. The last chapter concludes with one more implication for policy and practice.

Acknowledgments

Writing the acknowledgments for a book is a bit like preparing the guest list for a party—it is so easy to leave out someone who should be included. Thus, with some trepidation, I would like to thank all those who have helped me with this book, including those whom I neglect to mention by name. One especially important group that must remain nameless is the group of 25 professionals who participated in the study. They offered not only their time but also their words and insights. The best in this book came from them.

I would also like to thank the many students at both the University of Michigan and Rutgers University who helped with the research, especially Sally Wacker, Ed Egnatios, Bill O'Dowd, Bette Clark, Casey Kelliher, Kerry Klett, and Charles Reid.

Carole Herscheit and Laurie Lavine also assisted with the research. Laura Spitz Segal patiently typed the transcripts for the first study. Barb Strane and Judy Cox helped me track down the subjects for the follow-up study.

My colleagues at the Graduate School of Applied and Professional Psychology at Rutgers have supported and inspired me in many ways. I am particularly indebted to Dan Fishman, Lew Gantwerk, Sandra Harris, Milt Schwebel, and Alan Wiesenfeld for their guidance and suggestions along the way. I also appreciate the support I have had from my editor at Routledge, Philip Rappaport, who has always been ready to listen to my questions and find the answers.

Funding for the research on which the book is based came from Rutgers University and from the National Institute of Mental Health (Grant PHS MH 42457-01).

Seymour B. Sarason has contributed to this work in numerous ways, including the most important. He continues to be a source of inspiration as a teacher, mentor, and friend. I'd also like to recognize the contributions of my son, Joshua L. Cherniss, who has encouraged me through his example as well as through his words, and who also helped with the editing of chapter 1.

Finally, I thank my wife, Deborah Cherniss, who has helped in so many different ways, both tangible and intangible. She typed hundreds of pages of transcripts, she edited every page of the manuscript more than once, she offered suggestions and support whenever needed, and, most important, she always had faith in me and in this project. In my own life, she has been the best model of a compassionate helper I have ever encountered.

Part One

Setting the Stage

1

Introduction

Each year thousands of people enter one of the helping professions in order to serve others. What they do affects how we live, how we feel, even what we become, and their impact on our lives has been growing.

Professionals have always been important for the public welfare. One author called them "the agents by which society dealt with its major problems" (Schein, 1972, p. 2). In the last century, however, the professions have become even more significant. Just in sheer numbers, the proportion of professionals in the population has grown enormously. In 1890, 3.8 percent of the adult population were professionals; in the next thirty years it rose slightly to 4.4 percent; but in the next 40 years, the percentage nearly tripled. In 1960 professionals constituted 13 percent of the adult population (Veysey, 1975).[1]

Professions have also proliferated in the last century. The health care field, for instance, was initially comprised of lay healers and then, with professionalization, physicians and nurses—and even nursing didn't emerge as a real occupation until the end of the nineteenth century. Today medical care is provided by a plethora of allied professions, including physical and occupational therapists, speech therapists, psychologists, chiropractors, social workers, and many others.

But numbers represent only part of the story. As the count of professionals and professions has increased, so too has society's reliance on them. Many of the caring and socializing functions formerly provided by family, church, neighbors, and friends have been assumed by formal institutions. Schools, hospitals, day-care centers, social welfare programs, and mental health clinics have multiplied as people

3

increasingly turn to them for help formerly provided by nonprofessional caregivers. We now use institutional help more than ever.

These formal helping agencies affect our lives in a variety of ways. Consider, for instance, the economic impact: between 1985 and 1991 the amount of money that Americans spent on food and tobacco increased 32 percent. The increase for clothing, accessories, and jewelry was 35 percent, while housing expenses increased 42 percent.

But the amount Americans spent on medical care during this same period increased 100 percent—more than three times as much as the increase in food expenditures. Costs for education and research increased even more: 116 percent. Expenditures for religious and welfare activities increased 89 percent. In other words, the amount of money we spend for health, education, and social welfare has increased at a much higher rate in recent years than the amount we spent on food, clothing, and housing.[2] In economic terms alone, helping professionals are becoming more important in our lives. What Lynn (1965) wrote three decades ago is even more true today: "The professions are triumphant in American life."

The Fate of Professional Caring and Compassion

Entering a helping profession has always been regarded as a "calling." Those who turn their backs on more lucrative occupations to enter a field like nursing or teaching are doing so because they want to help others. Meaning is at least as important as money. They want to work for more than just a paycheck or a special space in the corporate parking lot.

And that is as it should be. Without idealism helping professionals become less caring and compassionate, and when that happens, the quality of life suffers.

The lay public has become increasingly critical of the professions, and research supports the growing belief that helping professionals too often lose their idealism and commitment (Sarason, 1985). For instance, Daniel Goleman of the *New York Times* reported on a study of 1,000 letters from dissatisfied patients at a large health maintenance organization in Michigan. More than 90 percent of the complaints arose from the way the medical staff communicated with patients. The most common complaint was that physicians "lacked compassion" (Goleman, 1991).

Nurses have also come under fire. When Truax, Altmann, and Millis (1974) assessed the degree of empathy communicated by various occupations, registered nurses scored lower than ten other groups. The only group they found to be less empathic was manufacturing plant supervisors. LaMonica, Carew, Winder, Haase, and Blanchard (1976), in a study of communication patterns, found that registered nurses on the average fell at the mid-point between "hurting another person" and "only partially responding to superficially expressed feelings" (p. 450). Nurses, like physicians, have not fared well in tests of caring and compassion.

Medical personnel aren't the only ones found to be lacking in empathy. All of the helping professions have come under attack at one time or another for failing to provide the caring and compassion that the public expects. Teachers, school psychologists, and other educational personnel, for instance, have also been viewed as insensitive and intolerant (Turnbull & Turnbull, 1979). Many parents believe that professional educators care more about their paychecks and vacation time than about education.

A recent example was a news article reporting that many teachers are refusing to write letters of recommendation, tutor students, or perform other duties not specified in their contracts because they are angry about budget cuts and meager pay raises. One teacher quoted in the article admitted that he and his fellow professionals have put their idealism "on hold" and that the students are suffering. While the teachers' grievances are often legitimate, "many students and parents do not sympathize with the teachers" (Celis, 1992, p. D2). One parent-teacher association president was quoted as saying, "We need teachers who are completely committed. I understand the teachers' outrage. But their priority should be the kids" (Celis, 1992, p. D2).

In the case of lawyers, one need only consider popular lawyer jokes that depict lawyers as venal, insensitive, and self-serving. Mental health professionals are sometimes viewed as cold, analytical, and more eager to get their share of health insurance reimbursement than to do what is in the best interests of their clients. The public has become profoundly disappointed with all of the helping professions.

To some extent, the human service professions seem to fall short because the public expects more from them now than they did in the past. Gow (1982), for instance, argued that the ideal in nursing care has changed considerably in the last two decades. A caring and committed nurse was formerly "responsible, orderly, tidy, neat, prudent, industrious, disciplined, and sensible." Now nurses are supposed to be "empathic, giving, and in tune with the emotional lives of their patients." Standards for caring and compassion have risen. We expect more of helping professionals than ever before.[3]

Not all human service professionals are guilty of the insensitivity and callousness that has been cited in popular news articles and caricatured in crude jokes. In fact most professionals are probably sensitive and caring most of the time, but too often professionals treat patients and clients as illnesses or problems rather than as persons in distress.

The professions are gradually coming to recognize the seriousness of the problem. Medicine provides a good example: both the American Medical Association and the Association of American Medical Colleges report that significantly more attention is now being given to the issue of empathy in the curriculum (Belkin, 1992). Organizations that accredit medical schools and grant licenses now require that medical students be taught how to communicate with patients. The National Board of Medical Examiners plans to add a section on doctor-patient relations to the licensing exam as early as 1995. Caring and compassion are becoming mandatory.

In response to this increased pressure, many new training programs are being created. Mount Sinai Hospital, for instance, launched a $1 million training program for doctors in response to concerns that "today's doctors are more adept with technology and jargon than with compassion" (Belkin, 1992, p. A1).

But how much does training influence professional practice later in the career? Becker, Hughes, and Strauss (1961) argued that medical school socializes students to be medical students, not physicians. They conjectured that once formal training is over and physicians start practicing, they are exposed to a completely different set of social forces that influence caring and compassion in unknown ways. Training may have little impact on later attitudes.

Subsequent research on how professionals' attitudes change following training has tended to support Becker et al.'s cautions. For instance, Gray, Moody, and Newman (1965) studied physicians during the three years following graduation from medical school. They found that the new physicians became less cynical and more concerned about human welfare. There was also considerable variability: many physicians became more positive in their attitudes, but others didn't. Situational factors, such as the types of settings in which the physicians practiced, seemed to strongly influence their attitudes following the completion of schooling.

Blackburn and Fox (1983) took an even longer time perspective. They studied the social values of physicians who were at different stages of their careers, and they found that humanism and idealism increased during the first part of the career (when the physicians were on average between 32 and 43 years old), then dropped during the next five-year period, and then steadily rose for the remainder of the career.

In other words professionals don't emerge from their training as "finished products"—they continue to grow and change as they respond to the role pressures of practice. Their perspectives shift as they make the transition from student to practitioner, and, as Blackburn and Fox (1983) discovered, they may continue to change throughout their careers.[4]

A Tale of Two Studies

I first became interested in the plight of helping professionals—and the fate of their idealism—during my graduate school days. As part of my training in clinical and community psychology, I worked in high schools, community mental health programs, and other "human service" settings. I consulted with the staffs, helping them to better understand the psychological dynamics of their most troubling cases. As I got to know many of these helping professionals, I saw what it was like for them at work. It wasn't easy.

Many of the people in these settings were novices, and they found it difficult making the transition from student to professional. New teachers, for instance, were overwhelmed with the realities of public schools. Actual teaching wasn't what they had expected. They felt unprepared for the demands that they had to face daily, and as these new teachers tried to cope with these demands, their attitudes changed. Many went from being committed, idealistic helpers to exhausted, cynical functionaries who simply tried to make it through each day. They began to do things that they vowed they would never do.

There was no word at that time for what was happening to these professionals. Later it would be called "burnout."

When I completed graduate school, I took a position in a new, experimental program struggling to survive in a hostile environment. I experienced the same stress that my professional "consultees" had encountered, and, like them, I began to lose some of my own enthusiasm and commitment during those difficult first years. But I did have one advantage: as a faculty member in a university that valued research, I could step back and study the process. That was when I began to study the work lives of human service professionals. I have been studying them ever since.

This book is based on two of those studies. The first study focused on the stresses and coping efforts of new professionals, those who had just completed their formal training. I wanted to see how much stress these novices experienced, what the sources of stress were, and how these fledgling professionals coped with it. I also wanted to learn more about how this coping influenced their attitudes and behavior.

I focused on human service professionals who worked in public institutions because these settings seemed to be playing an increasingly important role in society. More professionals were going to work for large organizations, and fewer were going into private practice. Also, professional values and organizational demands tend to clash in public institutions. I wanted to learn more about what happens when they do.

Other than focusing on public service settings, I wanted the study to be as broad as possible. Human service professionals in public service face common problems. I didn't want to study just one field. I eventually included four different fields: high school teaching, mental health, public health nursing, and poverty law.

In any research project, there's a trade-off when it comes to deciding how many subjects to include. If you have a large sample, you can be more confident that what you find is generally true and not just an anomaly. But you can't study the people in as much depth. On the other hand, if you have a smaller sample, you can study each person more intensively, but you can't be as sure that your findings are valid for those not studied.

I decided to study each individual in depth over a period of time. This meant that the sample couldn't be a large one, yet I still wanted to make it as large as resources would permit. The sample eventually contained 26 professionals—six lawyers, seven high school teachers, six public health nurses, and seven mental health professionals.[5] There were 17 women and nine men. (Two of the occupations—nursing and social work—have traditionally been made up primarily of women. Thus it is not surprising that women outnumbered men in the sample.) The participants were recent graduates of local training programs.

Most studies in the social sciences use structured interviews and questionnaires. I preferred unstructured interviews because I wanted to discover how these new professionals felt about their experiences and how they saw their worlds. I was afraid that if I tried to guess what was most important to them and then designed structured instruments for measuring it, I might lose some of the most interesting facets of the experience. Structured research methods often get in the way of a penetrating exploration of how people truly feel about their lives. It was important that our subjects be able to tell their own stories in a relaxed and supportive setting that encouraged candor.[6]

When we had completed the interviews, I was faced with the awesome task of interpreting the material we collected. I spent a year poring over thousands of pages of transcripts. At last I identified a small set of themes that best characterized what it was like to be a new professional in public service—what was most stressful, how people coped, and how their attitudes and behavior changed.

The first year of practice was extremely stressful for most professionals. As a result the professionals lost much of the idealism that they had when they began their careers. In the face of unfulfilled expectations and a multitude of misfortunes, most of the novices became less caring and committed. Many seemed to burn out, victims of their own idealism and of the nonsupportive institutions in which they worked. There were some notable exceptions, and they helped us to learn how professional burnout could be prevented, but in general the picture was one of unmitigated stress, strain, and disillusionment. (Chapter 2 contains a more detailed summary of the results of the initial study.)

The original study culminated with a book (Cherniss, 1980), and I thought that would be the end of it. I never planned to contact the participants again for any follow-up research. In fact I carefully destroyed information that could identify the subjects in order to protect their privacy.

Then, about a year after the book appeared, a reader asked me if I planned to go back and see what had happened to the professionals after their first year of practice. Initially I demurred. "I'm burned out on burnout," I protested, only half in jest.

But the seed had been planted. The more I thought about it, the more intrigued I became with the idea. As the tenth anniversary of the first study approached, I decided to give it a try.[7]

There was, however, the problem of the destroyed records. How could I track down a group of highly mobile professionals when all I had was their first names and last initials, and the places where they had worked ten years before? It seemed hopeless, especially because colleagues who had done follow-up research warned me about how hard it was to track down subjects even when a wealth of identifying information was available. I had been trained as a psychologist, not a private detective.

Fortunately, my original interviewers turned out to be pack rats. We discovered that we still had our daily appointment books from ten years before tucked away safely in our attics, and in those books we found the last name of every subject. I had been less diligent in destroying identifying information than I thought!

Tracking down the subjects still proved difficult. I initially contacted the agencies where they had worked. Most had left years before, but sometimes there was a person who remembered the subject and could give me a current address or phone number. I found other subjects through university alumni offices or professional directories, but in a few cases I had to try numerous leads before I finally found them.

A former colleague of one subject, for instance, remembered that she had moved to another city. He also remembered that her husband was a physician, and after a minute or two he recalled the husband's first name. (Their last name was an all-too-common one.) I got the phone number for a physician in that city with that name, called him—and found another subject.

An even more tortuous case was that of a clinical social worker whom no one remembered. The director at his first agency had no idea what had become of him. The alumni offices at his college and graduate school had no current information on him. I despaired of ever finding him. Then I went over the old interview transcripts, looking for some kind of clue, and I discovered that his wife had been in graduate school. I contacted the alumni office of her school. They did have a current phone number and address for her. I thought I had succeeded.

Unfortunately, when I contacted the wife she told me that they had divorced several years before, and she had no idea where her ex-husband was. However, she did have the name of someone she had never met, whom her former husband told her she could contact if she "ever had to get in touch with him." She gave me the person's name and phone number.

When I called the contact person, I tried to explain as best I could why I was interested in finding his friend. He was understandably suspicious and reluctant to give me the information, but he agreed to contact his friend to see if it was okay. I eventually did make contact with this long-lost subject, and when I did, he was quite willing to participate in the follow-up study. Another quest had ended.

I ultimately managed to find every subject. Many didn't remember the original study, but they took it on faith that they had been in it. And all agreed to be in the follow-up study. One of the poverty lawyers had died the year before, but I was able to interview her husband. Another lawyer had to be dropped from the study because he had contracted multiple sclerosis, was severely depressed, and couldn't remember much about the period when he was still working. I did try to interview him at his home, but I terminated the interview after 40 minutes when it became clear that he just couldn't remember enough about his past life.

I personally conducted all the interviews for the new study. The participants had scattered across the country, so I spent a lot of time in planes and airports. I even interviewed one subject in a boarding lounge at Chicago's O'Hare Airport as we were en route to different destinations.

As I prepared for the first interview, many questions began to form in my mind. But the most basic was: How had these public service professionals changed over time? Did they eventually leave public service and enter private practice? Did they change occupations? And if they remained in public service, how had their attitudes changed? Were they as caring and committed as they were when they began their careers? What about openness to change—had they become more conservative and set in their ways? And were work-related rewards such as challenge, autonomy, and making money more or less important now? All of these questions related to one fundamental concern: what was the fate of the idealism and commitment that the professionals had when they began their careers?

Friends and colleagues frequently had their own predictions about what I might find. One chuckled and said, "I'll bet a lot of them are making sandals in Soho now." Another remarked wistfully, "I guess they all went back to get MBA's and now are pulling down six figures." People assumed that most of the helping professionals had left for greener pastures.

Interestingly, no one predicted that any subject was still caring and committed. People seemed to assume that it would be difficult for public service professionals to remain idealistic in the face of budget cuts, lay-offs, and the lack of support for human service programs.

The people who offered predictions also assumed that change would be simple and straightforward: from poverty lawyer to tax attorney, or from social worker to organic farmer. No one considered that some subjects may have made two or three changes during those years—and in different directions.

One colleague made a request rather than a prediction. She was a human resources consultant who conducted burnout prevention workshops. She said, "I want find out how I can help professionals regain their satisfaction and commitment. It's so hard to feel fulfilled in this kind of work. There are so many stresses and frustrations. So I hope you will find out what helped people in your study to avoid burnout."

What I eventually discovered was far more complex—and interesting—than anything that my friends and colleagues had predicted. Some of the subjects had made radical career changes. There was, for instance, the poverty lawyer who became a Beverly Hills tax attorney. And there was the social worker who became a prosperous real estate agent. These radical career changers were the ones my colleagues had predicted I would find.

But then there were others who did, to some extent, recover from burnout. They never completely regained the kind of idealism, caring, and commitment that they had when they began their careers. Once burned, they were cautious about investing too much of themselves in either their careers or their clients.[8] They gradually came to feel, however, more confident about their abilities. They found ways to avoid some of the more disagreeable aspects of professional practice—they changed jobs, they returned to school to acquire new specialities, they invested more of themselves in nonwork interests—but they were able to remain in a helping field and to make a worthwhile contribution to society. They had survived.

Finally, there were a few who managed to sustain—or regain—the idealism that they had as novices. They continued to work in public service, helping the needy, advocating for social change. There was the poverty lawyer who still represented the disadvantaged and worked for social reform. There was the high school teacher who chose to teach less-motivated students because she felt that they were the ones who needed her most. And there was the clinical psychologist who passed up opportunities to go into private practice because he found working in the public schools so meaningful. Somehow these professionals were able to resist the forces that undermined the commitment of their colleagues. They hadn't just survived; they prevailed.

What I found especially intriguing about these different outcomes was that I wouldn't have predicted many of them. I frequently discovered that the people who "should have" dropped out—because of how arduous their first year of practice was—hadn't. And the people who initially thrived sometimes dropped out anyway. For instance, consider two of the teachers.

The first year of teaching had been a nightmare for Eugenia Barton.[9] Just about everything that could go wrong did go wrong for this high school business teacher. Discipline was a major problem. She became frustrated and angry with her students because they were "rude to each other and wouldn't listen." She hated to go to work because one class behaved so badly. But she was reluctant to ask for help—it might reflect badly on her, and she might not be rehired.

Eugenia also felt "bowled over" by the heavy work load. After the first two months, she said she was "too tired to give a damn." Other teachers didn't give her any support because of the "tendency to grab what you've created and not share it." The principal also didn't help—in fact, he totally ignored her.

Eugenia found teaching hard even when things went well. Her natural shyness made group discussions sheer agony. She said that she was "frantic thinking up what to say next." In sum, her first-year experience was a "day-by-day struggle." Only one other professional was rated as more frustrated and stressed out than Eugenia.

Given her difficult start, I expected that Eugenia would soon leave teaching. It would have been easy for her to do so: her husband made a good living as a manager in a large corporation; and, with her business background, Eugenia could easily have found a more rewarding job elsewhere. Yet Eugenia had remained in teaching. In fact, 12 years later she was teaching in the same school, and she was one of the most satisfied and compassionate professionals. What had kept this harried new teacher from dropping out?

Alice Harris, on the other hand, should have remained in teaching. She had decided on a teaching career earlier than most—while still in high school. And she had the best experience of any new teacher. She worked only part-time during her first semester, which gave her "lots of time during the day to spend preparing." She taught in an exciting, innovative program. She didn't have the discipline problems that plagued the other new teachers. Only the brightest and most motivated students took her classes. "They want to know," Alice said, "and they're curious. They're just terrific!"

Alice had done her student teaching in the same school and so "felt right at home" from the first day. She received continuous help and support from four experienced teachers who team-taught in the program with her. They were "really great," fun and stimulating as well as supportive. "If all else goes bad, you can always count on the team to cheer you up," Alice said.

Alice had little contact with the administration but felt she had their support. Her principal had taught in the same program before he was promoted. He had been the mentor of her critic teacher and referred to Alice as "the third generation."

Alice was surely the kind of teacher, working in the kind of situation, that led to long-term commitment. Even if her enthusiasm waned, her training in the humanities left her with few career options. She might take some time off to start a family, but I was sure that her commitment to teaching would continue.

It didn't turn out that way. After teaching in the same school two more years, Alice quit and eventually decided to change careers. When interviewed again 12 years later, she said she would never consider teaching again.

What accounted for these different outcomes? And what factors helped a few of the public service professionals to remain committed and caring after 12 years of practice? As I pored over the thousands of pages of transcripts, these were the questions that most interested me, and the answers proved to be more elusive than I had anticipated.

But eventually, some clues began to emerge. Those professionals who had remained caring and committed seemed to share certain qualities and experiences that set them apart from the others. In the last part of this book, I present those factors. But first I return to that initial year of practice and describe what it was like to be a new public professional.

2

The First Year

"Thought I'd Died and Gone to Hell"

In the beginning they were idealistic, caring, and committed. They had lived through the tumultuous demonstrations of the sixties. They had heard the cries for social justice. Then they had decided to commit their lives to helping others. After completing years of schooling, they were professionals—teachers, nurses, therapists, lawyers.

These new professionals were enthusiastic—their time had finally come. But the real world wasn't what they had anticipated: There were unexpected frustrations, and the collegial support they hoped for never came. Their formal schooling had left them unprepared for the challenges they faced.

They wished for their situations to improve, and sometimes they did. But for many, the strain was unremitting. They became disillusioned. They lost much of their compassion and commitment. They began to burn out.

The new professionals came to their careers with unrealistic expectations, and this was one source of their difficulty. They were victims of the "professional mystique"—an overly romanticized view of professional work. It was a view built from countless media images—the competent physician, the dedicated teacher, the clever attorney. These stereotypes came from movies, books, and television programs (De Fleur, 1964), and the new professionals believed them.

Unfortunately, public service jobs didn't measure up to these images, and this discrepancy between how things were and how they were supposed to be—what Kramer (1974) referred to as "reality shock"—was a major source of stress.

Sources of Stress

The "Crisis of Competence"

In the movie, *Stand and Deliver*, a dedicated and inspired teacher, Jaime Escalante, manages to teach calculus to a group of disadvantaged high school students. The movie conveys an implicit message: Good teachers can reach even the most difficult students. Those who fail to do so are uncaring, incompetent, or both. This kind of heroic expectation was the burden that the new professionals brought into their first job.

Professionals are supposed to be competent. When we refer to a thief as a "real professional," we don't mean that he received an advanced degree in stealing, or that he has a license. What we mean is that he's good at what he does.

The dictionary defines competence as "having all the natural powers, physical or mental, to meet the demands of a situation or work." One of the new professionals, Sherman Reynolds, a clinical social worker who worked in a family counseling agency, expressed it this way: "A *real* professional, not just someone with the title, would be someone who feels right on top of things." Sherman and the other new professionals felt that they should know what to do in most situations. They should be "on top of things."

But it didn't work out that way. The new professionals often *didn't* know what to do. Teachers found themselves in front of a class on the first day of school without a clue as to how to start. New attorneys knew their way around the law library, but they literally got lost the first time they entered the courthouse. The public health nurses and mental health professionals were better prepared; but they, too, felt inept much of the time.

Achieving an acceptable level of competence thus became the overriding goal for the novice professionals. Their commitment to other goals—helping the needy, working toward social change, promoting social justice—receded in importance. The feelings of inadequacy that plagued the professionals during the first year made it difficult for them to think about anything else. Idealism, altruism, and compassion became unaffordable luxuries. How to avoid failure and humiliation was what dominated their thinking.

Competence meant different things for each profession. New teachers saw *control of student behavior* as the critical measure of competence. Nothing was more upsetting than to have their students act up. Chemistry teacher Calvin Miller was typical. He couldn't stop ruminating about a student who frequently spoke out of turn and bothered other students. "This is where I feel I fail," Calvin said. "My job is to try to deal with this kid and get him to learn.... It has really upset me when he's disrupted the class because there are a couple of people in that class who really want to learn. And then they get upset. And then they go home and say something about how the class was just in an uproar today and Mr. Miller couldn't keep John settled down. So I get a reputation as not being able to keep control of the class."

The neophytes soon learned that reputation is important in the professional world. Poverty lawyer Jean Chalmers described how casual conversations between attorneys often turned into evaluation sessions. "When you talk to lawyers," Jean complained, "the first thing they say is, 'She's a bad lawyer, she's a good lawyer. He's a bad lawyer, he's a good lawyer....' They want to know, Are you good at what you do?"

Jean noted that it didn't matter whether you were a "nice person"; all that counted was how competent you were. And evaluation went on continually—in the office, after work, at cocktail parties.

A professional might fail for a number of reasons, but the inexperienced tended to blame themselves. Sarah Prentiss was a young and idealistic public health nurse. She was especially bothered by what happened with one of her clients, an older woman who was sick, poor, and alone. During their last contact the woman had said, "I don't know why you're bothering with me. I just want to die."

This statement upset Sarah because she heard it as a testament to her own failure. "You know," Sarah said, "I think about her. I can't help it. She's in this big house, the plumbing doesn't work, no hot water ... she'll probably just stay in her house and die.... And I thought, 'Gee, what's wrong with me?' or 'What did I do?' And you know, I might have done something wrong. Maybe I just turned her off. Maybe it was just a personality conflict. But I didn't see it, and that's the thing that bothered me—that I didn't have enough insight to see the problem. So yeah, it bothered me."

Even skilled veterans make mistakes. And new professionals still have much to learn. But the expectations are high, and so are the costs of failure for a nurse, teacher, lawyer, or psychotherapist. Professionals, no matter how new they may be, are supposed to be competent. But often they don't *feel* competent. And the new professionals weren't prepared for this "crisis of competence."

The Professional vs. the System

Professionals are also supposed to be independent. The new professionals expected that their training and credentials would give them the right to make decisions without others second-guessing them. In fact, this autonomy was one of the major attractions of professional work. They could have made more money in business. But they chose to enter a profession because they valued independence and believed that as professionals they would have it.[1]

Autonomy proved to be elusive as well. The new professionals suffered numerous indignities and encountered many constraints in the institutions where they worked. And they became upset when others didn't treat them like the competent professionals they wished to be. Sarah Prentiss, the new public health nurse, became irate as she described a run-in she had with a public school principal.

> The principal mentioned to me about a "growing-up" program. So I went down and talked to the teachers who were going to be involved in it, and I set up a date, and I told him the date. . . .
>
> Okay, I walk in there last week and he says to me, "Well, we set up the program for Wednesday at 7:30." It was just like, "Okay, you do this, this, and this." And I looked at him and I. . . . First of all, fifth- and sixth-grade boys and girls in two hours? He's crazy! You know, there's no way. I said, "First of all, we need more time than that," and he says, "Well, we've gone for two years like that." And I said, "Well, I know how much time I need to spend with these kids, because they have a lot of questions. Fifth and sixth grade kids know a lot; they're doing a lot of things that we weren't doing."

And this man says to me, "Well, if they have questions, they can go home and ask their parents."

And I said, "Well, what's the whole philosophy of education?" I got into a big discussion with him. We were out in the hall, and I was just burning. I just had had it. He was putting me down.

Sarah was upset because she believed that the principal's plan might be harmful to children. But even more distressing was the feeling that he had slighted her and that she didn't have the autonomy and respect due a professional.

Incidents like Sarah's confrontation with the principal weren't unusual. Nick Fisher, a school social worker, was even more tormented by infringements on his autonomy. Nick had taught in an urban classroom for two years. He left teaching and entered social work because he wanted to help his students overcome the personal problems that made life so difficult. When he returned to the schools as a social worker, he thought he would be a caring and compassionate helper. But administrators and teachers saw his role differently: they wanted him to help make the system run more smoothly.

"I get a lot of feeling from other people," Nick complained, "that my role is to handle discipline, which is something I don't want to do at all. I'll be walking through the office, and if there are a couple of kids that have just been brought in from a fight, the principal will say to me, 'You'd better talk to these kids.' I don't like that."

Nick thought it was inappropriate for him to get involved in student discipline, but the principal had put him on the spot. Nick resented this infringement on his autonomy, and he felt it would harm his relations with the kids if he did what the principal asked. But he worried about what would happen if he refused.

Nick wasn't satisfied with the way he attempted to resolve the dilemma. "I usually try to take that middle ground," Nick explained, "sort of doing it, but doing it my way. . . . I still feel uncomfortable, like I've done nothing. It's hard because if you don't have the backing of the administration, you can't do anything anyway. The last social worker that was here got in a fight with the administration over one kid, and he just lost total effectiveness.

"It really is a trade-off. The demands put on you by the job mean that you have to be doing things that you're opposed to. How do you do that and still remain idealistic? It's hard."

Then Nick ruefully added, "The principal here just told my boss that I'm the best social worker they've ever had. I don't know whether that's a compliment. At least it means I still have some sort of effectiveness. It really is a trade-off." There was a pause. Then he quietly added, "It means I don't feel real good."

The problems that the professionals encountered in working with complex organizations were related to their training. Not only had their teachers and supervisors neglected to teach them how to handle the constraints and dilemmas that they would face, their teachers hadn't even alerted them that such problems would occur. The professionals had been trained to do their work in ideal environments—or perhaps it would be more accurate to say that they had been trained to practice in a social vacuum. They hadn't been taught about the organizational craziness that they would encounter. And they had no idea how to deal with it.

School social workers, for instance, are often put in the position that Nick Fisher found himself in, yet he was totally unprepared when the principal asked him to be a disciplinarian. Nick blamed the principal for being "unreasonable" and "dictatorial." He also blamed himself at some level for not knowing how to deal more skillfully with the situation. But his difficulty in dealing with that incident also pointed to a basic flaw in the training program that failed to prepare him for such problems.

Even though Nick felt that he was being less assertive than he wanted to be, he eventually clashed with a principal about how to handle a student. The principal wanted to put the student in a special class for the emotionally disturbed. Nick believed it would harm the child to be placed in that class. He wanted to help the student stay in his regular classroom. Nick's anger was palpable when he said, "You know, I don't like to be put in a corner, but if I'm put in a corner, I can fight pretty good. I mean, I could really dish it out to those assholes."

But then Nick calmed down, apparently alarmed by his own feelings, and added, "But I don't want to do it because these are people I have to work with."

Matters had not improved by the end of the year. Nick still felt overwhelmed by the constant discord. And he now tried to avoid it rather than confront it.

"I feel a lot like I'm in a battle zone," Nick protested, "with bullets whizzing over my head, always keeping my head low. And I really feel like I'm avoiding problems. I often find myself not wanting to talk to people, planning my day so that I don't have to be around the office, just trying to stay out of people's way when they're looking for somebody to be angry at."

Nick felt burned out. Laying low and avoiding problems had become the only apparent means of escape from bureaucratic obstruction and troubling value conflicts.

The new professionals valued autonomy in part because it was linked to achieving a sense of competence. When others imposed restrictions on the new professionals, it not only limited their autonomy—it also called into question their ability. Competent professionals are supposed to enjoy a high degree of autonomy. So a lack of autonomy made the novices feel less competent.[2]

Lack of autonomy also made it more difficult for the professionals to do their best. When public health nurse Sarah Prentiss wasn't allowed to structure the sex education program in the way she thought best, she felt that she couldn't do an effective job. The professionals often felt they couldn't succeed unless they had more autonomy. And if they didn't succeed, they would feel terrible.

Difficulties with Clients

A third major source of stress for the novice professionals also impinged on their sense of competence. The professionals encountered unexpected problems in working with clients, and these problems were especially exasperating because they made it more difficult for the professionals to be effective.

At the climax of almost every good melodrama about a professional, the person who has been helped turns around, looks at the professional hero, and with admiration and appreciation says, "Thanks." Such expressions of gratitude are reserved for the professional helper—the nurse, the attorney, the therapist. People usually don't become so emotional when they thank the news carrier for delivering the paper on time every day. This kind of appreciation and gratitude from clients was something that the novices expected to find when they began their careers.

The novices thus were disappointed when they discovered that their clients usually didn't appreciate what they were trying to do for them. Many clients were resistant. They seemed to feel that the professional was an adversary rather than an ally.

Legal aid attorney Perry Curtis talked at length about the problems he had with clients. Perry had just spent three years in lecture halls and law libraries. He had had no contact with a live client during that time. He had not had any instruction on how attorneys can most effectively communicate with their clients. But Perry believed that his clients would recognize his good intentions. He expected them to be cooperative and grateful. Perry's expectations were wrong.

"They just harass you and make impossible demands on you," Perry complained a few months after he began working at legal aid. "They won't follow your advice. 'Are you a real attorney?' I've had that asked. They think they know more than you do. They'll say, 'Well, my neighbor told me I could do this.' And then there's the person who, because you're not there holding his or her hand every minute, is calling everyone and complaining about the attorney who isn't doing this or that for them."

Perry identified all of the ways in which clients rankled the new professionals. First, he mentioned the "impossible demands." The new professionals found that no matter how hard they tried, there were times when they simply could not give their clients all that the clients wanted. Second, clients were resistant—they wouldn't follow advice. Third, many clients were unimpressed with the professional status that the novice had worked so hard to attain. They didn't treat their lawyer, nurse, or teacher with the kind of deference and respect that the professionals expected. And finally, there were the clients who complained—the carping critics who could cause real trouble. It was hard for the insecure neophyte to discount client criticism.

But the hardest thing to bear for many new professionals was being lied to and manipulated by their clients. Margaret Williams was an activist poverty lawyer. She had gone to a prestigious law school with the intention of becoming an advocate for the poor and disadvantaged. She had been active in radical political groups all through college and law school. She was prepared to give up all of the opportunities and privileges available to a child of the upper middle class in order to help bring about social change. She initially idealized her poor, disadvantaged clients. To her, they were the vanguard of the revolution. She respected and admired them. But her views soon changed.

"Oh, let me tell you about clients lying to you," she exclaimed, rolling her eyes in exasperation. This was said in an interview that took place after she had been working in legal aid for less than six months. "They lie like crazy. I can't stand anything more than clients who lie to you. I had no idea that I would be lied to as badly as I have been."

Merton Douglas suggested that high school teachers were also lied to by students, and, like Margaret, he found lying particularly hard to tolerate. "I don't like being chumped by students," he said emphatically. "I really don't.... That's one of my pet peeves, I think, not only with my students, but in associations with people in general. I don't like to be taken, and I don't think anybody really does."

In the face of such resistance, manipulation, and frustration, the new professionals found it hard to maintain their initial idealism and enthusiasm. In their minds, they were making a commitment, even a sacrifice. And they would have done so gladly if their clients had been cooperative and appreciative. That was the way it was supposed to be. And when it turned out to be different, the new professionals became frustrated, demoralized, and disillusioned.

But even lack of appreciation might have been tolerable if the new professionals had felt more confident and secure. And achieving a sense of confidence was difficult when clients lied, when clients were resistant, or when clients lacked basic skills. Difficult clients merely exacerbated the professionals' already shaky sense of self-esteem.

Boredom and Routine

Professional work in public service settings may not pay well, and it may be frustrating at times. But it is supposed to be meaningful and interesting. What could be more stimulating than arguing a case in court? What could be boring about helping a troubled adolescent overcome her problems?

Those were the thoughts that many of the novices carried into their first professional jobs. Unfortunately, many found that the work they had spent years preparing for soon lost its fascination. The intellectual stimulation and learning that they had taken for granted in school seemed to end with their formal education. Sometimes, their work was not much more challenging or varied than clerical work. In fact, much of it *was* clerical work.

Margaret Williams, for instance, discovered that grappling with difficult and interesting legal issues was something that lawyers did in law school, not in legal aid. "I spend more of my time on the phone than anything else ... a lot of welfare and social security problems. A lot of times, there's nothing that's at all a legal question, but the person just doesn't know what's happening or doesn't know how to sit tight and wait.... I spend a lot of time doing routine things like name changes and guardianships. At first, I was so happy that I got a job, I wasn't going to criticize anything at all. But recently I started getting sick of doing all of this real diddly shit and not getting into any big cases."

Margaret disdainfully referred to much of her activity as "diddly shit" and "crap." In law school, she wrote and edited for the law review. In her new job, she made phone calls to see why someone's welfare check was delayed. She complained that much of what she did could have been done by a paralegal. But the paralegals in her agency did work that was even more routine.

New high school teachers were similarly disillusioned. Merton Douglas reported that after the first two months, the routine of daily teaching was becoming deadening. The work itself was uninteresting, and his own role in the learning process seemed insignificant. He said, "I just think that after awhile, I'm going to start to feel like a TV set spewing out information. I'm going to get to feel like my function isn't necessary. They could get a PA system to repeat what I repeat each day.... I just kind of feel like I'm a robot."

Lack of Collegiality

Many of these disappointments and frustrations would have been tolerable if the new professionals hadn't felt so alone. Another expectation that proved to be illusory was that they would find stimulating and sympathetic colleagues who would help them to cope, learn, and grow. The professional community was supposed to be just that—a community of like-minded people who helped one another and provided a united front against a sometimes hostile world. But few found the help and support that they expected from their colleagues.

Sometimes it was simply the structure of the job that prevented the novices from becoming part of a community of peers. Public health nurse Sarah Prentiss said, "You go from family to family or school to school, and you really aren't working with people as you would in an office. And you get kind of lonely, or you want to talk about something because you're listening to all these problems that other people have, and just venting a few of your own feelings sometimes really is important. . . . It's nice to be able to communicate with people you work with, especially if there's a problem. But you're not in the office that much. You come here to do paper work or make phone calls, and then you just leave and get on your way."

New professionals expected that colleagues, especially more experienced ones, would be a source of emotional support and reassurance for new professionals. They would provide invaluable information and advice on how to handle difficult situations. The novice professionals also looked to colleagues for feedback on how they were doing; this was especially important because it was often hard to get much feedback directly from clients.

Finally, colleagues were supposed to be an important source of stimulation and encouragement. As Douglas Furth put it, "I don't feel anyone is there who is encouraging me to try new stuff and be creative. . . . There's no one doing that. There's just no direction or encouragement. So any encouragement has to come from me. . . . That's all right. It's not horrible. But it's not the same as someone coming and talking to me occasionally. 'What's going on? Have you done this? Have you done any family work?' There's no one there saying that to me. It all has to come from me."

The professionals ultimately needed colleagues to achieve a sense of competence. They found that they needed information and advice from colleagues to perform competently, and they needed feedback to determine how well they were doing. When the professionals failed to find collegial relations in the workplace, it became that much harder to feel capable.

The Social Historical Context

These stresses were related to larger social forces. In describing their experiences and searching for meaning, the new professionals focused on their clients, their coworkers, their supervisors, the programs in which they worked, and of course themselves. But all of these concrete entities were part of a larger culture, a culture with traditions, values, and patterns of social organization that strongly shaped the structure of the human services and, consequently, the experience of each new professional.

The Bureaucratic Ethos

The bureaucratic mode of organization represented one of those factors that were part of a larger social context. Weber (1947) described bureaucracy as a form of social organization in which abstract and impersonal rules define the responsibilities of members and the relationships among them. The purpose is to ensure that tasks are done uniformly, at the right place, and at the right time. Hierarchy of authority, in which every person has a superior, and specialization of function are two other prominent features of the bureaucratic mode of organization.

The bureaucratic system is hundreds of years old. The Roman armies and the early Catholic Church utilized aspects of bureaucracy. Business enterprises began to use features of bureaucratic organization during the industrial revolution of the early nineteenth century. Later in that century, when schools and social welfare programs became larger and more complex, they adopted the bureaucratic mode as well.

Bureaucracy has taken on negative connotations in modern life. Modern writers depict it as alienating, dehumanizing, and inimical to creative and spontaneous activity. But bureaucracy, as Weber pointed out, has some positive virtues. It is a way of coordinating diverse activity in large, complex enterprises. While it sometimes seems cumbersome, it often ensures a certain level of efficiency. In human service programs, bureaucratic rules and regulations may ensure a certain level of care. For instance, Foner (1994) has pointed out how accident reporting requirements in nursing homes, which most staff find burdensome, have promoted more humane care and prevented some of the abuses that reached scandalous proportions in the mid-seventies.

Bureaucratic procedures can also minimize favoritism and ensure a certain degree of fairness. Professionals and clients often become frustrated with bureaucratic routines that prevent the professional from giving a client too much individual attention. But too much concern for one or two clients may adversely affect others. If an aide in a nursing home, for instance, spends too much time talking with a depressed patient and consequently falls behind schedule, the other residents will suffer. The routines and schedules that are so much a part of bureaucracy provide a way of ensuring a certain degree of uniformity that is consistent with fairness and good care.

Nevertheless, bureaucracy often seems to be at odds with compassionate, effective helping. When speed, efficiency, and conformity to rules become the overarching concerns, compassionate care suffers. Foner (1994), for instance, observed two aides working in a nursing home. One was particularly callous and brusque with patients—sometimes even cruel. The other was kind and compassionate. But the first one received more positive evaluations from her nursing supervisors because she always followed orders and finished assigned tasks on schedule. The compassionate aide was slower and sometimes circumvented rules to help individual patients. As a result, the kinder aide was often in trouble. Her ratings were much lower.

This situation existed in a good nursing home with a progressive, committed administration and a reputation for providing quality care. Thus it shows that even in the best institutions, a bureaucratic structure encourages a loss of perspective in which speed, efficiency, and conformity to authority have higher priority than quality of care. Means become confused with ends.[3]

When human service programs are organized along bureaucratic lines, the caregiver is often caught in a dilemma. Caregivers want to be responsive to clients' individual needs. In fact, professionals usually have an ethical and legal obligation to do so. But administrative rules can prevent them from providing this kind of treatment.

The new professionals soon encountered these hard truths as they tried to help their clients while working in a bureaucracy. When the principal told Sarah Prentiss that she had to fit her program into a limited period of time, he was doing so out of a concern with efficiency and smoothness of functioning. He had hundreds of students and numerous academic programs to juggle each day. In order to cope with this complexity, there had to be a schedule that allowed for little variation. To accommodate Sarah's needs, the learning program for all of the students and teachers in the school would have to be disrupted. At some level Sarah could probably appreciate the principal's concerns. But she was also painfully aware of how inadequate the time allotted was. As a public health nurse, she had been taught that her first responsibility was to do a good job of teaching health practices to the students.

It was no accident that this conflict between two sets of concerns—efficiency and orderliness vs. professional standards—ultimately manifested itself as a personal conflict between Sarah and the principal. In a bureaucracy, administrators are given authority over others in order "to unify and coordinate diverse and conflicting organizational participants and units" (Brager & Holloway, 1978, p. 8). But people at different places in the chain of command have access to different information and are subject to different pressures. This was the case with Sarah and the principal. Not only was the principal aware of conflicting needs in a way that Sarah was not, but also he was the one who would be blamed if the schedule was disrupted. Sarah would be unaffected by the disruption; not so the principal. In such a situation, conflict is inevitable.

Similarly, Nick Fisher was caught in a dilemma that inevitably occurs in bureaucratic systems. The principal whom he described may have been concerned about the emotional well-being of students who were sent to the office for discipline or who had behavioral problems that made it difficult for them to learn in a normal classroom. But he was even more concerned about making the system run smoothly. The principal was concerned with maintaining an environment that minimally met the needs of the majority of students; Nick, on the other hand, saw himself as an advocate of the individual student who was having particular difficulty.

Sarah and Nick's problems were exacerbated by the specialization of function that is another characteristic of bureaucracies. Sarah was responsible for health education, while the teachers were responsible for teaching the basics. If Sarah got more time for her sex education program, the teachers would have less time for their function. Because different groups in a bureaucracy assume responsibility for different and potentially competing functions, conflict is inevitable. And over time this conflict has increased, because specialization of function in the human services has accelerated with the growth in knowledge. As more is known about sex education, teachers gradually relinquish it to specialists like Sarah. As the number of different specialists grows, the potential for the kinds of conflicts that Sarah and Nick experienced also grows.

Bureaucracy, as well as the problems associated with it, tends to grow over time. Increasing specialization is only one reason for this growth. Another reason is that those who conform to bureaucratic values are the ones who are promoted to positions of greater influence. In her nursing home study, Foner (1994) observed a supervising nurse who was especially liked by the administration because she was so well-organized and efficient. Her floor was the most orderly in the institution. Foner discovered that this nurse was also aloof and mean to both residents and staff, but this did not seem to affect her status with her superiors. In fact, she was eventually promoted to a higher-level position where her emphasis on orderliness had an even greater impact on the setting.

Once bureaucracy takes root, it grows. But why does the bureaucratic mode of organization take root initially? Schools, mental health clinics, and other human service organizations do not need to be organized along bureaucratic lines, but most are. Bureaucracy has come to be the dominant form for several reasons.

One is simply the effect of past abuses. There has been enough corruption, neglect, and incompetence in the human services to make some degree of regulation seem necessary, and with each new scandal, the degree of bureaucratic regulation increases. The nursing home scandals of the seventies, for instance, led to stricter government regulation, which led in turn to greater bureaucratic control and reduced autonomy for the staff of nursing homes. More recently, growing awareness of corruption in local school boards in New York City is leading to calls for increased monitoring and control by the central office. In responding to this call, the administration will undoubtedly develop additional rules, regulations, and procedures that are designed to increase accountability but that will also have the effect of increasing the deadening weight of bureaucracy.

Another source of increasing regimentation is labor contracts. Work rules that are designed to protect workers from unfair and vindictive management practices usually have the unintended consequence of further restricting autonomy and flexibility. But there are other factors that are even more deeply ingrained in American society.

American Ambivalence Toward Helping the Needy

As a society we are ambivalent about supporting human service programs. We want to make sure that we receive adequate health care, schooling, legal aid, and other services when needed. We also feel compassion for others who clearly need such help, as witnessed by the prompt and generous public response when there is a hurricane in Florida or an earthquake in California, but we also do not want to pay for "freeloaders" (Brager & Holloway, 1978). We become outraged when we hear stories of fraud in the provision of benefits. We want to help, but we do not want to be "taken."

Part of this ambivalence is related to Americans' strong commitment to the value of self-reliance. We want to help people who really need help, but we are loathe to help others unless they have done everything they can to help themselves. We continually worry that if we help people too much, they will become dependent. Our discomfort with dependency reflects our commitment to self-reliance.

Our generosity is also diluted by our belief in individualism and free will. When people become unemployed, need legal help, or develop emotional problems, we tend to see the cause as a lack of individual motivation. We recognize the influence of economic, political, or social factors, but we tend to think that people can "rise above" such obstacles if they just try.

Our desire to help the needy is also diluted—some might even say compromised—by another motivation: social control. Welfare programs, services for the mentally ill, and even public education are supported in part to maintain social order (Brager & Holloway, 1978). We support schools partly to keep unruly children off the streets. We support mental health programs to prevent the mentally ill from creating disorder in the workplace, in the street, and in our families. The commitment to help is sometimes undermined by the social control motive.

Our support for education, welfare, and other human services is also diminished by materialism. Since the industrial revolution, our society has had an enormous surplus. Even people of modest means can afford to buy far more than they need for adequate food, shelter, clothing, and even entertainment. With this surplus of wealth, we could permit people to work much less, or we could use the surplus to provide better education, mental health care, legal aid, and other social services. But most of this surplus is used on personal consumption. We complain about higher taxes, even though our taxes are among the lowest in the world, because we want to keep our money to spend on *things.* We want to help the needy, and we want a good education system for our children; but we want even more to accumulate material possessions that will enhance our status, entertain us, and make our lives even more comfortable.[4]

This ambivalence toward human service has a profound impact on the work environments of helping professionals. The most obvious effect involves resources. Public human services never receive sufficient resources for fulfilling their mandates. Whether teachers have 30 students in their class, or 25, or even 18, the task of providing a quality education to every child is impossible. As de Grazia (1962, p. 361) observed, "Mass education is a contradiction in terms. There must be a one-to-one or at least one-to-a-few relationship." The same can be said for health care, psychotherapy, legal aid, and virtually any other human service that we can imagine. Foner (1994), for instance, observed that nursing home aides would be less stressed out and more responsive to the patients' needs if they had fewer residents to look after. The ideal would be just one or two patients per aide. But she could readily see that such an arrangement would be impossible. The public is simply not willing to invest additional billions of dollars in long-term health care to secure such an arrangement.[5]

With limited resources, the sense of inadequacy that plagued the new professionals is inevitable. First, their training was less effective than it might have been because the training programs from which they came did not have the number of teachers and field supervisors necessary to provide all students with a good education. The student teachers, for example, spent a mere 12 weeks in the classroom receiving, in most cases, a minimal amount of coaching and guidance from a mentor. To provide all student teachers with better preparation would require a significant increase in the amount of money allocated to teacher training programs.

And even if they had been better trained, the new teachers would still have felt overwhelmed by the task of maintaining control in the classroom *and* presenting the material in an engaging way, given the large number of students for whom they were responsible. Calvin Miller could probably have been successful in maintaining order in his class if he had only five or six students to worry about. But with more than 20 in a chemistry lab, the task seemed overwhelming. With time, of course, most teachers learn how to maintain better control in the classroom. But they often do so by sacrificing other goals, such as individualization of instruction for each student. Students may conform to the rules, but they also learn much less than we would like.

Public ambivalence also makes the clients more irascible. Lack of adequate funding for the human services means that clients are frequently short-changed. Over time, they become increasingly resentful and mistrustful. When a legal aid lawyer meets a client for the first time, that client may have a long history of frustrating contacts with professionals who simply did not have the time to be warm, responsive, and helpful. As a result, the client is more difficult to engage and quick to complain.

Inadequate public support for the human services also contributes to the lack of collegiality. Legal aid lawyer Margaret Williams noted that her colleagues were not available to help her because they were so overwhelmed trying to keep up with their own crushing case loads. "I get thrown out of people's offices all the time because they're busy," she complained. When professionals do not have enough time to help many clients, it is difficult to find the time to help a new colleague.

Lack of public support also leads to greater bureaucratic constraint. As resources diminish, more emphasis is placed on speed and efficiency. Administrators who are trying to stretch every dollar are likely to impose more restrictions on professional staff. Sarah Prentiss's principal, for instance, felt compelled to limit the amount of time she had for her sex education program because his teachers already did not have enough time to cover the basics. While Sarah blamed the principal for the limit that was being placed on her, in fact both the principal and Sarah were victims of society's ambivalence about supporting public education.

The Impact of Recent History

The societal factors that I have discussed thus far have been present for a long time, but in addition to these, there are others that are of more recent vintage. Social changes in the sixties and seventies increased the tensions that adversely affected new professionals.

First there was the growing discontent with all social institutions and forms of authority. Rothman (1978) has noted that until the sixties, our society was dominated by the "progressive" ethos, which included the belief that social institutions were benign and that conflicts between different groups could be resolved through rational discussion. This view began to crumble with the rise of the civil rights movement, the Vietnam War and the antiwar movement, the assassinations of popular leaders, and the growth of the "counter-culture." These events led to a growing belief that the various interests in society are not in harmony, that conflict is inevitable, and that groups suffer or prosper to the extent that they press assertively for their interests. The buzz word that became increasingly popular was "empowerment."

The empowerment ethos eventually spread to the human services where a powerful "consumer" movement developed. This led to increased demands for accountability, restrictive legislation, and the involvement of the courts. People working in education and the human services responded in kind: they unionized and pressed for their own interests through collective bargaining. All of these changes eventually contributed to decreased autonomy and flexibility, a greater emphasis on following the rules, and reduced public support. Clients were also more resistant and suspicious as they came to believe that professionals were not there to help clients but to protect themselves.

At the same time that the public became more mistrustful of the human services, they also expected more of them. The "War on Poverty" of the sixties was intended to eradicate poverty and the social ills associated with it. The Community Mental Health Centers act, established at around the same time, was intended to do the same for mental illness, while mandatory special education legislation, which came only a few years later, had similar lofty goals for handicapped school children. The schools and other human service programs were supposed to solve many of society's problems, and when they fell short, people lost faith in them. Disillusionment contributed to a further decline in public support. Helping professionals were no longer viewed with the same respect and admiration. The heroes of the eighties were not idealistic teachers or physicians; they were stockbrokers and corporate executives.[6]

Economic changes also contributed to professional stress. The fifties and sixties were a period of unparalleled prosperity in this country, but they eventually gave way to the "stagflation" of the seventies. People had to work harder and harder just to keep up. This put enormous strain on individuals and families, which inevitably led to greater demands on human service programs. Clients became needier and more difficult to help, and the numbers needing help increased. At the same time, support for the human services declined. Thus professionals had to do more with less.

The professionals in my study were only vaguely aware of these larger social forces. They talked mainly about the more immediate and visible sources of stress in their jobs, such as resistant clients, inadequate resources, insufficient time, and stifling rules. Most of the people who have written about professional stress and burnout have also restricted their attention to these more proximal influences. But we cannot fully understand the sources of the professionals' frustration without considering the social context in which their struggles occurred.

3

From Stress to Burnout

In the process of coming to terms with the stresses and frustrations of their work, the new professionals began to change. They became less caring and committed. They began to see many of their clients as adversaries rather than innocent victims of misfortune. What began as a calling became nothing but a job.

These changes in outlook seemed to be self-protective. For instance, the new professionals adopted more modest goals in order to reduce the sense of failure that haunted them. The more modest their goals and standards, the more likely it was that they would begin to feel competent. And when they failed to achieve even scaled-down goals, blaming someone or something other than themselves also helped bolster their sagging self-esteem. Finally, if all else failed, they could reduce their psychological involvement in their work. For if work became only a small part of who they were, the new professionals could tolerate less achievement there and still retain some self-respect.

The problem with these self-protective changes is that they ultimately led to a decline in caring and commitment. Adopting more modest standards, blaming others for failure, and limiting involvement in work inevitably meant that the professionals cared less—and gave less.

Adopting More Modest Goals

Most of the new professionals came to believe that their initial goals were unrealistically high, and they lowered their sights. In many cases, for instance, the new professionals decided to con-

centrate their efforts on just a few of the most rewarding and deserv-
ing clients, virtually ignoring the rest. This was something that
many would have considered anathema just a few months earlier
when they were still idealistic students. But in the face of the frustrations that they were experiencing, such a maneuver seemed to be
quite sensible.

Nick Fisher was one of those new professionals who coped by
lowering his expectations and concentrating on just a few clients.
When Nick became a school social worker, he had hoped to do more
than just help individual students make a better adjustment to
school. Initially, Nick had believed that the whole school system
needed to be changed, and that was one of his goals. He hoped to
make the system more responsive to students. He planned to organize parents into a positive force for change. But Nick continually
encountered more resistance and conflict than he had expected, and
this resistance wore him down. After a few skirmishes with the
administration, he withdrew and concentrated on individual counseling with just a few students. Looking back on what had happened
to him, Nick admitted, "What I found myself doing was getting
involved in two cases and sort of ignoring everything else that I
promised to be doing."

Nick could not completely justify such a narrowing of focus in
his work. Near the end of the first year, he said, "I'm deeply
involved with maybe three kids at the high school, and the other
social worker is maybe involved with six. So what does that do for
the other 300 kids who need help?" He said that teachers and
administrators were getting to the point where "they don't depend
on me an awful lot, and that's frustrating. I don't have that much
effect. All I can do is give platitudes, accentuate the positive sort of
stuff. That gets kind of bad." Changing his goals made Nick's work
less frustrating, but he had settled for less—much less.

Concentrating on just a few clients was not the only way the
new professionals began to lower their goals. Most began to cut
corners in various ways. High school chemistry teacher Calvin
Miller began his teaching career with high aspirations. He was
determined that he would reach all his students and stimulate
their thirst for learning. Single, with no family or hobbies to distract
him, Calvin felt that he could devote all of his time and energy to
his calling.

But after only three discouraging months in the classroom, Calvin admitted that he found himself doing things that he had pledged never to do. "I had some real dingbats for teachers in high school, and I said to myself, 'I'd never do that,' or 'I wouldn't want to be like that. . . .' But now, when I'm facing the reality of the situation, I catch myself at times doing some things that they would have done and saying, 'Wow, here I am doing exactly what I said I would never do,' and yet having to do it." An example that Calvin gave was "having kids do things just for the sake of doing them—the 'busy work' idea."

Public health nurse Sarah Prentiss explained why she and so many other new professionals adopted more modest goals. "I think that enthusiasm and idealism are good as long as they don't hurt you. But they were hurting me. They were. It was really bugging me because I expected things to be like I wanted them to be, and they weren't that way. But I realized that, and I'm glad I did."

The new professionals were often reluctant to give up what Sarah referred to as "the idealism thing." But when the gap between real and ideal remained wide, and their ideals seemed to be a source of pain rather than inspiration, most of the novices adopted more modest goals. By lowering their sights, they made it easier to succeed.

Blaming Someone Else

Even when the new professionals adopted more modest goals, they frequently failed to attain them, and such failure continued to be painful. How could they lessen the pain associated with falling short? One way was to blame others.

Initially, most of the novices were more likely to feel that what happened in their work was primarily the result of their own efforts. If a student did not learn, the teacher must be using the wrong approach. If a neurotic client continued to engage in self-defeating behavior, the therapist lacked the necessary skill or sensitivity. If an innocent client went to jail, the attorney had not done enough in his defense. After a few months of being buffeted by the realities of practice, many of the professionals modified this belief. Rather than blaming their own lack of skill or motivation, they would increasingly blame the client when their efforts to help fell short.

Public health nurse Sarah Prentiss revealed how the new professionals' thinking about personal responsibility changed over time.

In the last chapter, I described a situation in which Sarah felt guilty because she had been rejected by an elderly patient who was slowly dying alone in her home. She worried at that time that she "might have done something" to "turn off" the woman. The implication was that her own behavior may have contributed to the woman's response and that a different approach might have been more effective in reaching her.

A few months later, Sarah's sense of personal responsibility for failure seemed to have diminished. When asked if she still felt bad when a patient rejected her, she quickly responded, "I don't do that anymore. When things don't work out, I really don't think that it's me because I think that I've had too many positive experiences and I don't come on too strong."

Sarah still seemed to feel the need to attribute responsibility to someone, so now she tended to blame the client. She described a recent case when she had gone out to a home and the mother met her at the door and said, "I don't know how you got our name. We don't need you. We don't need anybody." Sarah said that she did not pursue this case any further because the woman's response was probably caused by her "low mentality." Sarah then decided that "no way could I get anywhere with them." With some probing from the interviewer, Sarah conceded that the woman's rejection of help might have been due to a sense of pride. But then she added, "Of course, I don't know if it would even be pride in *her* case."

Although there may have been many factors contributing to the client's initial hesitation and resistance, including something Sarah had done or said, Sarah now chose to attribute the cause primarily to the woman's alleged mental deficiency. By attributing the cause of resistance to something like "low mentality," Sarah got herself off the hook and avoided the painful self-doubt and guilt she had felt a few months earlier when she considered that other factors might be involved.

A more charitable way of avoiding personal responsibility for failure was to blame the system rather than the client. High school teacher Calvin Miller initially blamed himself for his failure to reach all of his students and for the discipline problems that plagued him during the first semester. Near the end of the first year, however, he had shifted the blame—but not onto the students. He attributed his students' lack of interest in learning to the extracurricular activities that came to dominate high school life: "It's hard to get them interested in your class when they've got all these other things going on. How can you be interested in school when you've got swimming coming up and gymnastics. So that helps me realize they're not always going to be enthusiastic or interested."

The professionals were not altogether wrong in "blaming the system" for their troubles. As I pointed out in the previous chapter, there was a larger social context that did contribute to the stresses and strains they encountered. But in blaming the system for *all* the problems and shortcomings, they abrogated any personal responsibility for making things better. Thus, while there is no disputing Calvin's claim that extracurricular activities compete for students' attention, a change in his approach could have made a difference in how receptive his students were. And it's likely that after less than a year in the classroom, there were many ways to motivate students that Calvin still hadn't learned. But if Calvin thought that another teacher could do a better job of motivating his students, then he would have to assume some personal responsibility for their resistance, and this could further undermine his already precarious self-esteem. Blaming others made failure tolerable.

Liking Clients Less

As the new professionals encountered unexpected difficulty in working with clients, and as they began to blame clients rather than themselves for these difficulties, their feelings about clients changed. Idealistic, trusting attitudes gave way to mistrust, cynicism, and even hostility.

High school teacher Eugenia Barton was one of those who became especially disillusioned with students. Raising three children of her own had not prepared her for the behavior problems she encountered in the classroom, and her education courses proved to be virtually useless. As Eugenia struggled to find the solutions to her problems, she became increasingly bitter. Near the end of her first term, she said, "High school kids will do you in. . . . I wouldn't count on my high school kids to help me at all." She felt that initially she had been too considerate: "I was gullible and stupid . . . too easy."

Eugenia referred to the old maxim in the teaching profession, "Don't smile until Christmas," and said that she had refused to accept it when she began her career. She earnestly believed that if she treated kids with respect, they would reciprocate. But by November, there had been a revolution in her thinking. She vowed that in the future she would not be as "flexible" or "trusting." She would have strict rules and allow no deviations. Her trust in students had been shattered.

Several other new teachers responded in similar ways, and the teachers were not the only group to become more cynical. Reginald Smith became a public defender because he believed that many poor defendants accused of a crime were victims of injustice and poverty. But after working in the criminal justice system for six months, he had to admit, "This job has made me less trustful of people." Margaret Williams, another poverty lawyer who entered the profession with high ideals and compassion, complained bitterly about being "chumped" by many of her clients and said, "Now I don't expect the clients to be telling the truth."

Looking Out for Number One

Those who enter a helping profession and then go into public service are usually altruistic; they want to serve others. That was certainly true of my subjects. During the first year or two of practice, however, many of the professionals began to focus more and more on their own needs, and they increasingly came to resent how little those needs were being met. They came to feel that they were being exploited and that they had to put their own needs above those of others. Self-sacrifice lost its appeal.

Attitudes about financial remuneration were a particularly good indicator of this shift from altruism to self-interest. Many of the novices initially displayed little concern about their salaries, but this began to change. What seemed to be ample compensation when they were hired came to be viewed as rather paltry just a few months later.

Shana Phillips described the process that many of her peers went through: "I think you could generalize about a lot of people who get out of law school. In the first year or two, they are very idealistic and they want to help folks. The next year or two, they want to help folks *and* make money. The next year they just want to make money. And I can see that process happening to myself."

This growing preoccupation with money—and more generally with one's own interests—seemed to be tied to how demanding and frustrating the job was. When the interviewer asked Shana why she thought people's attitudes about making money changed over time, she answered, "Well, public service law doesn't pay that well, but I think that it's more than that. It's just the reality of practicing law. . . . When you're getting hassled by everybody from the judge to your client, and working as heavily as you're working and burning out, you say, 'Why am I doing this?' Maybe if there was more money there it would be more worth my while. I could see putting up with what I'm putting up with for $25,000, but I can't see doing it for $15,000."

Many new professionals became increasingly reluctant to make sacrifices for others and more concerned about protecting their own interests. Extrinsic factors like pay, hours, and additional duties became more important as they became more frustrated with how unrewarding the work itself was.

Dropping Out

As the novices lowered their goals and lost their initial compassion and idealism, as they no longer felt so responsible for the outcome of their efforts, and as they became preoccupied with their own needs, their commitment declined. They consciously stopped devoting so much of their time and energy to work.

The motive again was to protect themselves from the stress and strain that they were experiencing in their jobs. Dropping out was a way to cut the emotional losses.

Poverty lawyer Shana Phillips began her career with a high degree of commitment. Like Margaret Williams, Shana had been active in radical politics while still an undergraduate. She had been arrested in student protests. She even considered joining the Weather Underground—a radical terrorist group—before deciding that she would instead work for social change by becoming a lawyer. When she graduated from law school and passed the bar, she threw herself into her first job.

Shana's clients were convicted felons, and her job was to help them appeal their sentences. She typically worked six and a half days a week. Her work was the most important activity in her life, but the job proved to be frustrating and unrewarding. Many of her clients were unappreciative and manipulative. She received little support from her competitive colleagues. She felt unprepared and uncertain about her own abilities. She became increasingly frustrated with the bureaucratic constraints of her own agency and of the judicial system in general. Shana felt that she was putting much more into her job than she was getting out of it.

At this point, Shana's life began to fall apart. She began to use alcohol and drugs heavily. She acted out her conflicts in her sexual life. "For awhile, I was nuts," she recalled as she looked back on this period a few months later. "I was seeing five men and I was hustling everyone. I was even hustling the gay women I know, and I'm not gay."

Finally, Shana reached the breaking point. She took some vacation time and went away to spend some time on a commune with friends. When she returned, her philosophy of life had radically changed. She now believed that work should not be the most important thing in her life. She sharply reduced her involvement in her work and invested much of her time and energy in other activities. In discussing the role that work now occupied in her life, she said, "It's not a big fulfilling thing for me anymore. . . . It's just part of my life. It's not anything that keeps me so much in touch with my feelings, my opinions, my values." When the interviewer asked if this new outlook represented a major shift for Shana, she responded, "Oh yeah. I was going to be a big radical lawyer. I was going to be the female version of William Kunstler. . . . But I've learned a lot about just broadening my horizons and having other interests. Law is not everything."

Shortly after this major change in her priorities, Shana changed jobs, taking a position with less client contact and less pressure. She strictly limited herself to a 40-hour work week and spent much of her time and energy outside of work in a new hobby—yoga. Her aspiration for the future was to devote even less of herself to work than she was already doing. She mused, "I have a fantasy. I have a whole new fantasy life. It consists of someone giving me $50,000. I go to California. I would do yoga half a day for four days and then I would practice law maybe four half days."

By the end of her first year as a poverty lawyer, the most fulfilling and important activity in her life was her hobby. "Yoga has become a real big part of my life. . . . It's a whole life style. . . . It's part of me." Unfortunately, as Shana withdrew psychologically from work, it became more difficult for her to maintain her motivation. She found herself cutting corners at work and taking advantage of the flexibility in her new job. "There's a supervising attorney at my new agency who is just a big teddy bear. Sometimes when you're in a situation like that, you tend to abuse the other person's flexibility. Occasionally I see myself slipping into that. I even start having motivational problems where I just don't want to do anything. After awhile, I get bored."

Most of the other new professionals also became less involved in work during the first year of practice. This drop in commitment, as was the case with Shana, was a response to frustration and disillusionment. In fact, it was another way of coping with a difficult and frustrating work experience. Like reducing their goals and expecting less from their clients, withdrawing psychologically from work was a way of cutting the emotional losses.

Conclusion: Professional Burnout and the "Me Decade"

The changes that occurred in this group of idealistic new professionals seem to be what many see as the defining characteristics of the eighties. In general, the idealism and concern about the disadvantaged that characterized the sixties and early seventies seemed to give way to a preoccupation with the self in subsequent years. Terms such as "the Me Decade," "the new narcissism," and "looking out for number one," were used to label this shift in public attitudes. Applications to social work schools, nursing programs, and medical schools plummeted while applications to business schools and MBA programs skyrocketed. A decade characterized by social awareness was followed by a decade dominated by increasing materialism.

Most attempts to understand why this change occurred have focused on large-scale political and economic factors, such as economic recessions, inflation, the rise in oil prices, and the influence of conservative political leaders like Ronald Reagan. For instance, ethicist Michael Josephson has noted that after the assassinations of charismatic political leaders like the Kennedys, Martin Luther King Jr., and Malcolm X, many young people became disillusioned (Moyers, 1989). They felt that positive social change was an impossible dream and that the best thing to do was to focus on their own needs. "The next movement," according to Josephson, "was a kind of self-concern, the feeling that you have to take care of yourself first. Then, the economy became a huge problem. And when the economy becomes a huge problem, people start thinking of their pocketbook, and of making things better for themselves" (Moyers, 1989, p. 14).

Without discounting the importance of these "macro-level" influences, my findings suggest another perspective on why selfish materialism seemed to become such a dominant force in the last decade. The young helping professionals I studied went through the same metamorphosis that an entire generation seemed to go through during these same years. The cause of this change was the "reality shock" that they experienced when they began their careers —the stresses and strains, the frustration and disillusionment, the lack of support, and the aggravating obstacles.

As a result of these frustrations and disappointments, many of the new helping professionals began to lose their compassion and commitment. They began to withdraw psychologically from the vocation that no longer seemed like a calling. They began to think more about their own self-interest. Most of the new professionals lost their idealism very early in their careers, and this change seemed to be caused by the imbalance between what the professionals put into their jobs and what they got out of them. When people are under great stress, when their self-esteem is threatened, and when their efforts are constantly frustrated, they become more concerned about themselves and less concerned about others.

Why then did America turn its back on the poor and needy in the eighties? Why did America lose its sense of idealism and compassion for the disadvantaged? Maybe it was in part because individual Americans who came of age in the sixties expected so much and accomplished so little when they attempted to put those ideals into practice. The changes that these new helping professionals went through early in their careers not only mirrored the changes in national consciousness that began to occur at that time; they also contributed to those changes. To the extent that professionals collectively help define the historical climate of modern society, the plight of these new public professionals influenced a whole decade. Their disappointments and failures changed their outlooks, and this change in outlook affected relatives, friends, and acquaintances.

People who didn't share the professionals' frustrating experiences did come to share their pessimistic views. Personal history shaped social history.

But personal careers, like social history, do not stand still. What happened to these new professionals during the decade following their first year of practice? At her last interview, for instance, poverty lawyer Margaret Williams was so burned out that she was seriously thinking of quitting legal aid and going to work for the prosecuting attorney's office. She wanted to get some of her former clients "behind bars where they belong." Did Margaret in fact follow through with this threat? Or did she begin to recover some of her lost idealism and commitment as she came to feel more confident and comfortable in her job?

And what about another poverty lawyer who became less idealistic and committed—Shana Phillips. At our last interview with her, it was difficult to keep her on the topic of work. She was much more interested in talking about trips to California communes and yoga classes. Did Shana remain one of "the uncommitted," or did she eventually become re-invested in her work? If she did become more committed to law, how did this change come about?

In short, were these helping professionals able to recover from burnout? And if they did, what helped them to do so?

Part Two

The Next Decade

4

The Flight from Public Service

One of the cornerstones of President Bill Clinton's domestic policy is to promote public service. In his inaugural address he called for a renewed emphasis on commitment to the public good. He asked Americans in all walks of life to consider making a more significant contribution to their communities.

Promoting public service is a laudable goal. But in order to accomplish this goal, we need to ask, what has made public service unattractive in the past? Why do so many people avoid public service? Why do some who enter public service choose to leave?

When we think of public service, we tend to think of volunteer programs, but public service is also an option for professionals. Each year thousands of professionals choose to work in public service jobs, and each year thousands leave public service. Some move into full-time private practice; some become full-time homemakers; others change occupations.

All of the professionals in my study began their careers in public service jobs. When I finally tracked down all of the original subjects in my study, I found that most had left public service during the previous decade. At the time of the follow-up interviews, only 10 of the 26 subjects in the original study were still working as helping professionals in public institutions. (Thirteen had left public service, two were at home full-time caring for young children, and one was permanently disabled.) Of the 10 who remained in public service, two were no longer working directly with clients. Thus, out of 26 professionals who began their careers serving the needy in public service, only eight continued to do so most of the time.[1]

Although some of the professionals changed occupations, the majority continued to work in their original profession—or a closely related one. It was the setting and nature of their work that changed: A legal aid lawyer left to go into private practice, as did a clinical social worker whose first job was at a community mental health center. A public health nurse became a health care planning consultant.

Even those who abandoned their original profession often ended up in similar fields. A mental health counselor became a career counselor. A legal aid advocate went back to school to become an urban planner. A high school art history teacher became a museum docent.

The new "professions," in fact, were sometimes so similar to the old ones that it was difficult to determine whether they were really new. When Anita Warren left public health nursing to become an oncology nurse practitioner, was that a new profession or merely a shift in specialization? And what about Margaret Williams? She began as a legal aid lawyer and eventually ended up working in a city attorney's office, specializing in municipal bankruptcy work. She readily admitted that she no longer pursued her liberal political and social ideals through her work. The nature of her work and the setting were very different, but she was still working as an attorney—in public service.

Ultimately, however, the trend was to move away from their original callings. These professionals began in public service jobs helping the poor and disadvantaged. Twelve years later, most had left public service, and many of those who remained would have left if circumstances permitted. Yet it would be wrong to assume that all of those who left public service had become cynical and burned out. There were different reasons for leaving public service and different paths taken.

Different Paths Out of Public Service

Going for the Gold

Some of the professionals who left public service did leave because they had become burned out. They had lost all of their idealism. They had become more concerned with making money or gaining status. They left to achieve conventional career success.

Shana Phillips, for instance, followed a career path that increasingly moved away from social action toward greater financial rewards. As we saw in chapter 3, Shana had been a student activist who chose law as a profession because she saw it as a vehicle for social change. But she experienced frustration and disillusionment at every turn, and she eventually changed jobs, reduced her psychological involvement in work, and devoted much of her energy to yoga. Her dream was to move to California, make a lot of money, and practice law half-time.

When I tracked Shana down more than a decade later, I discovered that at least part of her dream had come true. Shana had moved to California, and she had made money—lots of it. But the life of leisure that she had imagined proved to be elusive.

Shortly after our last contact in the initial study, Shana took the California bar exam and passed it. She quit her job, moved to California, and did almost nothing for a few months. Then she heard about a job as an associate in a small private law firm. She got the job and worked there for a year or so, but she was dissatisfied. She took a similar job with another small firm, but this, too, proved to be unrewarding. Shana then decided to strike out on her own and set up her own practice.

Shana's practice was successful. Within a couple of years, her annual net income was more than $100,000, but the pace was grueling. As she put it, "I was like an automaton. I worked so hard I kept four secretaries busy full time just keeping up with me."

Shana finally broke down—just as she had earlier in her career. She stopped working completely for more than six months. She decided that she would never return to law. She even took the exam necessary to become a real estate agent. But after intensive therapy, reflection, and rest, Shana decided that she had invested too much time and effort in her legal career to "throw it away." She still wanted to make a change—she had no desire to return to the pressures of a solo practice, but she also wanted to make a lot of money again. So she returned to law school to secure the additional training necessary to become a specialist in tax law. When I interviewed her for the follow-up study, she was almost finished with her course work and looking forward to becoming a tax lawyer.

Searching for Greater Intellectual Stimulation

Shana was the kind of public service professional my colleagues had predicted I would find. She had been an idealistic, young social activist who went into law to change the world, became frustrated and disillusioned, abandoned public service, and moved into private practice where she became consumed with making money.

But not all the professionals who left public service did so to make more money. A more common reason for leaving public service was a desire for intellectually stimulating work.

Anita Warren began her career as a public health nurse working in a visiting nurse's agency. After a couple of years, she moved west with her husband to work on an Indian reservation. She taught nursing to native Americans in a small community college for about three years.

Anita enjoyed aspects of the work, but she became frustrated with the limited impact she was having. No matter how hard she tried, many of her students failed to pass the state nursing exam. And as her frustration mounted, her values began to change. Helping the poor and underserved was no longer as appealing as it had once been. What Anita wanted most was challenge and intellectual stimulation. Status was also becoming more important to her, and there wasn't much status associated with teaching in a small, two-year community college located on an isolated Indian reservation.

Anita began to think about returning to school for advanced training in a specialty. "I like having a specialty," she said later after she had made the change. "In my opinion, that's the nature of nursing, as it has been the nature of medicine for many years. The knowledge is exploding at such a rapid rate. For me, it's rewarding to know a lot about an area. I like being an expert. It does a lot for me personally."

Anita had become especially interested in oncology, and one day she learned about a special fellowship in oncology nursing. The training program would enable her to become a clinical nurse-practitioner—a specialist. It seemed to be exactly what she had been looking for. "And so I decided, 'Well, what do I have to lose?' So I applied, and I was accepted."

The move wasn't an easy one. She would have to leave her husband and two small children for several months to study in a different state. "It set up a lot of personal dilemmas for us because I was ready to leave, but my husband was doing well with his job. And the children posed another dilemma. . . . But I did decide that I wanted to have this fellowship. And so my husband stayed with the kids for the first semester, and then he quit his job and joined me." After completing her training, Anita returned home and secured a job as head nurse in a prestigious oncology treatment center.

In leaving public health nursing to become an oncology nurse practitioner, Anita had moved away from her initial commitment to public service and helping the disadvantaged. Professional status and intellectual stimulation had become more important. She was still not interested in making a lot of money, but authorship on a research publication had become more attractive than helping an elderly patient learn to walk again. Working in a prestigious teaching hospital had become more appealing than teaching native Americans on a reservation.

The Status Seekers

Status was even more important in Merton Douglas's decision to leave public service. If there is such a thing as a natural-born teacher, Merton would qualify as one. He had loved working as a camp counselor during his college years, and teaching seemed to be a logical extension of that kind of work. He admitted that he liked to perform in front of a group of kids, to wisecrack with them and hold them spellbound with his stories, and he did.

Merton experienced many of the same frustrations and uncertainties as the other new teachers during his first year, but he overcame these more quickly than most. He was comfortable in the teaching role before the first year ended.

Merton continued to teach for the next five years, and his joy with teaching increased. He became the junior varsity football coach in his third year, and this experience taught him some motivating strategies that he was able to adapt to the classroom. As a result, he felt even more successful and stimulated as a teacher during the next two years.

Then Merton began to date a woman who was an accountant working for a large corporation, and they eventually became engaged. Merton was still satisfied with teaching, but his fiancé seemed to feel that he was capable of something "better." She began to question him about his career choice, and Merton became more aware of some of the things he disliked about teaching.

"I don't know," Merton recalled, "it never really happened one day where I said, 'By God, we're going to make a change.' But we had these conversations about, you know, 'Are you really happy doing what you're doing?' And I guess the bottom line for me was, I certainly was not unhappy, but I foresaw the limitations."

Merton began to identify many things about teaching that he didn't like, and the low status was one of them. Merton initially had not been bothered by the low status accorded to high school teachers, but his fiancé was. She felt that Merton should be in a higher-status occupation.

Merton finally made the decision to explore career options during a fateful visit with his fiancé's family: "I guess I had always thought about going to law school, off and on. But at that time, law school was the furthest thing from my mind. For Thanksgiving, we planned to visit Brenda's brother and his family. The purpose of the trip was to meet the rest of the family before we got married. And his wife, Karen, had just finished law school, and I think *that*, more than anything else, rekindled the thoughts of law school."

Merton went on to describe how they spent the rest of the vacation talking with his future sister-in-law about how to apply to law school. He was still not completely sold on the idea, but Karen pointed out that if he wanted to go to law school the next year, he had to act right away. Merton's reservations were finally dispelled when his fiancé said that she would support both of them for the next three years if he decided to go to law school. Merton applied, was accepted, and eventually became a lawyer.

Becoming One's Own Boss

Other professionals left public service out of a desire for greater autonomy. Public health nurse Angela McPherson had worked several years as a field supervisor in a visiting nurse's association. Then she was promoted to a staff planning position in the agency's central office. "I was ready for a change. And then an opportunity opened up in the administrative offices of the agency ... a health care planning position. It became a very broad role, a real interesting role."

When a new director took over at the agency, however, Angela found it difficult to work with her. "The new executive and I just—well, we just didn't see eye-to-eye. So I was a little uncomfortable because of that. When we had to communicate, it was awkward."

Angela began to think about career alternatives as the conflict with the new executive director persisted. "I was starting to get a little restless at that time. I had a sense that because of this discomfort, dissonance, whatever, that I was not going to be moving up. And I wasn't sure I wanted to, either." Angela quit a few months later.

Angela initially thought that she would look for a similar position in another public health agency. But there were few openings within commuting distance, and her husband was reluctant to quit his own job.

"Once I decided that I had to leave, it was interesting. I forced myself to say, 'What else could I do?' I started pushing my mind to see what else I could do." Angela had been receiving many requests for information from other agencies because of the special expertise she had developed in her job. "I saw a market there for that information," she said, "so I decided that I would take the summer off and then consider starting a business in the fall, in consultation, to help people do program development."

Ultimately Angela was successful. After two years, she had enough clients to earn a decent living, and she had never regretted the change. "It's been excellent. Like everything, it has its little problems. But generally, it's been a wonderful opportunity. I love the way of working." One of the aspects that made private consulting so appealing was the autonomy. Angela no longer worried about having a difficult boss. She *was* the boss.

Looking for Less Difficult Clients

Douglas Furth was bothered more by the clients he had to work with than the lack of autonomy. Douglas had thought it would be rewarding to become a psychotherapist. He had earned his master's in clinical social work so he could work as a therapist in the mental health field, but during the next three years he worked in two different agencies and never found the fulfillment he had expected. It took him some time to figure out what the problem was, but finally he realized: it was the clients.

"They were tough cases," Douglas said when I asked him why he left the mental health center where he had been working. "We didn't see a lot of progress with many of them. . . . Dealing with the kinds of personal problems that people were bringing in was draining. After a point I just decided I didn't want a steady diet of that. I didn't feel that way about all the clients. But in general it just didn't seem suited for me."

He went on to explain what he meant: "I like to do short-term work. I like to see some things happening quickly. I like to go right in there and kind of facilitate some change and then have the person go on their way. I didn't like having to just give people support when I didn't see anything particularly changing in their lives. . . ."

Douglas thought that if he went into private practice, he would be able to work with more rewarding clients, but the work still wasn't rewarding enough. "I did get a certain satisfaction from working with people who were more together, in my private practice. But even there, you'd get some who had really hard times, and you had to be with them through those hard times. I could do it, but it was taxing. And it wasn't rewarding enough, even with the ones that I liked."

Douglas's father was a career consultant, and he had been urging Douglas to try it for years. When Douglas realized that the mental health field wasn't for him, he was ready to listen to his father.

"It's such an interesting family story," Douglas said. "All those years my father was doing career counseling, and all those years he wanted me to come into his business. But I didn't. Who knows for what reasons? Probably too much father-son stuff.

"And then at that point, it was probably one of the first times I was really asking, 'What am I going to do?' It would have been a great time for me to go to a career consultant! Anyway, I approached him and said, 'Tell me more about this.' I felt I had to do something, and I hadn't latched on to anything in mental health that I wanted to pursue."

Douglas spent several days with his father and decided that he would give career counseling a try. The more he learned about the field, the more he liked it. "It was a counseling relationship," he explained, "and I knew what that was about. And I knew the people were more intact."

Douglas had been a career counselor for eight years when I interviewed him for the follow-up. He had his own business and was financially successful. He enjoyed the work and was sure he had made the right decision. "It's very stimulating work. It's very challenging. Everyone's a new case. None of them are the same. It fits my style well. And I really enjoy most of the clients. I think that's one of the reasons I've stayed with it and why I do well with people. In this kind of work, I deal with what's best in people. It's not that I don't help them with weaknesses. I do that, too. But I'm always looking for what's strongest, and helping people to learn how to talk about themselves in the most positive way. It's a very nice relationship to have with people."

Those Who Stayed: Cutting One's Losses

Even some of those who remained in public service might have left if there hadn't been some obstacle. Several, for instance, had remained in public service careers to minimize stress in their lives. They saw career change as a potentially stressful experience, and they felt that they were coping with too many other stresses to take on still more. It was easier to remain in a "comfortable" job—even if it was no longer satisfying or meaningful.

Gloria Bennett, for example, knew that she was not happy in her job as a nurse, but in order to minimize stress she consciously chose not to leave. "I was not interested in totally disrupting everything," she confessed. "It became the lesser of all evils to think of staying. I mean, for good or bad, it was familiar. I knew the people. I had another year or so to go to school, and I still had my thesis left to do."

Even when Gloria finished her master's thesis, she remained in the job for two more years. She still couldn't face the stress of change. "I got done with my course work and just sat for a year. Classic burnout. I think I withdrew. I think it was just easier to stay."

"Burnout" is often seen as synonymous with quitting, but Gloria's statement about why she remained in an unsatisfying job suggests that, paradoxically, burnout can be a reason to stay rather than leave. Those who are burned out feel that they are carrying a heavy load, and they may choose not to make a change because they believe that they couldn't handle the additional stresses it would bring about.

Professionals who were juggling the demands of work and family were also likely to remain in their jobs to minimize stress. This was especially true for those with young children under the age of five. But even when the children were older, and stress levels had subsided, family obligations could continue to keep some helping professionals from making a career change. High school teacher Eugenia Barton found her first year of teaching particularly stressful. I thought that she would have left the field by the time I conducted the follow-up study. In fact during the follow-up interview, she said that she had thought about quitting many times during the first two years, but she remained because the schedule allowed her to be available to her children. "After the first year," she explained, "I looked at that calendar and saw that it couldn't be beat for a working mother. And I told myself that I would like that job—or else! And eventually I did."

Many of the professionals who remained in public service had become too dependent on their jobs to consider making a change. Public health nurse Jessica Andrews, for instance, explained how a relatively good salary kept her from leaving: "Unfortunately, my divorce was final in June," she said with a sigh. "That's another reason I'm staying at the health department and doing what I'm doing. . . . I need to stay here. I need the insurance, I need the pay. . . . I don't want to go through the risks of setting up my own business right now. I want Blue Cross, and I want orthodontic care and eyeglass care and all that. And you can't do that privately."

Conclusion: Individual Choice and Cultural Values

Most of the professionals ultimately left public service, and many who stayed would have left if they thought it were possible. Of those who left—or wanted to—few were motivated by greed alone. They were influenced by multiple motives. All of the factors I've mentioned were usually involved to some extent: money, status, autonomy, intellectual stimulation.

But what is most notable is that altruism played a relatively small role in the professionals' decision making, and that was just as true for those who remained in public service as for those who left. The professionals had not become callous and indifferent to the plight of the needy, but compassion was not a dominant factor in the decisions they made concerning their careers.

The career changes we have examined in this chapter seemed to be individual choices, but when we look at them together, it becomes clear that the professionals' decisions reflected the values of the larger society. Helping the needy, by itself, is not associated with status. A few of the most heroic helpers, the Mother Teresas and Albert Schweitzers, do achieve a certain degree of fame, and those who dedicate their lives to helping others do earn a certain amount of admiration. But the therapist or teacher who is relatively successful never receives the monetary rewards or the social respect that a moderately successful business executive or sports figure receives.

Helping professionals come under the influence of these social values early in their careers, if not before. A young, idealistic Anita Warren soon learned that in nursing, there are more institutional rewards associated with publishing articles than with helping elderly patients to walk again. Merton Douglas learned that he would earn more respect as a lawyer representing large insurance companies than as a teacher working in a public school.

Professionals, like other workers, seek success. Career decisions, to a great extent, represent attempts to maximize success and avoid failure. If a person does not feel successful in a particular job, he or she will make a change—if this seems practical. But conceptions of success are also influenced by cultural values. Like most Americans, helping professionals are impatient with slow progress. If most of their students do not make visible and significant improvements during a certain period of time, if most of their clients do not undergo dramatic changes in their psychological functioning, if most of their patients do not improve markedly in their physical status over the course of a few days or weeks of care, the professionals feel frustrated and ineffectual. Douglas Furth was not unique in becoming impatient with clients who did not change quickly and who needed support just to remain at their current level of functioning.

Infused with the Western idea of success, most of the professionals were unable to see their clients' problems over more than a limited period of time. As part of a highly individualistic society, they were not able to see their own individual efforts as part of a larger, evolving social process in which immediate gains are often small. Professional career changes thus reveal much about the kind of society in which we all live.

In this chapter we have focused primarily on career change, but the professionals didn't just change jobs and careers. They also changed the way they viewed the world. The social forces that led to career change also triggered changes in the professionals' attitudes and values. And these changes in outlook—changes in idealism, caring, and compassion, changes in commitment and social philosophy—were just as important as whether or not the professionals remained in public service.

5

More Compassion—
For Those Who Deserve It

The professionals were still neophytes at the end of the first year of practice. Their beliefs and feelings were in flux. I wasn't sure what would happen to their attitudes toward clients during the subsequent phase of the career. And the answer proved to be more complex than I anticipated. In some ways the professionals recovered: they became more sympathetic toward clients *in general* during the next decade of practice. As they overcame many of the tribulations associated with the transition from student to professional, and as their sense of efficacy increased, they came to feel more positive about most of their clients.

But while the professionals became more compassionate toward the *typical* client, many became less so toward the difficult ones. They became less willing to extend themselves for clients who seemed unmotivated. They became less tolerant of clients who refused to fit the mold. And they began to routinely "weed out" such clients.

The Return of Compassion

High school teacher Eugenia Barton is an example of how attitudes toward clients rebounded as the professionals overcame their initial difficulties. Eugenia had a particularly hard time with her students during her first year of teaching. By the middle of that first year, she had lost almost all sympathy for them: "High school kids will do you in. . . . I wouldn't count on my high school kids to help me at all." She complained about how little respect they had for her or each other. "Little children in big bodies" was how she derisively referred to them. They had become the enemy, and she was determined that they would not defeat her in the future.

Twelve years later, Eugenia was still teaching high school students, and her attitudes had softened considerably. In fact, she was rated as one of the most compassionate professionals.[1] When I asked Eugenia how she felt about her students, she answered, "I like them. I think I like them more every year. As I get to know them and have them in two or three classes, I become very close to them and very warm about them."

As Eugenia looked back, she realized that the problems she had with her students were not their fault: "Over the years, I've learned to see them as children who don't like themselves sometimes, and don't like others sometimes. And I've learned not to take what they do or say personally. I recognize that it's not a personal attack on me, that it's their level of maturity. And so I've become much more tolerant of 'monkey business.'. . .

"And I've also learned that the kids that are annoying are a very small percentage. When you start out, you may have trouble in a class, and you may say, 'This class is awful.' But if you look at the class, out of 30 it probably isn't more than four who are doing mischief. . . . And so my perspective has changed. I can recognize why they do things, and that it's not everyone."

Eugenia later added, "Kids come from very troubled situations and have troubles of their own, and they bring those things into the classroom. And you learn that what they do is out of their immaturity and frustration."

During her first year of teaching, when her own self-confidence was low and her sense of frustration high, Eugenia saw the students' misbehavior as pervasive. But 12 years later, as a confident, seasoned professional who loved her work, she saw the same misbehavior as limited to a few students, and she attributed it to something that the students had no control over and that they would probably outgrow. Consequently she felt much more sympathetic toward even the more difficult ones.

Public health nurse Sarah Prentiss described how she went through much the same process. In retrospect, Sarah blamed herself for the problems she had with patients early in her career. During the follow-up interview she talked with candor about how her naive sense of superiority made her impatient and unsympathetic toward them: "Initially, I would go into these situations where I would say, 'Okay, this is what you should eat, and this is how you should feed your children.' I mean, I had definite opinions on how one should be a mother, based on what I had read and how I was raised. I think I had an attitude like, 'Well, here I am, look at me. I'm going to save you.' I mean, it makes me laugh, because people must have looked at me and said, 'Oh Lord, here she comes again, this young, vivacious girl who's gonna solve all my problems.'

"That was another thing. I didn't have kids. You know, I was a 22-year-old girl. And I'd say, 'Well, the book says this. I know all these things because I've been to school and I have a college degree.'"

After describing how unrealistic her attitudes had been, Sarah went on to say that with greater experience and maturity, she became more accepting and sympathetic toward her patients. She began to realize that many of their defects were not their fault.

You hear stories, and you say, "Oh my Lord, how can a woman put a baby down with the bottle every single night? They come in with their teeth decayed all the way down to the gum line. How can that happen?" Well, now I know. It's ignorance. And they come from situations where their families were the same. Their mothers did the same thing. Their grandmothers did the same thing. It's just a cycle.... And these women are so frustrated. They don't have money to have a baby-sitter. They don't have any money to go out, to have nice clothes. Their husbands are spending their money. So I can understand how it can happen. Now I can see how frustrated people get. It's just—life situations.... They're in this little niche, and they think that's where they'll stay. They have no dream of anything more than what they have....

As a 34-year-old mother of two young children, with 10 years of experience as a public health nurse, Sarah could look at her patients' behavior with more compassion. Experience and maturity brought understanding.[2]

Becoming Less Tolerant of the "Bad" Clients

There were limits to the sympathy that the professionals felt toward their clients. As they became confident practitioners, they became less patient with clients who were more difficult or resistant. They divided the world into good clients and bad clients. While they now saw most clients as "good," they believed that a minority were "bad." And over time they became increasingly intolerant of the bad ones.

Public health nurse Sarah Prentiss showed how the professionals developed a double image of their recipients. After talking with great sympathy and understanding about why many of her clients acted in self-defeating ways, she then began to express more impatience. When I asked her what it was like to work with the most disadvantaged clients, she admitted, "I probably reached a point of saturation, a total feeling of helplessness. I felt like, 'Why am I even going into these houses? What influence do I really have on them?' I did have people who cared a little more. So those were the people I probably put my energy into."

Sarah even reached the point where she began to doubt the value of her calling: "When I started working at the health department, I thought that public health nursing was just about the cat's pajamas. It was wonderful. But I changed. I began to think, 'What are we all doing? Why are we hitting our heads against a brick wall?' Now I think it's better to just have people come to us, rather than pounding on their doors. Because the people who want our services are going to seek us out."

High school teacher Calvin Miller also became less tolerant of those who caused difficulties. When I asked Calvin how his attitudes toward students had changed since his first year of teaching, he replied, "Well, in some respects I'm more understanding, and in other respects I'm less understanding. I think I'm more understanding of what they need as individuals. I'm able to like individual students more. I'm more relaxed. But I'm also . . . less understanding of undisciplined behavior. I'm less tolerant of the 'Mickey Mouse' stuff. I lose patience with kids who don't do their work and stuff like that. I'm tired of trying to spoon-feed people sometimes."

The professionals, not surprisingly, were reluctant to talk about what they did with clients whose behavior they couldn't tolerate, but there was evidence that they sometimes acted in ways that were not necessarily in the best interests of the clients.

Career counselor Douglas Furth, for instance, had become increasingly intolerant of clients who seemed to be "stuck." And he admitted that he found ways to avoid working with them. "We were everything to everybody," he complained, talking about how he saw most clients who came to him when he began his private practice. But after two years, he had discovered ways to "cool out" potentially difficult, resistant clients. "Now, if I have any hesitations about someone, often I'll steer them away."[3]

When Professionals Become Administrators

When the professionals became supervisors of others, they went through a similar change in attitude. They usually began with a positive and trusting attitude toward their subordinates, and they were determined to treat them better than they themselves had been treated by supervisors. They were going to be democratic and tolerant. They were going to respect the opinions of subordinates. They believed that if you trusted a subordinate to be motivated and loyal, that would be the kind of behavior you would get.

They became less optimistic over time. After experiencing an initial reality shock, followed by disillusionment and cynicism, the professionals-turned-administrators recovered some of their trust and positive regard for subordinates. But they came to believe that there were good subordinates and bad ones, and they learned to act tough with those who seemed to be the bad ones.

Jessica Andrews was a positive, progressive nurse who went into administration so that she could make the health care system better. She was attracted to the humanistic management theories that she learned in her administration classes, and initially she went out of her way to be considerate toward her subordinates. Jessica expected that her subordinates would be dedicated and committed if she treated them with respect and kindness.

When I interviewed Jessica 12 years later, she was the assistant director of nursing in a large county health department. She described how years of working with difficult employees had made her "grow up." Initially, Jessica hadn't made distinctions between staff people. She believed that everyone was capable of being a good employee, and that a supervisor should treat them all the same. But she had come to feel that there *were* different kinds of people, and that a supervisor had to treat some of them with great firmness. This was especially true, in Jessica's opinion, of nonprofessionals.

> It's more difficult to supervise nonprofessional people because you have to be a lot more directive and . . . I don't want to say threatening, but bordering on the disciplinary action

level—directive and confrontive.... My attitude toward supervision has changed. I now believe there are times when it's okay to be very directive and ride herd on them very tightly, just like a parent. In my theory classes, I was taught that the best type of management was participative. But in order to be participative, your employees have to have some self-control and self-direction. They can't do it without that. So you, as their supervisor, have to step in.

Jessica had come to believe that some people are just "lazy," and that the only way to deal with them as a supervisor is through firmness. "Why would people screw up on their job?" she asked at one point. Then she answered her own question by saying, "There are lazy people. There are frankly lazy people. And I'm intolerant of them when I've given them every chance. When that happens, I will lower the boom."

As Jessica became a seasoned administrator, she also viewed "minorities" as more potentially difficult: "I've become more careful about working with minorities," she said. "I don't want them to have a grievance against me. And I never thought about that before. I walk into situations when, for example, the Hispanics complain about each other. The first couple of times I was real open-minded about it. But when they complained for the third or fourth time, I decided I wasn't going to be open-minded about it. I was more quick. So I think, yeah, my attitudes about people have changed."

It's not surprising that professionals react so negatively to difficult clients or, in the case of administrators, difficult subordinates. Social psychologists have found that altruism and empathy decline if helping becomes too costly. In such situations, the would-be helper might even come to deny the other person's need and derogate the needy person, just as some of the professionals in my study derogated the difficult clients who made their work so stressful (Batson, 1991).

Helping professionals, like most other people, see helping as a social exchange. When professionals feel they are giving more and getting less in return, they begin to feel resentful. They especially resent clients who demand much and give back little in either gratitude or meaningful improvement.[4]

Another important factor in the professionals' intolerance of difficult clients seems to be a sense that they're undeserving. Cooperative, appreciative students, for instance, "deserve" more sympathy and compassion from a teacher than do unmotivated, complaining students.

The Crucial Role of Professional Self-Efficacy

One factor that seemed to be especially important in the professionals' mixed responses to clients was their need to feel competent and effective. Several of the professionals explicitly said that it was growing self-confidence that enabled them to become more open and compassionate toward clients. As they felt better about themselves, they began to feel better about their clients. Self-confidence led to self-tolerance, and self-tolerance helped them to become more tolerant and compassionate toward clients.

Further, a positive spiral was created in which self-confidence led to more positive attitudes toward clients, which in turn contributed to greater effectiveness, which in turn led to even greater self-confidence.

Teacher Eugenia Barton succinctly described how this positive spiral had worked in her own case. When I asked her if she felt she had a greater impact on students now than during the first part of her career, she answered, "Oh I think I probably have a greater impact now. The more I learn to like kids, and the more comfortable I am, the better are the results in my interaction with them. So I suppose I see my impact as more positive and greater."[5]

Difficult clients, on the other hand, threatened the professionals' sense of efficacy. The professionals couldn't feel as sure of themselves when working with difficult clients. Self-doubt is painful, and difficult clients stimulated professional self-doubt.

Other studies also suggest that perceived self-efficacy influences how professionals will respond to clients. Mizrahi (1986), for instance, found that medical residents in a hospital were especially resentful and intolerant of patients who had chronic illnesses or terminal diseases—patients, in other words, whom they felt they couldn't help.

As concern about performance increases, caring and compassion decrease. Hughes and Carver (1990) found that hospital nurses who were more concerned about performance were less empathic toward patients. The researchers suggested that empathy, in the nurses' minds, was associated with loss of control; and any loss of control became intolerable when the fear of failure was high.

Social and developmental psychologists have also noted a relationship between self-efficacy and empathy. Maas (1989) proposed that those who are "successful in modifying their surroundings" develop greater social responsibility. Fiske and Chiriboga (1990) concurred: they presented the case of a man who became more tolerant and caring when he finally achieved his life plan. Frustration and uncertainty led to negative attitudes toward others, while the accomplishment of important life goals led to acceptance and caring.

In reviewing social psychological experiments on the determinants of helping behavior, Batson (1991) reported that people with high self-esteem are more likely to help a person in distress. Berkowitz (1970) found that when the subjects in his experiment were made to feel more concerned about success, they were less likely to help someone else. (That seems to be precisely the state in which professionals find themselves when working with a difficult client.) Berkowitz also reported that when tasks involve evaluation, heightening the subjects' concern about self-worth, they are less likely to help another person. Fear of failure undermines altruism.[6]

Can Difficult Clients Be Rewarding?

For most professionals, resistant and difficult clients represent a major source of frustration, but a few of the professionals didn't mind working with such clients. Their experience suggests that when professionals have the appropriate tools for working with such clients, they can remain compassionate toward them.

Having the Appropriate Tools

Helping professionals in the last two decades have been asked to take on many new challenges. Teachers, for instance, have had to work with learning disabled children from dysfunctional families. Mental health professionals have had to do outpatient therapy with patients whose problems are so severe that in the past they were institutionalized. Public health nurses have had to take on new roles as they work with patients who have problems undreamed of ten years ago.

It takes time for professional training programs to catch up with these changes. New professionals often find that the skills and perspectives they acquired in school are insufficient for meeting these new challenges. What they have been taught sometimes even impedes their functioning. Many students in clinical psychology and social work programs, for instance, are still taught long-term, insight-oriented therapy techniques, but such techniques are often inappropriate for work with the chronically mentally ill. New techniques, based on rehabilitation principles, seem to be more relevant, but few mental health professionals have received training in these new approaches. The same lag in technical innovation can be found in the other professions.

In some cases, it's difficult to know whether the problem is lack of training in new techniques or just inadequate training in general. Probably both factors contributed to Douglas Furth's difficulties. Douglas, as we've seen, finally left mental health because he found the clients needy and resistant to change. Most of his comments essentially "blamed" the clients, but at one point, he acknowledged that part of the problem was that he lacked the skills necessary for working effectively with such clients. Douglas realized that he became frustrated with his difficult clients because he was "new" and "didn't feel that skilled." So the problem wasn't that many of the clients were unmotivated or didn't change that quickly. It was that Douglas often felt unsure about what he was doing or how quickly change should be occurring. His training had been inadequate.

A realistic time perspective is a particularly important "tool" for professionals who work with difficult clients. Many professionals find difficult clients burdensome simply because the professionals' time perspective is unrealistic. The professionals either expected change to occur more quickly, or they couldn't be satisfied unless it did. When change occurs more slowly than professionals expect or want, there's a natural tendency to blame it on the client. Thus a realistic time perspective is an important tool that many professionals lack.

Supportive Work Environments and Difficult Clients

Professionals are also more likely to find it rewarding to work with difficult clients if their work settings are supportive. In fact, it's almost axiomatic that the more demanding the clients, the more supportive the work environment needs to be.

The work environment can provide support in a number of ways. One way is by providing more structure and positive feedback. Eugenia Barton, for instance, didn't mind working with less academically able students because she was able to see the impact of her efforts. She could see the impact because she taught concrete skills such as typing. With good planning and supervision, even professionals whose work is more ambiguous can be helped to see the impact of their efforts.

Colarelli and Siegal (1966), for instance, described an innovative mental hospital program in which staff morale improved when a new system for monitoring client progress was introduced. The system was designed by the staff members themselves, and it made it easy for any one of them to recognize the small, subtle signs of progress that were characteristic of that kind of work. The staff working in this environment found it easier to work with resistant, slow-to-improve clients because the monitoring system provided structure and direction. The system also gave the staff a framework for assessment and evaluation that made it easier for them to see where they were, where they had been, and where they were going with each client.

The supervisor's attitude and behavior are also important. More experienced professionals need much less support from supervisors than do novices, but when professionals work with difficult, unrewarding clients, they need support. Sensitive supervisors can provide it.

Public health nurse Sarah Prentiss, for instance, blamed the clients and their lack of motivation for her decision to leave the field after ten years. But she recognized that the situation was exacerbated by a demanding, unsympathetic supervisor who took a personal dislike to her. "She didn't understand the frustration," lamented Sarah in thinking back on that period. "She was in her office, and she just had unrealistic expectations for the staff. She'd say, 'Oh, come on, try this, go back and try this.' And I'd say, 'No, we've tried that.' 'Oh, come on,' she'd say. She just had no idea." A more sympathetic supervisor might have helped Sarah develop the kind of perspective necessary to work with more difficult clients.

Bureaucratic constraints or indifference can also make it more difficult for professionals to sustain efforts with resistant clients.

After talking about how rewarding it was to take her students on field trips when she worked in a smaller, more supportive school district, teacher Charlotte Noble described how difficult it was to do the same in a larger district: "In the big district, to do something like that ... there was just too much paperwork and red tape. And people in the central office would say, 'Well, that's not really your job. The guidance counselor should be doing that.' So I didn't do any more of that." Bureaucratic resistance discouraged a dedicated teacher from developing more rewarding, personal relationships with her students.

When the conditions are right, therefore, professionals can enjoy working with less able and motivated clients. They entered their fields to help the needy, and "difficult" clients are among the neediest, thus working with these clients can be especially meaningful and rewarding. As teacher Eugenia Barton said, "I guess I get my biggest satisfactions from working with the less able, less affluent segment of the population. I kind of think of that as a challenge. I feel good when they're successful."

The Larger Context: Who Gets "Stuck" with the Difficult Clients?

In the professions difficult clients tend to be distributed unevenly. Some practitioners must work with large numbers of difficult clients, while others are able to spend most of their time working with the more rewarding ones.

Some teachers, for instance, work in schools where the students tend to be compliant and able, if not outstanding. Other teachers work in schools where most of the students are apathetic or defiant. The same uneven distribution of difficult clients can be found in other professions.

The professionals who spend much of their time working with difficult clients are more likely to burn out. Public health nurse Sarah Prentiss had always worked in programs where most of the clients were grateful and cooperative. Then she transferred to a program where most of the clients were ungrateful and uncooperative. Sarah soon lost her enthusiasm for the work: "When I went to work in the inner city, three-quarters of my caseload were resistant. I mean, it was just ... you were scratching for people that wanted to see you. Because it was so much of the ... just the *pits.*"

This uneven distribution of difficult clients is neither an individual nor an organizational problem—nor is it an accident. It has to do with the way human services are organized in our society. Inequality is built in. The professions deal with difficult social problems in the same way that the rest of society does: they allow the bulk of the problems to become concentrated in certain types of institutions, and then they let the practitioners who work in such settings carry the burden for the whole profession.

Conclusion: Toward a Caring Society

Changes in the way the professionals viewed their clients mirrored changes that were occurring in the larger society. The eighties were a period when we, as a society, became less concerned about the plight of those who didn't fit the mold, who couldn't keep up— who were more "difficult." Affirmative action policies became increasingly unpopular. Attacks against homosexuals seemed to increase. The homeless, who refused to disappear as a presence in our midst, became more irritating.

Even George Bush recognized this trend when, during the 1988 presidential campaign, he called for a "kinder and gentler nation." In saying this, he acknowledged that we had become less gentle and less kind during the previous decade.

This growing antipathy toward the "have-nots" of society occurred within a context of growing concern about success, achievement, and self-worth. Gordon (1991) noted that competitiveness, assertiveness, and achievement came to be valued more than caring during the eighties. Economically, people felt they had to work harder just to keep up. Success became more important— and more elusive—for many people. And the more concerned we became with economic success, or just keeping up, the more intolerant we became toward those who had seemingly intractable problems—teenage parents, drug addicts, the homeless. By the end of the eighties, Gordon (1991) would assert that the United States was undergoing a "crisis of caring."

The eighties were also a period when we became less sure of ourselves psychologically. We became less confident about who we were and where we were going. We not only worried about economic success, we also wanted to be good parents, good lovers, and good workers. But what did this mean? And what was the secret of inner success? As each new self-help book addressed our preoccupation with inner worth, our compassion for the plight of the disadvantaged seemed to diminish. But the disadvantaged, in their growing numbers and visibility, called into question our worth as a society.

The professionals in my study avoided and rejected difficult clients because they posed a threat to the professionals' sense of efficacy. Working with difficult clients made the professionals feel less adequate and less sure of themselves. Perhaps the same dynamics were at work in our response as a society. Maybe we became less compassionate toward the neediest in part because they made us feel less sure of ourselves.

If the parallel is valid, this study suggests that such antipathy toward the neediest and most difficult members of our society isn't inevitable. When the professionals had the tools necessary for dealing with the more difficult clients, when they worked in a setting that was supportive of their efforts, and when they were able to see the clients as more than just "problems," the professionals felt compassion for them.

Compassion requires a supportive milieu. That milieu didn't exist during the eighties. But perhaps we can create it in the future.

6

More Open to Change—
On Their Terms

The quality of care provided in human service institutions depends in part on how caring and compassionate the professional care-givers are, but it also depends on their flexibility and openness to change. New problems and solutions are constantly emerging in education, mental health, nursing, and other fields. Professionals who have become set in their ways, who rigidly practice as they always have, aren't likely to provide effective—or humane—service (Schein, 1971).[1]

Reform was in the air in the late sixties and seventies. The new professionals in my study generally supported the liberal social policies that had become popular—policies designed to help the poor and the disadvantaged. Not all of the new professionals were equally ardent about social change and reform, but most tended to see themselves as "liberal," and most believed that some change in society was long overdue.

The civil rights movement and the war on poverty affected many areas of society, including the human services. Liberal reformers began to take a hard look at health care, mental health, education, and the law—and they found these fields to be rife with inefficiency and injustice. Leaders in these fields responded to these critiques and began calling for reform.

The new professionals in my study had been exposed to many of these critiques in their classes. They had learned about the short-comings of traditional practice in their fields, and many had been schooled in new ways of thinking. They were determined to change their professions. They were to be the "agents of change."

But what would happen to these young idealists once they began practicing in the "real world"? One criticism often made about the human services was that practitioners tend to become complacent and set in their ways. Once they have been practicing for a while, they are threatened by change and quick to undermine efforts at reform.

The new professionals in my study were determined to be different. They would remain open and flexible. They wouldn't become like the burned out veterans they had heard about. They would resist the pressures of older colleagues to socialize them into the old ways. They would hold fast to the new ideas they had learned in their courses. They would be innovators—and they would remain that way no matter what.

Ten years later, as I was preparing for the follow-up study, I asked the students in one of my seminars to make some guesses about how these professionals might have changed over time. One of the students said, "I'll bet that they have become more rigid and resistant to change. They'll be much more cautious and reluctant to 'rock the boat.' They may have been innovators when they were young and idealistic, but now they'll be defenders of the status quo."

As I listened to this 23-year-old student offer her predictions, I recognized a stereotype that many of us have about those who are approaching middle age, and yet I found it hard to dis agree with this view. Back in the sixties, it was the young who advocated for change, while those who were older and more established seemed to block change at every turn.

People are supposed to become more conservative as they age. Radicals become moderates, liberals become conservatives, and human service professionals become more rigid and set in their ways. That is the conventional wisdom. But is it valid?

Research on creativity and innovation in science seems to support this view. Scientists and mathematicians tend to make their greatest contributions during young adulthood, and this would seem to suggest that flexibility is greatest in the 20s and early 30s.

Research on adult development, however, suggests that the conventional wisdom may be flawed. In reviewing several longitudinal studies of development across the life span, Haan (1989) noted that from early adulthood to early middle age, adults generally become more innovative and comfortable with uncertainty. Fiske and Chiriboga (1990), who have been involved with one of the most ambitious of these longitudinal studies, concur. They have found that both men and women become less rigid and more flexible over time.

But helping professionals, especially those working in the public sector, may represent a special case. Bureaucracies are supposed to be ossifying.[2] And public sector professionals are, among other things, bureaucrats (Prottas, 1980). Did the professionals in my study become more rigid with the passage of time, losing forever the desire to innovate, to experiment, and to change?

Different Responses to Change

In general, the professionals became more flexible and willing to experiment. Teachers became more inclined to try new things in the classroom. Mental health professionals became less rigidly wedded to a particular theoretical approach or set of techniques. The professionals were more willing to experiment and take chances than they had been as novices.[3]

Eugenia Barton put it well when I asked her if she had become more or less flexible since she began to teach: "Oh, much more, much more. I think the inflexibility comes out of fear. If you're scared to death of losing the class, or making mistakes, you tend to follow a very rigid plan. As you learn your subject matter and become more comfortable, it's much easier to experiment—not so threatening."

This greater willingness to experiment seemed to be related to the self-confidence that the professionals now felt. Clinical social worker Nick Fisher said, "I think I'm a lot more confident about myself, so I can try things. Like, I'll try emotional things that I would never have tried before because I'm just more comfortable with that area." And teacher Victoria Goble said, "I think as you gain self-confidence, then you're probably willing to take more risks. So to the extent that I've been willing to risk more, I've been willing to try new things."[4]

But it would be erroneous to conclude that the professionals had become more open to change in every respect. On the one hand, they seemed to be more willing to experiment, but on the other, they had also become more skeptical about the value of change. For instance, high school teacher Charlotte Noble said, "The older I've got, the more I've said, 'Well, in my experience I've done these other things that seem similar, and they didn't work. So I'm not going to try that.' I'll be flexible and try your idea *if* my experiences tell me that it might work."

Another teacher, Calvin Miller, sounded even more resistant to change when he said, "I was thinking the other day that maybe the problem in the schools has been we've been trying too many different things without sticking with one thing. It suddenly occurred to me that each year there's a different, new way of how to deal with discipline problems or attendance. It's like, 'What's the new philosophy this year?' And maybe the schools should go back to one consistent system or model or whatever."

It seemed at first that the professionals were contradicting themselves. The same individuals who professed to being more open to change at one point in the interview would seem to be more resistant to change at another point, but then I realized that the professionals had become more open to *some* kinds of change and less open to others. More specifically, the professionals seemed to be less willing to try new ideas that came from others but more willing to experiment with their own ideas.

Clinical social worker Nick Fisher helped clarify the complex way in which the professionals reacted to change. First Nick said that he was more willing to experiment because he was more self-confident. Then he said that he was more cautious and less willing to "go off half-cocked, just saying, 'There's a neat idea, let's do it.'" The apparent contradiction was resolved when he said, "In some ways, I see myself as real leery of doing anything flexible. I'm kind of rigid. I think to myself, 'I'll do my thing that I know about. . . . I'm not sure I like this idea of doing something new that *you* do.' So I think a lot of times I shut myself off to new possibilities. If somehow or another I can get *ownership* of the idea, then I'll probably be willing to take chances."

The professionals were more willing to experiment, but their willingness to experiment was restricted to what came from their own imaginations. Given that the experience of one individual is always limited, one must wonder how meaningful such openness to change really is for professional progress and renewal.

Sustaining Openness to Change: Some Implications

How, then, can we make professionals more open to change, more willing to experiment? How can we foster creativity and innovation in the helping professions? One way is to involve professionals more meaningfully in the process of innovation. The key is *ownership*: if another person suggests a new idea, the experienced professional is likely to respond with skepticism. If the professional is the one, however, who thinks of the new idea, then he or she is more willing to try it.

This is not, unfortunately, the way in which reform in schools and the human services is usually implemented. The reforms are typically formulated by administrators, politicians, or academics, and then they are imposed on experienced professionals. If, however, teachers and human service professionals were allowed to play a greater role in planning change, there might be more meaningful reform in the human services.

A second way to make veteran professionals more open to innovation is to make them novices again: to put experienced professionals in novel, challenging situations, and to do so every five years or so. This is what happened fortuitously to Carol Potter. She had worked as a resource room teacher for several years and was comfortable in this role. As a resource room teacher, she would work with students individually for one or two hours each week.

Then one day she was told that she would be reassigned to a self-contained classroom for the next year. She was dismayed. Now she would be working with a large group of children all day, five days a week. It was a very different kind of role, and one she didn't welcome. She almost quit. But eventually she decided to try it.

Desperate for help, Carol found another teacher in the district who had worked in self-contained classrooms for several years. Carol went to her and enlisted her aid. Carol said it was as though she had become a student again. She was hungry for any advice that this other teacher could give her, and she was fortunate that the other teacher was willing to help. For the next year, Carol met with the other teacher at least once a week to discuss how things were going and to get help with problems that came up.

Carol exemplifies how an experienced professional can be encouraged to become more flexible and open to learning. She readily admitted that she wouldn't have volunteered to make the change, but that in retrospect it had been good for her. It kept her interested in her work, and it helped her to become more open to learning new ideas and techniques.

Pelz and Andrews (1966) reached the same conclusion in their research on engineers and scientists working in industry. After studying the factors that contributed to creativity in research and development settings, they concluded that a change in job assignments every five years or so is one way to keep technical people fresh, excited, and involved in their work. Periodic changes in job assignments can also promote flexibility and creativity. Social workers, teachers, and nurses—like engineers—can benefit from periodic changes in roles and responsibilities.

But there's one important qualifier: professionals who are thrust into new roles need more support and guidance to keep stress at manageable levels. As Nicholson (1984) has noted, high levels of psychological stress engender conformity and resistance to change. Changes in role won't make professionals more open to new ideas if the professionals aren't helped to cope with the stress that accompanies change. Carol Potter was fortunate in receiving that kind of help, so ultimately her role change was a positive experience. Without support, forced change may lead to greater rigidity. To remain flexible, professionals need change, challenge, *and* support.

7

Why Work? Shifting Priorities

The ideal professional is not only caring, compassionate, open to new ideas, and flexible; professionals should also be dedicated and committed to their work. They should regard it as more than just a job. It should be a calling.

A certain degree of commitment is important for any job, but it's especially important for the work of helping professionals.[1] Alienation among professionals is harmful because they have so much discretion in performing their jobs, and the potential for social upheaval is greater when the professional social class becomes disaffected (Korman, Wittig-Berman, & Lang, 1981; Sarason, 1977).[2]

In the beginning, dedication was no problem for most of the professionals in my study. Work was of central importance to them. They were glad to be finished with their formal training, and they were eager to put into practice what they had learned. They wanted to be as good as they could. Unsure of themselves, afraid of failing, they spent long hours trying to make up for gaps in their skill and knowledge. Work was everything.

By the end of the first year, however, their commitments had changed. Frustration and failure had led many to reassess their priorities. They cut back their involvement in work, investing their energy and time in other pursuits. They became less willing to spend extra time on work-related projects—unless they were compensated for it. They became more concerned about extrinsic rewards such as money. No longer were they idealistic professionals. They had become alienated workers.

When I returned to interview them 12 years later, I found that many had recovered, to some extent, after that first year. As they became more self-confident, and as they found ways to make their jobs more rewarding, they became more interested and involved in their work again. But they never became as committed as they had been in the beginning, and their reasons for working had changed.

The professionals wanted their work to be interesting and challenging. They did not want to give up meaning for status, security, and money. On the other hand, these "extrinsic" rewards of work continued to become more important over time. They hadn't gone into nursing or social work for status and fortune, but somewhere along the way many had started to seek it out.

The Growing Importance of Status and Prestige

Feeling competent continued to be important for the professionals. As clinical social worker Nick Fisher put it, "When things work out well during a session, it really validates me. There's a feeling of confidence and almost—it's starting to sound mushy—there's a kind of a sense of art, almost like an artist would talk about, manipulating their work and feeling like they can express . . . workmanship, yeah, that would be a good way to put it, craftsmanship. And there's a real sense of satisfaction . . . a sense of craftsmanship."[3]

Performing competently—and avoiding the humiliation associated with failure—was still important to seasoned professionals after more than a decade of experience.[4] High school teacher Victoria Goble admitted, "I still have nightmares in the fall about telling a class to do something, and then they all look at me and say 'NO!'" At this point she giggled and then added, "So I infer that the anxiety is still pretty high."

Given that achieving a sense of competence was still important for the professionals, how did they come to feel successful? For teachers, mental health counselors, and other helping professionals, work with clients often provides only a fleeting sense of self-efficacy and impact. Status and prestige among colleagues provide more tangible marks of success.

Certain individuals stand out in any professional community because of their accomplishments. Some even attain "national visibility." As the professionals in my study mastered the basics, they began to dream about success on a larger scale.

It can be difficult for professionals to become aware of—much less talk about—their aspirations for status and prestige. Preoccupation with such matters violates cultural norms. As Sarason (1988, p. 75) noted, "If engaging in competition, tournament style, is encouraged and rewarded, it is also true in America that we are taught that it is unseemly to parade one's competitiveness, and we cloak it in a variety of garments that hide from us and others how much we want to be better than everyone else, how deeply we want to stand on the mountain of success."

The in-depth, biographical interviews used to gather data for this study were particularly helpful in uncovering these attitudes about status. As the interviews progressed, the professionals came to realize that I was more interested in learning from their experience than making judgments about it. And gradually they began to reveal things about themselves that they normally wouldn't reveal. It was then that comments about their need for status were likely to emerge. The biographical interview facilitated the development of rapport and trust, which made it easier for the professionals to talk about how important status had become.

When clinical social worker Nick Fisher began his career, prestige was of little importance to him. But during the follow-up interview 12 years later, he admitted that it had become much more important as time passed. At some point in his career, it had become important to him to be a "recognized expert," a person with visibility and stature within the professional community.

As Nick put it during the interview: "I really like having people's regard. I like the people that I work with to know my name and to feel that I do good work and to get positive feedback from that. I like it when I go down to the court system and they say, 'Well, you're the expert in this stuff, and you know exactly what you're doing.' And, 'If Fisher says such-and-such, that's the way it's going to be.' That feels real good."[5]

One of the most striking examples of how attitudes toward status and prestige changed over time came from Margaret Williams. Margaret had originally become a lawyer to help the poor. Poverty law was a way of making society more just and humane. Even though she had attended a prestigious law school, Margaret refused to interview for any prestigious jobs.

But Margaret experienced a severe case of "reality shock" during her first year of practice. As her idealism and commitment diminished, her desire for status and recognition increased. When I re-interviewed her for the follow-up study, she was aware of how her priorities had changed. She was now practicing in one of the more conservative specialties of the law, one dealing exclusively with financial matters. In talking about her current work, she said: "I now supposedly am the national authority in my specialty. I've been named chairman of a national bar association committee, and I'm getting big cases and all of that stuff, and calls from all over the country from other attorneys who want to know what to do. I now have some expertise in something that's recognized. And it may not pay off financially, but I have some respect from a lot of people."

Later in the interview, Margaret acknowledged that securing recognition and prestige had become more important than helping people: "It's a game. I hate to put it that way, but that's all it is. . . . If I win my big cases, that's going to be a feather in my cap. It's certainly not going to change the world, or make life better for anybody. It's merely going to be a feather in my cap. And that's all I care about right now."[6]

Margaret no longer cared about "changing the world" or pursuing justice. The primary motive at this point in her career had become "winning the game" and acquiring "feathers in her cap." Those feathers represented status and prestige within her profession.

Publishing articles in professional journals and giving presentations at conferences are prime ways for professionals to achieve greater visibility and status. At this point in their careers, the professionals in my study increasingly sought out opportunities to enhance their reputations by publishing or presenting. And when they succeeded, the gratification was substantial. Nurse Jessica Andrews said, "I've published one article. It was in a prestigious journal. And I'd love to do more writing. . . . I've presented at APHA twice since I've been here, and people came up to us after the presentations and said, 'This is wonderful,' and I'm still getting requests for my article from ten years ago, from places like Egypt, and Canada, and Israel."

For the mental health professionals, becoming a nationally recognized expert who gives workshops around the country is another route to higher status and prestige. For instance, clinical social worker Jennifer Talmadge had a successful and intrinsically rewarding private practice, but she admitted that she had dreams of "becoming rich and famous" by doing "these huge workshops all over the country" and becoming a "hit star."

Income is another indicator of one's relative status in our society. As the professionals moved into mid-life and took on more obligations, their pecuniary needs naturally increased, but their growing concern about money went beyond financial necessity. Income is a tangible way of measuring status, success, and, ultimately, self-worth. If they were making less money than their peers, they had to struggle against feelings of shame.

Margaret Williams had initially been nonchalant about money. Early in her first year as a legal aid lawyer, she said she didn't mind the low status and salary associated with her work. She felt that she could "live fine" on what she earned, and she had "no complaints."

Margaret's views had changed 12 years later. She explained why her income had become more important: "I'm still getting paid the same as somebody a year or two out of school. And it has kept me from getting a job in the outside world because people just wonder, 'Hey, somebody who was on law review, been practicing for 12 years, does the kind of work you do, and is only making $30,000—what's wrong?'"

But Margaret wasn't just concerned about her income because it might keep her from getting a better job. She couldn't stop talking about how much people judged her on the basis of her low income. And as she repeatedly proclaimed that she wasn't bothered by that, it became apparent that she was. Her self-esteem suffered because of how little she earned.

At one point, for instance, Margaret said, "This society judges you on how much money you make. So if that were that important to me, I'd think my life was a complete failure. So I just can't think of it as very important, and I don't."

A few minutes later, Margaret spontaneously returned to the theme of money and self-worth: "I think it's very sad that society thinks there's something wrong with me because I don't make a lot of money. . . . It's very hard to deal with people who think I must not be a very good attorney because I don't make a lot of money."[7]

Margaret tried to think of income as unimportant—with mixed success. So many of the people with whom she associated did believe that income reflected how competent one was. Because Margaret's salary was so low, she had to fight off feeling that her life was a "complete failure."

Teachers ultimately have much less earning power than attorneys, but they, too, seemed to feel a strong link between income and self-worth. High school teacher Eugenia Barton's husband was a manager who worked for a large corporation. The family could live well on his salary alone. But the size of her salary was still important to Eugenia because of what it said about her status: "I believe that the respect that a teacher gets is directly related to the salary. And I understand that more clearly than I did before." Status, and the symbolic value of money in conferring status, had become more important for Eugenia as well.[8]

Theories of adult development suggest that as people move beyond early adulthood and approach mid-life, status and recognition become more important. For instance, Levinson (1978) has proposed that between the ages of 33 and 40 (which is the phase that most of my subjects had entered by the time of the follow-up), the focus is on "climbing the ladder." The main task for this period is "becoming one's own man (or woman)," and affirmation from others is important in achieving this task. Gould (1978) has noted that between the ages of 35 and 45 there is the first emotional awareness that time is running out for one's dreams. This tends to make the individual even more determined to achieve status and recognition in whatever endeavor has become the focus of one's life work.

Career theory also emphasizes the importance of status and success at mid-career. Hall (1986), for instance, has stated that the need for recognition is the most important of all career-related needs during the "advancement" stage of the career, the period that begins when a person has settled into a particular occupation, usually in the late 20's or early 30's.

Empirical research on adult development has supported these theories. Several longitudinal studies have found that as people move from early adulthood to middle-age, their needs for achievement and recognition increase (Haan, 1989). In one study of young managers, for instance, Hall and Nougaim (1968) found that the subjects became increasingly concerned about achievement and esteem during the early part of their careers. Bray, Campbell, and Grant (1974) found that managers at AT&T became more achievement-oriented after the first eight years of their careers.

Maturation wasn't the only force contributing to greater concern about status and recognition in the professionals I studied. They were also influenced by historical change—more specifically, the increasing emphasis placed on "fame and fortune" as important life goals during the eighties. Surveys of workers, and of college students preparing to become workers, detected a strong shift in attitudes during this period. In the early seventies, college students were more concerned about doing work that was "meaningful." By the mid-eighties, however, college students had become more concerned about "being very well off financially" and "opportunities for advancement" (Stark, 1988). Thus the helping professionals were pushed by a variety of psychological and social forces as they became more concerned about status and prestige.

The Growing Importance of Challenge and Stimulation

If *extrinsic* rewards like money, status, and prestige had become more important for the professionals, then it seemed that they would be less interested in *intrinsic* rewards like challenge, stimulation, and opportunities to utilize valued skills—at least that's what I expected.[9]

The actual results, however, were different. I discovered that one can continue to value intrinsic rewards at the same time that one comes to value extrinsic rewards. Even though status and financial compensation had become more important, most professionals had also come to value even more the intrinsic rewards. In some cases, when confronted with a choice between the two, the professionals chose to give up greater status, prestige, and money to work in more intrinsically rewarding jobs.

Former high school teacher Alice Harris gave a particularly clear and vivid description of what it is like to do intrinsically rewarding work. In discussing her career options, she said, "For a while, I thought that if I didn't do something in art it would be okay. If I were doing something in publicity or in PR for some company or some small business or something of that nature, it would be okay. But every time I go to the museum and give a tour, I am so happy, I love it so much. I'm in my element. I come to life. It's like something happens to me, and I'm so happy to be doing that. When I come home from those experiences, I always say, 'I can't just be a publicist. I really want to be doing something that involves art.'"

When Alice talks about how much she "enjoys" giving talks at the museum, how she "comes to life" when she does this kind of work, and how "happy" it makes her feel, she gives us a good description of what intrinsically rewarding work is like. It's work that's fulfilling just in the doing of it.

Before they began their careers, these professionals had wanted to do work that was intrinsically satisfying, but during the first year of practice, survival took precedence. They were so caught up in trying to establish themselves and to feel competent that they had little time to worry about whether their work was enjoyable.

But as time passed, they were more likely to experience intrinsic enjoyment in their work; and when they did so, they realized how important it was for them. In fact, the more intrinsic fulfillment they experienced in their work, the more they wanted that fulfillment—and the more important it became as a reason for working.

Nurse Angela McPherson, for instance, talked about how important it was to do work that was intrinsically satisfying. When I asked her if it always had been important, she thought for a moment and then answered, "Well, I think I'm more aware of it because I've had more opportunity to work that way in the last four years. I think it was important before, but it's really tantamount now. I'm much more cognizant of it."[10]

Other researchers have also found that over time professional workers come to value both intrinsic and extrinsic rewards more highly. Adler and Aranya (1984), who studied CPAs, found that their needs for esteem, autonomy, and self-actualization increased over time, as did needs for security and social approval. Hall and Mansfield (1975) observed that during the "middle stabilization" stage of one's career, both achievement motivation and intrinsic motivation tend to be high.

Maturation and development weren't the only forces that led the professionals to value more highly both intrinsic and extrinsic aspects of work. Historical factors were also involved. Campbell and Moses (1986) noted that in the fifties, advancement was the prime motivator for managers. In the early seventies, new managers tended to be more interested in whether a job provided an intrinsic sense of accomplishment. The eighties saw a return to an emphasis on advancement, but achieving a sense of accomplishment continued to be important. Thus, for the newest generation of managers, both intrinsic and extrinsic rewards were important. The professionals in this study were part of the same cohort and were affected by the same social and historical forces.

The Balancing Act: Work, Family, and Leisure

The professionals also felt a growing need to strike a better balance between work and nonwork parts of their lives. Despite the importance of intrinsic rewards, they had become increasingly dissatisfied with how much of their time and effort went into their work. They wanted work to play a less major role in their lives.

Nick Fisher was one who strongly believed in the importance of balance between work and nonwork parts of life. Early in his career, Nick devoted most of his time and energy to his work. Work was his central life interest. No other goal was as important as establishing himself as a competent professional. But as time passed, Nick came to feel that other aspects of his life were as important as his work.

The importance of balance for Nick emerged most clearly when he talked about giving up fame for a saner life style: "I was at a point in my life about seven years ago where I could have 'gone national.' There's this guy down in Marin County who's written two good books now in my field, and he's into building an empire. He's running around the country and doing the workshops. And I don't want to do that. I was on the verge of doing that when I was doing all the stuff with the Air Force, and I realized I couldn't keep doing that."

When I asked Nick why he could not "keep doing that," he answered

Well, I see people who do that. And they spend a third of the year, easily, on airplanes, a third to half their year living in hotels, out of suitcases. Going in and doing this stuff to people who they don't know, shmoozing them up a little bit, and getting everybody to come up and say, "Oh how wonderful you are, you know so much, you're so smart," and all that stuff. I'm not that hungry for recognition. My ego's not that bad that I need all these strangers constantly coming up, not knowing me, and telling me that I'm the greatest thing since sliced bread. I know I can do that. I'm skilled enough at doing presentations so that I can win audiences over. I'm real good at it.

But when I was doing that, it was just lonelier than hell, it was really lonely. And I didn't like living out of suitcases, and I was tired all the time, bored. I wasn't being challenged worth anything. I didn't get a chance to feel anything. You go home to a hotel and watch TV or you go out and get laid with somebody. And that's a lot of what I was doing, and it was just nowhere. Seeing how hard people work, writing books, and how hard they work at getting to be. . . . This guy in Marin, for example, he is working real hard at this. And when you talk to him, he's so frenzied. And boy, I don't want to be like that. I want to raise my kid, and climb mountains, and have a good time, and just have enough money. . . .

For Nick, prestige and status were appealing—and attainable. But there was a limit to the price he was willing to pay. Maintaining a healthy balance between work, family, and leisure was ultimately more important than becoming "the greatest thing since sliced bread."[11]

As the professionals entered their thirties and forties, two changes in their lives contributed to this desire to find more of a balance between work and nonwork parts of their lives. First, they became parents. Many of the professionals had postponed having children until their late twenties or thirties. Before the children came, they were usually heavily involved in their work. But once they became parents, it was difficult to maintain the same high level of involvement in work. Parenting not only made demands on time that could not be ignored, it was also a compelling interest that competed with work.

High school teacher Charlotte Noble was consumed by her work for more than five years, but this changed when her daughter was born. "When I came back after my daughter, I took absolutely no extra duties at all. Bare minimum. So I went from doing a lot of extra work as coordinator of computers—which included ordering all the software and all the extra paperwork, and a lot of PO's [purchase orders] and calling suppliers and all that type of stuff—I went from that, almost having a job-and-a-half, to bare bones teaching."

Charlotte went on to explain that it was not just the amount of time she devoted to teaching that changed when she became a parent. The way she thought about her work also changed significantly. Teaching changed from being her central life interest to being merely one of several interests:

> I think I now consider teaching as more "my career" that's separated from "my personal life." When I was first teaching, I wasn't married, I wasn't dating anyone, all my friends were the other teachers I worked with at school. So school was my whole life almost. When I moved here and shortly thereafter got married and had a house, a husband, and other things that became my life, school became a nine-to-five with some extras—clubs or whatever. It was no longer my entire life. And I didn't socialize with students very much outside of the classroom. I didn't go to football games just to go to football games. I didn't have that kind of time to put in. When I was single and living alone, I enjoyed doing that. But things change. I have a lot of other responsibilities, and I'm not 22 any more.[12]

Acquiring family responsibilities was not the only force that led to a realignment of priorities. As the professionals entered early middle age, some of them became more aware of the passing of time and of their own mortality, which led to a reassessment of their priorities. This often led to a feeling that things weren't quite right, that there should be more balance between work, family, and leisure.

Public health nurse Angela McPherson was one of the professionals who went through this soul-searching process. She had married in her late thirties, and her husband was several years older than she. He already had children from a previous marriage. She had no children of her own and did not plan to have any in the future. Angela had always been career-oriented and very involved in her work, particularly after starting her own health care consulting business. She found her work to be rewarding—and time-consuming. She could easily invest most of her time and energy into her work, and she had done so for several years. But recently she had started to question whether it was such a good idea to put most of her creative energy into her work: "I think I've tried to tell myself, 'Work isn't everything.' I haven't done a very good job of that, but I think the idea of having some fun, and all that, is important. And I've been telling myself I have to do that some more. I'm just reading Kushner's book, *When All You've Ever Wanted Isn't Enough*. And I think that's the stage I'm getting to right now. Is this it? Is this all there is?"

Angela went on to explain that just a few months before, she had discovered that she had diabetes. She was now on insulin. It was the first time in her life she had to deal with a serious systemic disease, and it made her even more aware of her own mortality, the preciousness of life, and the feeling that she "should be doing some other things besides work."

Van Maanen (1977) noted a number of other factors that lead to a shift away from work and an increasing emphasis on nonwork aspects of life at mid-career. In addition to change in family structure, there is "plateauing"—the feeling that there are no more opportunities for advancement in one's job. Van Maanen suggested that this shift away from work as a central life interest may also be related to an increasing tendency for people to express nondominant needs in middle age—an observation first made by Carl Jung.

But change in the *zeitgeist*—the "spirit of the times"—is also a factor. Americans in general have become more concerned with balancing work and leisure during the last decade: Kerr (1991) reported on a survey of American workers, showing that 77 percent wanted more time to spend with family and friends and 72 percent wanted more time for self-improvement. In 1975, 60 percent of Americans polled said that they had enough leisure time. The feeling was very different by the end of the eighties.

Even though the professionals wanted to bring about more balance in their lives, many found it difficult to do so. When Angela McPherson said that she had "not done a very good job" of cutting back on her involvement in work, she expressed a common plaint. For instance, high school teacher Eugenia Barton spoke eloquently about how important it was for her to have a life outside of the classroom, how "you don't do your students any favor by getting in a rut, where all you do is lesson plans," and how "the balance is not only good for me, it's good for them." But then she added somewhat sheepishly, "I still have some trouble in things like reading. I always feel guilty. I can only read in the summer. I feel really guilty when I pick up a book that I enjoy in the winter. I keep thinking I should be working on school-related work. . . . That part I haven't worked through, where I can enjoy reading for pleasure."

In other cases, it was not guilt that kept the professionals from reducing their psychological involvement in work. Rather, they found it difficult to give up the gratifications that they received from work. Nurse Gloria Bennett, for instance, talked about how balance had become more important to her because of "all the years that have gone by." She had decided to cut back on her involvement in work and develop more interests outside of the job. But then, in order to get more stimulation, challenge, and status than nursing had provided, she decided to switch to law. When I interviewed her for the follow-up study, she was still working full-time as a nursing administrator and was also carrying almost a full course load at law school at night.[13]

In conclusion, the extrinsic and intrinsic rewards of work became increasingly valued over time. The professionals wanted more success, recognition, money—and fulfillment—than ever before. But they also wanted more opportunity to pursue interests outside of the job. Like many other Americans during the eighties, they had come to feel that they wanted to "have it all"—interesting and meaningful work that was enjoyable to do and that also provided ample pay and recognition, without interfering with other life interests and commitments. To what extent were they successful in finding this ideal state of affairs? I turn to this question in the next chapter.

Postscript: Are Men and Women Different?

In reacting to a journal article about this study, a reviewer took me to task for ignoring differences between men and women. I had to admit that I hadn't been looking for such differences. So I went back to the data to see if the women viewed their careers differently from the men. I still couldn't find many differences, and this surprised me.

Research studies have suggested that women are less invested in work and career advancement than are men, and more invested in home and family responsibilities.[14] But one problem with many of these studies is that they don't control for differences in occupation, status, and life circumstances. When men and women are working in the same occupations and facing the same constraints, demands, and opportunities, the differences in aspirations may not be as noticeable. In my study, all of the subjects began as helping professionals working in fields in which there is relatively less discrimination against women;[15] that may be why the differences in men's and women's attitudes toward achievement, status, and family were not as great.

Men as a group did seem to be somewhat more concerned about status and prestige than did the women. But even this difference failed to hold for the women who didn't have children. For lawyers like Shana Phillips and Margaret Williams, for nurses like Gloria Bennett, Angela McPherson, and Rebecca Simpson, and for mental health professional-turned-real estate agent Karla Adams, there was no discernible difference between their aspirations for financial success and status, and those of the men in the study. It was only when women assumed the role of primary parent in a family with children that their interest in career advancement and success sometimes became more tempered than it did for the men.[16]

If, in some studies, women appear to be less driven to achieve conventional success than men, it probably has less to do with their chromosomes and more to do with differences in the opportunities and supports they encounter in the workplace. Despite much progress in reducing discrimination, women in fields such as engineering and accounting still face many more obstacles to career advancement than do their counterparts in fields such as social work and nursing. Consequently, placing less value on traditional career success simply may be a rational way for women to adjust to an unfortunate reality.

8

Fulfillment and Regret

Given how much the professionals now wanted from their work—status, prestige, intrinsic fulfillment, and balance—one might assume that they would be frustrated much of the time. But this wasn't the case. Many of these individuals had managed to find work situations that met most of their needs and aspirations, at least to some extent. Several, in fact, proclaimed that this was the best period of their lives, that they had never been more satisfied.

Life and Work Satisfaction: No Time Like the Present

Youth is supposed to be the best time of life in our society, the time when we are not yet weighed down with responsibilities and constraints. Most of our lives are still ahead of us, and the opportunities can seem limitless. As we approach middle age, we are supposed to become more dissatisfied as the burdens of parenthood and jobs weigh us down, as we increasingly come to feel locked into our present jobs, and as we sense the passing of time and the closing off of options.

This popular conception of aging proved to be a myth for most of the professionals in my study. As they looked back over their lives, many were willing to say that the present was the best period. They were far more satisfied and content with life and career after 12 years of practice than they had been in the earliest years. To be sure, there were problems and worries, but, all things considered, life had never been so good.

High school teacher Eugenia Barton was one of those who had begun her career when she was already older. Eugenia had married while still in college, dropped out of school, and stayed home until her third child was well-launched. She did not return to finish her college degree and obtain her teaching certificate until she was 30, and she was 33 when she took her first teaching position. Thus, when I returned 12 years later to re-interview her, Eugenia was in her mid-forties. Her youngest child was 19, and she had recently become a grandmother.

Several times during the interview Eugenia stressed how satisfied she was with her career and her life. As we sat around her dining room table with her grandchild playing in the next room, Eugenia said: "I'm very comfortable. I'm real happy with my life, and my job, and I don't have any other ambitions. . . . I don't want to do anything but what I'm doing. I don't want to teach anything but what I'm teaching. I'm very comfortable."

One of the most important reasons that the professionals were generally so happy at this stage of their lives had to do with their work situations. Compared to the first few years of their careers, this period was far better in most cases. They usually had more autonomy, their relations with colleagues were closer and more supportive, and most important, they felt much more sure of themselves. Of course, not everyone I interviewed was satisfied with all aspects of work. But those who were very dissatisfied were a distinct minority. Twelve years before, it was the satisfied ones who constituted a minority.[1]

There were three reasons why the work situation had improved so much for most of these professionals. First, increasing seniority in most professions leads to better working conditions. For instance, more experienced teachers tend to be assigned more desirable classes than new teachers. Lawyers are usually able to work their way up to more meaningful and interesting cases. Second, the professionals seemed to become more satisfied because they lowered their expectations and aspirations. When they were idealistic novices, they had wanted many things from life and from work. Their expectations for intrinsic fulfillment, for supportive work environments, and for making an impact were often quite high. Over time, many of the professionals came to feel that those expectations were unrealistically high, and they began to adjust them downward.[2] As they did so, the gap between "real" and "ideal" diminished, and thus their satisfaction increased.[3]

Increasing Career Insight

There was one other reason that the professionals became more satisfied with their work over time: increasing career insight helped the professionals to identify the most optimal work situations. By career insight, I mean the extent to which one is aware of what type of work is most enjoyable, what type of work setting is most comfortable, and what types of work are most likely to lead to success.[4] Over time, the professionals' career insight increased considerably. Equally important, their willingness to make career decisions based on suitability also increased. During the earliest stage of their careers, they were more likely to choose jobs and work settings based on what they thought they *should* do rather than on what was most suitable for them, given their interests and aptitudes.

Douglas Furth originally went into mental health because he liked working with people and felt that it would be rewarding to help those with emotional problems. There was a strong sense of moral obligation in his choice of mental health as a career. It took him many years of increasing discontent before he realized that he wasn't suited for doing psychotherapy. He then became a career counselor, and he was much happier in his new career. In reflecting on what had happened to him, he admitted that earlier in his career he had had "a lot of blind spots" about himself. For Douglas, career insight led to a better understanding of what he liked and did not like in work.

For nurse Gloria Bennett, career insight involved the discovery of what she did best. Gloria began as a public health nurse and was relatively satisfied during the first year or two of her career. However, it did not take her long before she came to feel frustrated by the "lack of stimulation." She left public health nursing and went to work in a hospital. She worked in a number of different hospitals and in a number of different roles during the next few years. During much of this time she was frustrated and unhappy in her work. Most of her jobs were either too easy and lacked stimulation and challenge, or they were too difficult—"impossible" jobs that led to nothing but frustration and a sense of failure.

When I re-interviewed Gloria, she had given up on nursing and was in law school, preparing to make a career change. However, she said that her current job was by far the best she had ever had in nursing. It was challenging, yet she also felt a sense of accomplishment. When I asked her why she felt she had been so successful in her present job, she answered, "A lot of it was maturing and reflecting, and being able to articulate what fit for me, what I was good at, what I wasn't good at, that kind of thing." With increasing career insight, Gloria had developed a better understanding of what she was "good at," and this helped her to eventually find the optimal nursing job for herself.

Career insight often developed fortuitously as the professionals found themselves doing things they never thought they would do—and discovered that they liked doing them. In some cases, the professionals actively resisted moving into new roles and responsibilities, only to find that these new roles were far more satisfying than their previous ones had been. With this revelation, career insight increased.

A good example of this "involuntary" career insight occurred for lawyer Jesse Michaels. Jesse was one of the people who went into law to change the world. He worked in Washington for a few years, then tired of the "Washington scene" and took a job with a large insurance company. But he was still involved in the same type of work. His job was to follow closely what was happening in Washington to help the company anticipate important changes in federal regulations affecting the insurance industry.

Jesse continued to do legislative analysis and lobbying for a few more years. Then, a new president ordered a major reorganization of the company, and suddenly Jesse found himself transferred to a more traditional legal job. Initially he was bitter about the transfer. He felt he had invested many years in developing a specialized competence, and now he was being asked to throw it all away and do work that he had not done since law school. But the new job proved to be more rewarding than he had expected.

"Initially, I didn't really want to do it," he said. "I felt that my future was in the legislative lobbying area, and I didn't really want to switch to more of an in-house counsel role, doing traditional types of legal work. As it turned out, the more I did it, the more I liked it. I'd forgotten how much I liked certain things in law school, like contracts; how much I liked negotiating deals; how much I liked drafting contracts. The more I did it, the more I enjoyed it. And I really began to love it again. So it worked out quite well for me, frankly. It was surprising, because I wasn't really happy with the initial change. But I've really enjoyed it."

It was not that Jesse disliked legislative analysis and lobbying. But he had initially gravitated to that kind of work because he believed that he should do something that was socially relevant, something that would lead to positive social change. Thus, even though he enjoyed more traditional legal work, his social conscience led him to reject it. He probably would have continued along the career path he had been following had it not been for the involuntary transfer. That transfer helped him to see that there were areas of legal practice that were ultimately more stimulating and enjoyable for him.

Over time, the professionals came to realize that many of their career values and aspirations really were not *theirs*. Part of their growing career insight involved learning what preferences were really theirs and what had been picked up from others. As former social worker Sherman Reynolds put it, "I think I've defined my personal boundaries a lot more. I think I've come to understand what I truly desire, and what things I adopted . . . that were more externally presented and weren't really my own values."[5]

As working conditions improved with increasing seniority, as expectations became more realistic and attainable, and as greater career insight led to changes that improved the fit between the professional and the job, the professionals came to feel more efficacious in their work. And as their sense of efficacy increased, they felt more confident and assertive, which in turn led to even greater self-efficacy. This positive spiral made their work lives increasingly satisfying.

The Darker Side: Facing Career Constraints

Generally, the professionals were content, but there were some clouds in the picture. Those who had recently made a major career change, for instance, had to "start over" in some respects. They were once again experiencing some of the frustrations associated with being a novice. Also, some of the professionals expressed regrets about the past, even though they were relatively satisfied with their lives. Nurse Anita Warren, for instance, was delighted about the way her career had turned out, but she expressed some regrets about not having gone into medicine when she was younger and it was still a realistic option. But the most serious concern expressed by these professionals involved career constraints. Many were prevented from doing things that they very much wanted to do.

High school teacher Calvin Miller had been a varsity soccer coach for several years before moving to a new state. He wanted to coach soccer again, but he discovered that he couldn't.

"If I wanted to be a varsity coach here in this state," Calvin complained, "I'd have to get certification. That's irritating to me. I would have to go back and take like 18 credit hours. . . . I'm angry about that. I have 10 years varsity coaching experience, and a national coaching certificate, and I'd still be required to take some of these courses to get the thing."

Sometimes the constraints were as much internal as external. Jesse Michaels, the successful lawyer who now worked for a large insurance company, dreamed of leaving the law and starting his own business. He also wished he could spend more time on socially meaningful pursuits, such as developing low-cost housing for the poor. But he recognized the risks involved in starting new business ventures or working in a nonprofit housing corporation, and he was not willing to give up the security that his present work provided.

When I asked Jesse if he had ever thought of changing careers, he replied, "I haven't given it much thought. . . . I think I'd want to be involved with some non-profit type of work. I really don't know . . . housing, developing low-income housing, maybe something like that. . . . If I could just sit down and name my position, it would be something that would benefit a lot of people." After a long pause, Jesse added, "It probably wouldn't be in insurance, that's for sure. While it's been good for me, financially and career-wise, it's not exactly the stuff of dreams." At that point, Jesse just looked at me, smiled slightly, and shrugged. It didn't seem necessary for him to say anything more on the subject.

For several other professionals, family obligations detracted from the otherwise high level of satisfaction they felt at this point in their lives. Rebecca Simpson, for instance, would have liked to give up her job as a nursing administrator and return to school to work on a Ph.D. She had done enough research over the years to discover that this was what she most liked to do, but she felt locked into her present job because she was putting her husband through school.

Former high school teacher Merton Douglas felt fortunate to have the job of chief counsel for a large bank. It was unusual for a lawyer to secure such a prestigious position just two years out of law school, but there were many other things that Merton would have preferred doing.

When I asked Merton, a nonstop talker, how he liked his job, he suddenly became pensive. Finally he said,

> I don't dislike very much, really. I guess I yearn to be in some capacity, somewhere, either in my own business or at a certain level in a corporate structure, where I can truly just come and go as I please. . . . Frankly, how many basis points you're going to charge on a loan has never been on the top ten list of things that excite me. . . . I think the practice of law in general is . . . I don't want to say it's not my cup of tea, because it is—I do it well. I think I'm a good lawyer. But the day-to-day practice. . . .
>
> I think if I had to pick my ideal job, if I could have the choice of any job in the world, one would be to own and operate a golf course, because I love the game. . . . One of the other jobs would be to be a network sportscaster for baseball. . . . I'd like to own my own business some day. . . .

Then Merton thought about his previous career. "Will I ever return to teaching?" he asked himself. "I bet someday I do. I like to teach. I like to coach. I don't know if I'd be a classroom teacher, or what I would teach, but I would be teaching. . . ."

I asked Merton what prevented him from making a change at this point, and he said, "Too conservative, probably. . . . I don't want to start taking those kinds of risks until we have another income to fall back on, because of the obligation I owe to my family. So I think that for the next 10 years I'll continue to work somewhere in a salaried job, probably here. . . ."

Merton and his wife had just had their first child, and they had decided that his wife would stay home and care for their children while he worked and supported the family financially. So Merton figured he could do nothing to change his situation for the next ten years.[6]

Merton, Calvin, Jesse, and Rebecca weren't the only professionals who wanted to make changes but felt they couldn't. Others also experienced career constraints. But even if they couldn't do everything they wanted to do, the professionals were generally satisfied—certainly far more satisfied than they had been at the end of the first year of their careers.

While most of the professionals were content, a few stood out from the rest—not just because they were more satisfied, committed, and enthusiastic about their work, but also because they had initially been among the most frustrated and disappointed. These professionals were the ones who had recovered from early career burnout. In the next part of the book, I focus on their stories.

Part Three

How Some Overcame Burnout

Part Three

How Can I Overcome Anxiety?

9

Five Who Prevailed

The first year of professional practice was a difficult one, and many of the novices lost their commitment and idealism. During the next decade, there was some recovery as the professionals developed a sense of mastery. Few, however, managed to regain the excitement and dedication they had when they began their careers.

But there were some exceptions. A few of the professionals were able to recover most of their lost idealism. As their careers progressed, the impact of the first year diminished. Some of those who had difficult beginnings were able to turn things around, and 12 years later they were among the most satisfied and committed.

As I became reacquainted with the professionals, I was particularly intrigued by a small group who had been among the most burned out at the end of the first year of practice, but who were among the most committed and caring ten years later. These were the individuals who had truly "recovered" from burnout. There were five of them: two teachers, a public health nurse, and two mental health professionals.[1] What enabled these few to overcome early career burnout?[2]

Eugenia Barton, High School Teacher

Of the four professional groups that I studied, teachers scored highest in stress during the first year of practice. Eugenia Barton was one of the two teachers rated as most stressed during their first year of teaching. As I noted in my brief description of Eugenia in chapter 1, I was pretty sure that she would no longer be teaching when I located her 12 years later. But she was still teaching, and she was one of the most satisfied and committed professionals.

Eugenia had returned to school to secure her teaching credentials when her three children were old enough to be in school full time themselves. Thus, she was one of the oldest subjects in the original study—a "new" professional at the age of 33. At that time, she would have preferred to go into a field such as social work, but she settled on teaching because it would require the least amount of additional schooling. She felt that it would be a burden on her family to go to school any longer than necessary.

The first year of teaching in a public school was stressful for most of the teachers, but Eugenia had particular difficulty. She initially tried to "appeal to the better side" of her students, and she felt she had been "burned" by them as a result. She also had to work late every night at home just to keep up with her classes. This heavy workload put a strain not only on her, but on her husband and children as well.

Eugenia found little support from other teachers or her principal. Her efforts to secure assistance from another teacher were rebuffed. The principal was a shadowy figure who did nothing to make the experience of first year teachers any easier. Looking back on that first year of teaching 12 years later, Eugenia succinctly summarized how she felt, when she said, "First year, I thought I'd died and gone to hell."

One of the first questions I asked her when we met for the follow-up interview was, "Why didn't you quit teaching after that difficult start?" She replied, "After the first year, I looked at that calendar and saw that it couldn't be beat for a working mother. And I told myself that I would like that job—or else! And eventually I did."

The second year of teaching proved to be somewhat easier. Eugenia taught some of the same courses again, so she did not have to spend as much time on preparation. She adopted a much firmer stance with her new classes and found that she had fewer discipline problems. Eugenia was shy, but after the first year she began to develop some friendships with other teachers on the staff.

The organizational climate of the school was relatively positive, which also helped Eugenia adjust. It was a small high school situated in a predominantly stable, rural midwestern community where most of the parents respected teachers and backed them up if there was a conflict between a student and a teacher. Most students came from intact homes.

Over time the work itself also proved to be rewarding for Eugenia. As a vocational education teacher, she was able to see concrete results of her impact on her students, unlike teachers in other subjects such as English or social studies. As she put it: "I really enjoy teaching a skill. It's a much more measurable thing to teach. . . . You can see at the end whether you've taught them or not. . . . So I get a great deal of satisfaction from watching them grow." Eugenia said that she also felt good about working with less able students who needed the marketable skills she was teaching them.

As Eugenia mastered the craft of teaching, she also came to appreciate the autonomy associated with the role: "I like the independence. We can mumble and complain about principals and superintendents and all sorts of boards of education. But when you close that door to your room, you really are independent. I've never once had a principal ask me even the content of a class I taught. It's a very independent situation. And I like that."

By the end of her third year, Eugenia was able to move "beyond the survival level," as she put it, and "could look around and see that life existed beyond the lesson plans." She looked for something to do that would be interesting, and she became involved in the teacher's union. She eventually worked her way up to the presidency of a two-county region, and she readily admitted that her union work was a major commitment and source of satisfaction.

Another extra activity that Eugenia took on also proved to be an important source of gratification. Frustrated by the lack of resources available for her classes, Eugenia decided to start a student store. The store provided a meaningful learning experience for the students as well as a source of income that could be used to purchase equipment and materials for her vocational education program. Eugenia referred to the store as "the most wonderful thing I ever thought of."

Eugenia Barton eventually recovered from early career burnout. She summed up how she felt about her career when she said: "I'm very comfortable. I'm really happy with my life and my job, and I don't want to do anything but what I'm doing. I don't want to teach anything but what I'm teaching. . . . I never mind getting up, and I enjoy going to work."

Mark Connor, Psychologist

The second case study also involves a professional who works in the public schools, but as a psychologist rather than as a teacher. Like Eugenia Barton, Mark Connor had a particularly dismal experience during the first year of his career. In Mark's case, however, his first job didn't improve over time. He had to change jobs in order to recover from burnout.

Mark Connor was 29 years old when he took his first job as a school psychologist. He had previously worked for three years as an elementary school teacher in an inner-city school. He had gone into teaching primarily to avoid the draft during the Vietnam War. His first year of teaching was extremely difficult, but he eventually came to enjoy teaching. The most rewarding part of teaching, however, was the one-on-one contact with the children before and after school, when Mark was able to talk to them about their personal lives and problems. So his stint as a teacher ultimately confirmed his feelings that he should go into psychology. He eventually secured a master's degree, which enabled him to take a job as a school psychologist.

At first, however, psychology proved to be less rewarding than teaching. Mark remembered well the problems with his first job as a school psychologist when he spoke about it during the follow-up interview: "It was a very stressful job. I wasn't happy there. They gave us five schools for one psychologist, and I was responsible for close to 4,000 students. It was ridiculous."

In addition to the sheer burden of the work load, Mark also complained about interference from parents and other community members: "There was a lot of pressure from the community. And I didn't like that pressure. It's like everybody's looking over your shoulder, every minute."

Mark also didn't like the nature of his duties. He spent almost all of his time doing psychological testing or attending meetings to discuss the results of the tests. He found the content of the work especially onerous: "I really do not like to do diagnostic testing. That's why I was thinking of getting out of the field, because that was all that I was doing in the first job."

Mark stayed in the first job two years and then left. He thought he would be happier working in private practice, but he needed a doctorate for that. Mark, who was still single, decided that this would be a good time for him to try living in a different part of the country. He relocated and took another job as a school psychologist near a university where he could work on his doctorate part-time.

To Mark's surprise, the new job proved to be extremely rewarding. Even though he eventually did complete his doctorate, he continued working as a school psychologist in the same district. Nine years later when I conducted the follow-up interview, he was still there.

One of the things that Mark especially liked about the new district was the positive atmosphere. He described the people with whom he worked as "real positive, real helpful, supportive, and open." He was impressed that the administration sponsored regular meetings with organizational consultants to improve staff relationships and communication skills.

Supervision was also an important aspect of the new job. Mark described his supervisor: "He was so open that it just made the job a lot easier, because you could talk to him as a person, rather than as a superior. And I just really liked his creativity, his openness, and his honesty."

This style of leadership was very different from what Mark had experienced in his previous job: "It was more of a dictatorship. The director made all the decisions unilaterally and didn't ask for any input from the psychologists. . . . I felt powerless."

What Mark enjoys doing most is counseling students and their parents, and in his new job, he was now able to devote most of his time to counseling rather than testing. He also began to spend more time consulting with teachers on classroom management and curriculum problems, which also proved to be rewarding.

Like Eugenia, Mark's work experiences were greatly enriched by a special project that he initiated. When the school board removed counselors from the elementary schools because of budget cutbacks, Mark wrote a proposal to set up a counseling internship program. The board adopted the proposal. Part of the program involved Mark's serving as supervisor for the interns. Mark invested considerable time and effort in his supervisory responsibilities. He would tape the interns while they were counseling and then go over the tapes with them. This aspect of his work was particularly satisfying: "I love supervising. . . . I think doing that has kept me going."

Mark was able to do what he most liked to do because of the support and independence that he enjoyed in his job: "What's nice is the school district allows me to do basically what I want to do." Thus, as was true for Eugenia, independence seemed to be an important factor in Mark's recovery from early career burnout.

Mark did earn his doctorate, and he had a small private practice on the side, but he seemed to enjoy his work as a school psychologist even more than the private practice. After nine years, the job had not lost its appeal: "It still is wonderful. I couldn't imagine doing anything else than what I'm doing right now."

Angela McPherson, Public Health Nurse

Angela was 33 years old and single when we first interviewed her. She had worked for several years as a nurse before deciding to return to graduate school to receive the additional education necessary to move into administration. She had just taken her first job in nursing administration when the study began; thus, she really was a new administrator rather than a new nurse.[3] Her first job placed her in charge of a branch office at a large visiting nurse's association.

Much of Angela's difficulty during her first year involved the transition from practitioner to manager. She had been an energetic and "perfectionistic" practitioner, and it was difficult for her to step back and supervise other nurses who lacked her zeal and high standards. She observed: "I knew that if I went out and saw those patients myself, I had a great deal of confidence in the care I gave. And it was very hard for me. The hard part was sitting back and giving directions rather than doing. I wanted to go out and visit all the problem patients. . . . That was really a hard adjustment for me to make."

Angela was particularly unprepared for some of the testing behavior that she encountered in her staff, such as coming in later and later until she finally had to reprimand them. She was also unhappy with the more tedious administrative aspects of the job. She described an example that seemed to epitomize her frustration: "One of the nurses had brought in a pay stub and she wanted to check it. Something about personal time as opposed to vacation time. So I went looking through those little pieces of paper. The whole staff was laughing 'cause I had pieces of paper spread all over the desk. And I said to one of the nurses, 'For this I went 10 years to college!' But I don't know who else could do it. We don't have a business manager."

These kinds of administrative tasks added to an already heavy workload. She was responsible for 15 nurses as well as two clerical workers, she typically worked ten hours a day during the first year, and she complained that she received no feedback on her performance from anyone.

Angela had other complaints as well. Older staff members who had been at the agency for several years seemed to resent her. She became increasingly disillusioned with the agency bureaucracy that created barriers to what Angela believed was necessary change.

By the end of the initial study, Angela seemed to be moving into the more advanced stages of burnout. She admitted that her workload was lighter but complained bitterly that she was still working too hard. She reported that she was making an effort to reduce her investment in the job and was devoting more time to nonwork pursuits such as furniture refinishing and a tennis club. She was dissatisfied with the performance of some of her employees but felt that she could do nothing about it. She had become fatalistic about staff performance; feeling that nothing could make them change, she had just given up on them. She was considering changing jobs but felt that she would remain for a while because she was tied to the area (her fiancé could not relocate), and there was nothing else available.

Angela remained in that first job two more years. Then she was asked to take a staff job in the central office. It was a promotion, and Angela felt she was ready for a change. She found that working on her own was much more enjoyable than supervising others. The content of the work was challenging and interesting. Working on special projects seemed to suit her temperament much better than her previous job had. And she had a high degree of autonomy in the new job, even though she was still working in a large agency.

Angela remained in that second job for five years, and she might have remained even longer. But the situation became less satisfying when a new executive director took over: "The new executive director and I just didn't see eye to eye. So I was starting to get a little restless. I had a sense that because of this dissonance, I was not going to be moving up, and I wasn't sure I wanted to, either."

The conflict with the director came to a head when a new position was created—a position very much like Angela's. She applied for it and was rejected. At that point, she said, "I really felt it was untenable to stay . . . there was no way I could remain there."

For some time, Angela had been receiving requests for technical assistance from other agencies all over the state. That part of the job suggested a way out for her: "I saw a market there for information. So I decided that I would take the summer off and then consider starting a business in the fall, in consultation, to help people do program development. At that time I was unaware of anybody, at least in this state, doing consultation in that area."

Angela admitted that the whole idea was "a little scary," but her husband was working and they could live on his income for a while. With his encouragement, she took the summer off and attended several workshops and seminars on starting a business of one's own. That fall, she officially started the business. She and her husband agreed that they would give her two years to make the business financially viable.

At the time of the follow-up study, Angela had been in business as a private consultant for four years, and she loved it. She said, "It's been excellent. Like everything, it has its problems. But generally, it's been a wonderful opportunity. I love that way of working."

Angela liked being her own boss and being measured by what she did rather than what other people did. As a consultant she received more positive feedback than she had when she was working for an agency: "I really get a lot of nice feedback from people, and that really gives me a good feeling. I enjoy that feedback."

Angela McPherson made her initial recovery from burnout when she moved from a line to a staff position in her nursing agency. She might have become burned out again, however, when an unsupportive director became her new boss. At that point, Angela sustained her recovery by leaving the agency and striking out on her own as a private consultant.

Jennifer Talmadge, Clinical Social Worker

Like Mark Connor, Jennifer Talmadge began her career as a mental health professional working in the public schools. The oldest person in the study, she returned to graduate school to secure a

master's in social work when her own children were already in
school. Upon graduation, she took a job as a school social worker in
a district near her home.

Jennifer was frustrated by all the meetings and paperwork that
prevented her from doing the things that she most enjoyed: "All
you were doing was going to meetings, which was terrible, because
there were so many meetings to go to. Eventually, the things I liked
to do became almost like another part-time job. I was starting to
extend myself to do more work with people, even working nights,
just to work with some families—just to have time to do what I
liked to do."

Jennifer had become involved in the women's movement several
years earlier, and she worked as a volunteer at the local women's
crisis center. She began to discuss her job dissatisfaction with some
other social workers who also volunteered at the center. After com-
miserating with one another, they began to talk about the possibility
of creating a new kind of counseling "collective" that would provide
feminist-oriented counseling.

Jennifer could afford to give up her job in the schools and em-
bark on a risky new endeavor because her husband earned enough to
support the family. She was uneasy, however, about giving up the
security of her school position: "It was kind of scary because I was
pretty well into the school system at that time." Eventually, with
the encouragement of the others, Jennifer decided to take the
chance. The women rented space in an old house, fixed it up themselves, and waited for the clients to come in.

The venture proved to be successful in all respects. Clients
began coming to them almost immediately, and within a year or so
the practice was economically secure. Two of the original partners
eventually left; but the other three, including Jennifer, worked well
together and remained. They had been together for almost 10 years
when I did the follow-up interview with Jennifer.

The new setting proved to be ideal for Jennifer. She enjoyed a
high level of autonomy, and she also received much support from
her partners. Jennifer could also spend almost all of her time doing
the type of work that she most enjoyed. While working in the
schools, she had discovered that what she most enjoyed was working with groups, especially groups for women; the feminist counseling collective was an ideal setting for doing this kind of work.

The counseling collective provided the best aspects of private practice and a well-run agency. Jennifer could work as much or as little as she pleased. This gave her the flexibility to pursue many personal growth experiences outside of work, which she felt helped her to work more effectively with her clients.

Boredom never became a problem for Jennifer over the years, in part because the culture of the setting encouraged creative experimentation. "We've done a lot of things other than counseling," she explained. "We run groups, and we've worked on a simulation game for bulimia, and we've done a lot of different things other than just making this a counseling place. So that's kept up my interest."

Even though Jennifer was the oldest subject in the study, she had continued to experiment and change in her approach to work. She had recently become a grandmother, and this experience had inspired her to start leading groups for older women. She was also thinking of writing a book on the topic.

Jennifer Talmadge thus recovered from early career burnout by leaving a stressful and unrewarding work situation and creating a new one that provided all the autonomy, support, and stimulation that she needed. The emotional and instrumental support provided by friends and family seemed to be especially important in helping her to make the transition.

Carol Potter, Special Education Teacher

One reason that Carol Potter may have experienced so much discontent during her first teaching job was that she already knew that she didn't want to do what she was doing. Originally, she had planned to obtain a Ph.D. in Russian, but she dropped out of graduate school after receiving her master's. She spent the next four years wandering around the country, living in different places and working in a variety of jobs. Finally, she took a job as an aide in a special education class, and that experience helped her decide that she wanted to become a special education teacher.

To become a special education teacher, however, she needed to secure another master's. While she was working on that degree, she taught both Russian and French in a public high school, so when she was first interviewed for this study she was teaching, but not in her chosen subject.

Carol's first-year experience as a teacher was unique in other respects as well. Because so few students in her district took Russian, she had second-, third-, and fourth-year students in one class. This arrangement proved to be confusing and frustrating. Carol also had an especially difficult time because she taught in two different high schools, moving from one to the other each day. This made it harder for her to get to know people and made her feel more isolated than many of the other new teachers. Like most other new teachers, she received little support or encouragement from administrators.

After one year of teaching, Carol finished her special education training and moved to the West Coast where she expected to find a job easily. It proved more difficult than she imagined, and she finally gave up and went to Europe for eight months. When she returned, she again had difficulty in finding a job but eventually did so in a small, rural community. She was the first and only special education teacher in the district, and she taught all grades from kindergarten to 12th grade.

The first few months were difficult. Carol didn't know anyone with whom she worked. Then, just three weeks after school began, her father died. Carol almost quit.

> I went through a time there when I thought, "Maybe I shouldn't even be out here. I should go back and help my mom and forget this, and just start up back there, and help her out. . . ." But at the same time, I guess I'd come out here with so much more determination. "Yes, I do want to have a job. I want to teach. That's what I want to do." I talked to my mom about it, and we decided that this was what I needed to do. I'd found a job. Things were finally falling in place the way I had kind of hoped that they would.

So after a brief absence, Carol returned to work. She eventually made friends among many other teachers in the district. Many were young like Carol, and a camaraderie developed among the staff. Also, being the first and only special education teacher, Carol had "a lot of latitude" and was able to "try out" a lot of her own ideas with minimal interference.

Another teaching job, closer to where she lived and paying

more, opened up the following year, so Carol made a change once again. At this point, she finally settled down. She remained in the district and had been teaching there continuously for eight years when we met again. In the meantime, she had married and had two children.

Even though Carol had remained in the district, her job had changed periodically, and she felt that this helped to rejuvenate her and keep her from becoming stale. She worked in one school as a resource specialist for four years and was then transferred to another school and given a self-contained classroom. As a resource specialist, she worked with higher-functioning students one-on-one for a limited period of time each week. In the self-contained classroom, she had to work with a more difficult group of students all day long, every day. She faced this new assignment with great trepidation and resistance: "That was very upsetting to me. I didn't have a choice about it. It was called a 'Special Day Class,' where you have the same 10 to 12 students all day long. You're with these same students, most of them boys, often with learning disabilities, but also with accompanying behavior problems. And real different from the type of atmosphere and the type of student you have in a pull-out program, who isn't really so demanding emotionally or behaviorally."

Carol tried to change the assignment, without any success. She considered quitting, but she finally decided to give it a try.

The experience turned out to be better than Carol had expected: "I just lucked out. It was a good year. I prepped myself a lot, in terms of going and talking to other teachers. I went to some of the other specialized schools around here to get as much background as possible. And I got a lot of support from one of the staff members who'd become a real good friend of mine. She gave me a lot of ideas for organizing the classroom. And that set me up in terms of having tangible things and ideas, too, of how to deal with certain behavior problems."

Carol came to enjoy teaching in the self-contained classroom, and she learned that change, even when it is unwelcomed, can be a valuable antidote to career stagnation: "It worked out fine, it was a real good year. So I guess what I decided was, it was time for me. It was four years that I had done the other thing, and it kind of gave me a jolt and made me rethink things and learn some new techniques. It was stimulating. It was a real challenge. A little frustrating, but a good thing."

Carol continued to teach in the self-contained classroom for three years. Then she switched back to a resource specialist position, in part because it was a less demanding position, but also because, as she put it, "I needed a change again."

Carol seemed to be content at the time of the follow-up interview. She enjoyed teaching and had become comfortable in the role after many years of experience. Like Eugenia Barton, she worked in a small town school district in which there was considerable respect and support for teachers in the community. There were no major problems with students or other teachers, and she felt that her principal was involved, supportive, and helpful in dealing with parents. As a resource teacher, her schedule was somewhat flexible, and the hours were limited, which made it relatively easy for her to work full time and also handle the demands posed by two small children. Her husband was also a teacher, which meant that he, too, had more time to help out at home when needed.

Thus, Carol Potter had made a good recovery from early career burnout by changing specialties, relocating to a different part of the country, and settling down. Her family seemed to provide a source of balance and fulfillment in her life that complemented, rather than conflicted with, her career.

What Makes a Difference?

Five different human service professionals had five different histories—yet they did share one thing in common. All had been able to overcome early career burnout; all had become committed, caring, and satisfied in their work.

I wanted to find out what set these few individuals apart, what enabled them to overcome early career burnout. I studied the transcripts of all the subjects for several months, and eventually I discovered some clues: important ways in which the professionals who recovered from early career burnout—as well as those who avoided it altogether—differed from the others.

10

Antidotes to Burnout
Finding Meaningful Work

Some professionals were able to recover from early career burnout; finding out what helped them to do so became the most interesting aspect of the study. In learning how this group overcame early career burnout, I began to distill lessons that could help others to do the same. In this and the following two chapters, I present the facilitating factors in the work situation and in the individual that seemed most important for those who recovered.[1]

The first set of factors that seemed important in recovery from burnout involved the nature of the work itself. Of the five professionals who recovered from early career burnout, four made a significant job change within the first three years, and this change brought about a significant improvement in how meaningful their work was.[2]

For helping professionals to sustain their caring and commitment over a long period of time, there must be some balance between giving and getting. The more they give, the more rewarding the work must be for them, and meaningful work is intrinsically rewarding.[3]

As I noted in chapter 1, many helping professionals gave up more lucrative occupations because they wanted to do work that was meaningful. Doing psychotherapy or teaching social studies seemed more meaningful than selling real estate or designing one small part of a new automobile. But what makes work meaningful for a helping professional? A closer examination of the work of those who recovered from burnout, as well as that of others in the study, suggested that rewarding, meaningful work has several characteristics. The most important is the ability to make a significant impact.

Making a Significant Impact

Significance is a core motive for all people, but it's especially important for those engaged in a profession.[4] Professionals want to feel that they're making a difference in other people's lives. Work that gives them this opportunity seems "meaningful."

The professionals thrived when they were able to have a significant impact. Lawyers, for instance, talked about how rewarding it was to have "big cases." Margaret Williams, who didn't recover from burnout during the first decade of her career, never had a "big case" when she was a poverty lawyer working for legal services. But public service lawyer Jean Chalmers was able to work on "big cases" from the very beginning of her career. (Jean Chalmers was one of those subjects in the study who never experienced early career burnout and remained among the most dedicated and committed. She was still a dedicated reform lawyer when she died eight years after her career had begun.)

While Margaret worked in a neighborhood legal aid office that handled more mundane matters, Jean worked in a special branch of legal aid that specialized in reform work. Jean's clients didn't walk in off the street with the commonplace matters that Margaret Williams derisively referred to as "diddly shit." The lawyers in Jean's branch handled a relatively small number of class-action suits. A typical example would be a case that had the potential for significantly changing the way prisoners were treated in prisons throughout the country. Such a case could eventually affect the lives of thousands of people. Unlike the neighborhood legal aid lawyer working to help a single individual, Jean was making an impact on a whole system.

Jean's work was also more significant because she was one of the few lawyers in the state doing reform law, and she quickly specialized within her agency, making her own contribution highly visible and unique. She spoke with obvious pride about the many invitations she received to give speeches on a topic for which she had become one of the leading "experts." For a social activist like

Jean Chalmers, such work was extremely meaningful and rewarding. It was precisely the kind of work that she went into public
service law to do.

But often it's not enough for the professionals to have a significant impact; they must be able to *see* the impact. It must be tangible
and unambiguous. This is why high school teacher Eugenia Barton
liked her work so much. Most of her classes in vocational education
involved teaching a concrete skill. As she put it, "I really enjoy
teaching a skill. It's a much more measurable thing to teach. If I
teach a kid to take shorthand, or to type, or use calculators, or computers . . . you can see at the end whether you've taught them or
not. . . . And I need that. I get a great deal of satisfaction out of
watching them grow."

Angela McPherson expressed the same idea. In her work as a
health care consultant, Angela McPherson had many opportunities
to have a meaningful impact on health care settings, and she was
often able to see tangible signs of it. She gave a recent example,
implying that this sort of experience occurred often in her work: "I
went to New York last week to work with a large agency. And in
the time I was there, I was able to pick out some very important
issues. And the more I talked with the top administrators—I gave a
report on Friday, with my findings—the more I saw this recognition, you know, in their faces. At one point, I said something, and
the whole audience just recognized it right away, and chuckled.
And *that* felt good."

What made Angela's consultation in New York especially
meaningful was seeing the "recognition" in "the faces" of her
audience and hearing their "chuckle" of *appreciation.* In her work
as a health care planning consultant, Angela had many opportunities to get this kind of positive feedback—from the audience, as
in this case, and also from the work itself. This made the work
especially rewarding.[5]

Intellectual Challenge

Professionals also thrive on work that is intellectually challenging. Margaret Williams, who eventually began to recover from
burnout when she became a bankruptcy lawyer, alluded to this
important factor when she discussed one of her big cases. "It was

my first time going down to Cincinnati to argue a case," she said, "which in itself was great, dealing with judges who know what they're talking about. I got to use my brain, and I thought it was interesting to do. . . ." Unfortunately, Margaret had to wait almost 12 years before her work became this intellectually challenging.

Nurse Gloria Bennett also waited a long time—and finally gave up. She had decided to quit nursing just before we met for the follow-up interview. She had been successful; she had advanced to a high-level administrative position in a large, prestigious teaching hospital. But as she approached the pinnacle of her profession, she realized that it would never be stimulating enough for her. In explaining why she quit nursing and entered law school, intellectual challenge emerged as the prime factor.

"Nursing," she complained, "over the long haul, has not intellectually stimulated me, the way I would like to be stimulated. That's number one. Number two is, probably there is some deepseated need to meet a challenge in a way that I felt law would give me that nursing would not."

Jean Chalmers, in contrast, encountered intellectual challenge in her work from the very beginning. She noted that there was "something new all the time," and that she had the chance to sit down and think about challenging new problems. She and her colleagues were constantly breaking new ground in their work, and this made the atmosphere crackle with intellectual excitement. It also helped them resist burning out.[6]

"Nonprofessional duties" were particularly lacking in intellectual challenge. Every profession has a core of functions that are considered to be the essence of that profession's work. In mental health, it is psychotherapy; in law, it's legal research and litigation; in teaching, it's planning and delivering lessons in the person's subject matter. Professionals find it distasteful to perform functions that fall outside this core. Those who recovered from burnout began their careers working in jobs where much of their time was consumed by such work. When they changed jobs, they were able to spend much less time on nonprofessional duties.

Jennifer Talmadge, for instance, was forced to spend much of her time attending meetings and doing paper work in her first job as a school social worker: "The thing that definitely got in my way was the . . . administrative stuff. I just didn't like that." In order to do more meaningful, professional work, such as counseling, Jennifer had to work longer hours, which made the job even more onerous. When Jennifer left the schools to start a feminist counseling collective, she was able to spend most of her time doing work that was appropriate for a mental health professional.[7]

The Boredom Factor: The Importance of Change

Let's assume that a professional has found the ideal job. The work is meaningful and challenging. The clients are cooperative and grateful. There is a minimum of nonprofessional duties. Is this enough to prevent burnout?

Even when the situation is close to ideal, the professional may become restless if there is no change over time. Work that is rewarding today may not be as rewarding in two years because the professional continues to grow and change. In fact, meaningful work is often a stimulus to professional growth. Professionals who have ideal jobs may be especially likely to outgrow those jobs after a period of time.

Lawyer Shana Phillips was an example of how a job could lose its appeal over time. When she went to law school, she wanted to work as a criminal lawyer on behalf of the disadvantaged. She was fortunate to find a job that offered her everything that she wanted. But after a while, that type of work lost its appeal: "After 3 years of doing criminal appeals, I felt that I had basically run the gamut. Criminal law is different from civil law in that it's just not as broad. I handled everything from burglaries to murders, and I just basically got tired of them. I needed more of a challenge."

Change could be a mixed blessing. Even though Gloria Bennett knew that she needed a change after more than a decade in nursing and she found law school stimulating, she also found it difficult to be back in the role of student. Could she handle the course work? Could she be as successful in law as she had been in nursing? How long would it take for her to feel secure again? These were difficult questions. But even though change was stressful, Gloria rarely doubted the wisdom of her decision. Boredom was far worse than the anxiety she felt about how well she would do on the next exam.

Special education teacher Carol Potter expressed the same ambivalence about change, but she had learned that change was an antidote to burnout. After she had worked as a resource room teacher for several years, she was transferred into a self-contained classroom—involuntarily. She fought the transfer, but lost. The first few months were stressful, but with the help of an experienced colleague, she successfully mastered the challenge.

Looking back on that experience, Carol realized that change was valuable, even though it had been difficult. She hadn't been feeling bored as a resource room teacher, but in retrospect she realized that she had begun to stagnate. She probably would have continued to tread water for a long time if she hadn't been forced to make a major change. Making that change was an impetus to growth. Without it, Carol's commitment and satisfaction might have declined.

Doing meaningful work is thus a key to professional satisfaction. But finding the "right job" isn't enough. Many of the professionals in my study discovered that the right job today was no longer right after a few years. Even if the job remained the same, they didn't. Without change, boredom and stagnation are always potential threats.[8]

Cultivating Special Interests in the Job

Even in their first year of practice, many professionals found that the normal, day-to-day work of their profession was not as meaningful as they had expected. Some of the professionals resigned themselves to the situation, and their enthusiasm and commitment gradually diminished. Others, however, discovered a way to make their work more intrinsically rewarding. They began to cultivate a special interest in the job.

The professionals who made the best recovery from burnout developed, from scratch, a unique project, program, or specialty. In cultivating a special interest, the professional was able to focus on a work-related area that was particularly stimulating and meaningful. These special interests were often an important source of status and prestige.

For high school teacher Eugenia Barton, a special interest was developing a student store for her students to operate. For school psychologist Mark Connor, it was a "counselor intern program" that he designed and implemented in his district. For clinical social worker Jennifer Talmadge, it was an alternative counseling center that she created with three friends.

The positive impact of special interests became apparent when the professionals were asked to identify the most satisfying aspects of their careers. They often responded by mentioning a special interest that they had cultivated.

For instance, when I asked Eugenia Barton, "What have been the greatest sources of satisfaction as you look back over your teaching career?" she answered, "Well, there are a couple of things. . . . Personally, I guess probably I'm pleased with what I've done in the area of union efforts. I've gotten heavily involved in union things, and there are some nice satisfactions over the years." Eugenia had become involved in union activity during her third year of teaching, and it had become a particularly rewarding special interest. She eventually rose to the presidency of a region that encompassed eleven school districts.

The power of special interests to generate enthusiasm and commitment was revealed especially clearly when I asked school psychologist Mark Connor, "How involved are you in your job at this point?" He thought for a minute and then said, "Well . . . it depends upon which aspect of my job you're talking about. If we're talking about my intern counseling program—I say 'my' program because I developed it—I'm very, very involved with that. I'm always looking at materials to give to my interns in terms of counseling. I'm looking for filmstrips; I'm always looking for training programs for them. I'm *very* involved with that program."[9]

What all of these special interests have in common is that they provide the professional with a unique, personal way to experiment, to create, and to take a break from the more mundane activities associated with the normal role. Cultivating a special interest allows the professional to carve out one area of the job that will be characterized by high levels of autonomy, challenge, responsibility, and meaning. It becomes a significant source of ego gratification, providing a way of making an impact, of leaving one's mark on the world in a more tangible and permanent way than do day-to-day interactions with clients. In some instances, cultivating a special interest seems to compensate for other, less rewarding aspects of the job that, over time, might well lead to burnout.

Cultivating a special interest serves a number of other functions as well. Most important, it enhances self-efficacy. It gives the professional a distinctive competency. Second, cultivating a special interest can help the professional to earn recognition and respect from peers. Competent performance in the professional role alone rarely leads to special recognition for professionals. But professionals can often achieve recognition for a unique specialization or program that they developed.

High school teacher Victoria Goble achieved professional recognition by developing two special curriculum projects. One involved the use of computers in the schools. The other was a new program designed to make math more interesting for non–college-bound students. She became especially animated during our interview when she described the recognition she received from these projects:

> I enjoy the outcomes of the projects tremendously. There's a satisfaction in those projects that is very different from the day-to-day satisfaction associated with teaching. . . . I recently came back from this two-day task force, with educators from all around the state, and while I was there they talked about the general math project that I have developed. And I heard how excited they are about it. Realizing that I had been the instigator and the designer of that project was a real high for me, a real high. I felt really good about that. That's another . . . that's one more level up. . . . So the satisfaction from those projects is tremendous, simply tremendous.

Few teachers are able to achieve state-wide recognition for their work in the classroom. But Victoria did achieve such recognition for one of the projects she developed, and she was still basking in the glow of it when I interviewed her.

One of the problems with routine work in many helping professions is that there is little tangible feedback when professionals perform well. Special interests, however, can provide more tangible feedback more often, and this is a third important psychological reward provided by special interests. In Victoria's case, for instance, receiving $150,000 in grant money from the school district for her project was a kind of tangible reward that she rarely found in the classroom: "I was really excited when the school district was willing to commit $150,000 and a new staff person to coordinate the infusion of computer technology into our curriculum."

Unique special interests also give professionals more autonomy and control—at least within that part of their work lives. Victoria Goble, for instance, had fewer constraints in developing her special projects than she had in the classroom. Special interests provide an opportunity to be in charge of something—to be the undisputed leader. In cultivating a special interest, in starting something from scratch, professionals are able to work things out their own way. Special interests become oases of autonomous functioning.

Special interests can also be a vehicle for broadening one's horizons. They can add variety to one's work. They can become an antidote for stagnation and boredom. Finally, special interests meet one other need that professionals have as they approach mid-career. Erik Erikson (1968) referred to it as the "generativity" need, the desire to give birth to something and nurture it and see it grow.

Special interests, therefore, help professionals to become enthusiastic again about their work. They are an important source of commitment and satisfaction, but some special interests are more satisfying and meaningful than others.

Making Special Interests Rewarding

Special interests don't always foster caring, commitment, and satisfaction. Some of the professionals became bored and dissatisfied even though they were involved in special interests. In analyzing the data on special interests, it became clear that certain ingredients are necessary for special interests to have a positive impact on career development.

First, cultivating a special interest seems to be most beneficial when the project or responsibility is new and unique, when the professional is able to "start it from scratch." Teacher Eugenia Barton, for instance, *created* the student store at her school—she didn't just take it over from someone else. And school psychologist Mark Connor *designed* the counselor internship program that became such an important source of fulfillment for him. As public health nurse Jessica Andrews put it, "What's really satisfying is starting things from scratch—doing things that *nobody's* ever done before. I like doing that."

Another ingredient that makes special interests more motivating is their scope. Some special interests are limited in scope—they involve a small part of the job and last for only a few months. At the other end of the continuum are the special interests that become a new, full-time job. The special interests that serve best are those that involve a significant part of the job for an extended period of time.

An example of a too-limited special interest was one described by nurse Gloria Bennett: "Several years back I developed a patient classification system which was used to predict staffing needs. And that was kind of the current trend at the time, for institutions to get into those things. And our hospital did not have one. And so I worked on that with one of the engineers in operations research. That later became my thesis. I enjoyed that."

Unfortunately, Gloria spent only about six months on this special project. It still stood out as one of the most satisfying experiences of her career, but when the project ended, Gloria had developed no other unique and rewarding special interests. Her frustration and boredom increased over the years, and she eventually left the field to enter law. Perhaps Gloria would have found nursing more satisfying if she could have developed a more sustained special interest to pursue.

Other professionals did develop special interests with greater scope. Clinical social worker Jennifer Talmadge's special interest, for example, was a new feminist counseling center. It became a full-time job, enabling her to escape from a stultifying experience as a school social worker. And, not surprisingly, she was one of the most satisfied and motivated professionals after more than a decade of experience.

But even the most rewarding special interest can become stale after a number of years. Professionals may eventually outgrow their special interests. Thus, a final ingredient that makes special interests motivating is change.

Clinical social worker Jennifer Talmadge provided a good example of the importance of change. For nine years she found it rewarding to work in her feminist counseling center, but eventually

Jennifer became restless. She felt she needed to move into something new. Fortunately, she did. She was eager to tell me about it during our interview:

"So this is probably my new direction, which is more toward working with groups and doing some work with women and aging. And this is pretty recent. I would say this summer I realized, 'Oh, I'm going to write a book.' And I have a title, and I see the book—I know what it's going to be about."

Jennifer chuckled and then continued.

So I'm in this process of writing this book. And I'm giving two workshops in September—one on aging, and the other on first-time grandmothers. I would not have known this was going to be my direction. But I'm definitely ready for a career transition. . . .

I think now, in particular, I like the way I'm contributing again, because I'm excited about this new focus in my own life. I could still do things my old way, but I'm bored with it. And now I'm excited about this—it's added a lot more to the way that I'm working with people. It makes it, again, interesting to me.

Jennifer's new interest in aging shows that professionals can develop special interests at any point in their careers. In fact, for professionals who have reached a plateau in their careers and are starting to stagnate, a new special interest can be rejuvenating. (The word "rejuvenate" literally means "to become young again.") Jennifer's work in a feminist counseling center sustained her for a decade, but then she needed to get into something new. Her special interest in aging and in becoming a grandmother enabled her to do that without changing careers. The alternative might have been mid-career burnout.

Getting Started

Whether the professionals developed their special interests in a planned way or just "fell into them," they had to take the initiative to make them sustained, rewarding activities. Their experiences offer many lessons for others who would like to do the same.

The most successful professionals cultivated special interests that met an organizational need. Eugenia Barton, for instance, noticed that a colleague was having trouble with one of his classes: "We had a retailing class that was just the pits. And another teacher taught it, and it was really not a successful situation, and he wanted out."

Eugenia seized this opportunity to develop her student store idea: "I said I would take the class if we could put together a student store of some kind to occupy those kids.... And we went to the school board and got permission, and we have run it ever since." In this case, Eugenia found it relatively easy to secure the support of her colleagues and the school board because her "pet" project was viewed as a solution to an irritating organizational problem.

School psychologist Mark Connor used a similar strategy in securing support for his own special interest—a counselor internship program. Mark had been looking for ways to make his job more stimulating. When a budget crunch led to the elimination of elementary school counselors in his district, he saw an opportunity to expand his role while meeting an organizational need:

"I wrote a proposal to the board of education last year, to start a counseling-intern program for the elementary schools. Because there's such a tight budget crunch, they would not hire certified elementary counselors. But I really felt the elementary schools need certified people. So I wrote a proposal to have these interns work in the schools, and I would supervise them."

Mark's proposal actually met two needs: it allowed the schools to continue to have counselors in the elementary schools at almost no cost, and it provided Mark with an opportunity to add a whole new dimension to his role.

Thus, one important principle for getting started is to find a way to mesh organizational needs and individual interests. The most successful professionals looked at what their organizations did, and they asked themselves, "What are this organization's goals, priorities, and current needs or problems?" Then they looked at their own competencies and interests. Their new project or specialization formed at that point where their personal interests and their organization's needs converged.

This same principle is valid for professionals who aren't employed by an organization. Public health nurse Angela McPherson, for instance, developed expertise in home-care planning while working at a visiting nurse's agency. As her reputation grew, other health care agencies in the community asked her for information. When Angela became dissatisfied and decided to leave the agency where she was employed, she realized that there was a need for the kind of expertise she had developed. As she succinctly put it, "I saw a market there for information. So I decided that I would . . . start a consulting business to help people do program development." Within two years Angela had established an economically viable consulting business. She found a way to integrate organizational needs with her own occupational skills and interests.

Even when the professionals propose doing something that meets an organization's needs, they don't always find enough support to launch their special interests. Thus, professionals often need to take the initiative and negotiate for organizational support. Even when they're successful in establishing their special interests, they need to make sure that key decision-makers appreciate their efforts. Mark Connor illustrated this principle. After he had conducted his counselor internship program for a year, he undertook an evaluation of it. "I sent out a survey to parents, teachers, students, and principals. And I got the survey back, and it was really very positive."

Mark's survey helped secure the board's support for another year. It also enabled him to expand that support: "So the Board approved the program for the next year. And I requested that my interns receive a stipend. The Board agreed to the stipend. Plus, my supervisor asked the Board to hire a new part-time psychologist to take some of my duties—to do testing in the schools while I do supervision. And they agreed to that."

Without the survey's positive results, it might have been difficult for Mark to expand his program, and eventually he might have seen the program disappear. Special interests need organizational support, and professionals need to make sure that the support doesn't wither over time.

Conclusion

Some professionals cultivated special interests more readily than others. But any professional can do so. The "recipe" is one that anyone can employ; however, not all organizational settings are equally receptive. Organizations vary in how hospitable they are to the development of special interests, and it is difficult for even the most creative and savvy professionals to develop special interests without a certain amount of autonomy and support.

The work setting influences more than just the ease with which professionals can cultivate special interests. There are many ways in which the work setting encourages or inhibits professional caring, commitment, and satisfaction. The next chapter explores the role of the organizational setting in recovery from early career burnout.

11

Antidotes to Burnout
Finding Greater Professional Autonomy and Support

Meaningful work helps professionals remain dedicated. But it's difficult to make one's work meaningful in a setting that doesn't provide sufficient autonomy. As public health nurse Jessica Andrews put it, "The most satisfying work experience for me clearly is the opportunity to try to work problems out my own way.... I don't want to seem like a controlling person, but I like the chance to be in control. I think most professionals do."

Psychologist Mark Connor expressed the same sentiments. I asked him, "What are the things that affect job satisfaction most for you?" He immediately answered, "Feeling a sense of power in making decisions about what I do ... being able to have freedom of choice over what I do during the day, not having a boss over me on a daily basis." For both Mark and Jessica, autonomy emerged as one of the most important requirements for fulfillment at work.

The most satisfied and committed professionals had enjoyed a high degree of autonomy in their work environments. They were allowed to chart their own courses. This autonomy allowed professionals to design their jobs in ways that provided ample opportunity to utilize valued professional skills and do interesting work. Greater autonomy also gave the professionals more opportunities to cultivate special interests in their work, but not everyone in my study was so fortunate.

Bureaucratic Hassles and Organizational Politics

The professionals who eventually left public service most often cited "bureaucratic hassles" as the primary reason. The longer they practiced, the more they chafed under excessive red tape and interference from others.

In describing why she left public service to become a real estate agent, Karla Adams emphasized the red tape and lack of autonomy. She had been a social worker employed in a large, state institution for mentally disabled individuals:

"The main reason for my leaving and switching careers was just a total dissatisfaction with the mental health system, and civil service, and the bureaucracy. I got so frustrated with batting my head against a wall, and nothing really happening."

Bureaucracies seem to be rife with conflict, and this conflict—political in-fighting, jealous battles over turf, and other forms of bureaucratic warfare—took its toll over time. Several of the professionals became disgusted with what they derisively referred to as "politics." Public health nurse Sarah Prentiss was one of those who became disillusioned with the politics she saw. "I saw," Sarah told me, "the reality of all the channels, and the roadblocks and the . . . personality conflicts. A new idea might come from a certain individual, and for some reason it wasn't accepted; and then this other person comes along with the same idea, and it's accepted, and it's implemented. . . . And then you'd hear about some ridiculous political battle between these two people, and that's why the change didn't occur. I mean, it just seemed ridiculous to me. We know that that happens in every branch of our government. But I guess I just thought it was immature. And it was. . . ."

Sarah Prentiss thought that politics got in the way at her agency because it was a "government" agency, but attorney Jesse Michaels had similar complaints about his job in an insurance company. When I asked him, "What have been the biggest sources of stress and dissatisfaction?" he answered, "I suppose it's been, in terms of dissatisfaction, it's been the political goings-on. . . ." Jesse described a recent incident in which he had to spend several days gathering information just to defend his boss from criticism that had come from the senior vice-president for sales. "And to me," Jesse complained, "this is just political work. It's not going to sell one more insurance policy, it's not going to sell one more contract. All it's going to do is take up three days of our time to justify what we've done in the last year. And my *boss* doesn't want to do it, and *I* don't want to have to do it. But we *have* to do it. The guy says, 'Do it,' and we gotta do it. It's just a waste of time."

As political and economic support for the human services dwindled during the eighties, organizational conflicts and pressures became more intense. Gloria Bennett eventually decided to leave nursing and become an attorney because of these pressures. She described how budget cuts and layoffs had adversely affected the organizational climate in the last hospital where she worked: "We're having some very difficult times here now. Very, very difficult, because we've gone through our first set, ever, of layoffs.... That's been very painful.... Because of that, what has become more obvious is the bureaucracy at its worst. It's a civil service system, nurses are unionized, and that has taken the layoff situation and just made it ten times worse."

Of all the conflicts that professionals had to face, those associated with labor-management relations tended to be among the most frustrating. The professionals I studied often felt caught in the middle in these disputes. One of the former high school teachers, Merton Douglas, said that the high level of conflict and animosity between the teacher's union and school administration was a major source of stress for him. During the follow-up interview, he described one particularly bitter strike that had occurred seven years earlier:

I'll never forget. We were on strike one year in Perkinsville, and it was a miserable strike. We went on strike in March, and six weeks later, we're still on strike. It became very evident that the school board was just going to wait us out. So we went back to work, right where we left it, still working under the contract from last year. That move did nothing for us, other than extend the school year. The school board said, "Well, you guys were on strike for six weeks, so we're going to extend classes the final week of school. You'll have to teach a full day Wednesday and Thursday, not a half day, and then you'll have half a day of teaching on Friday as well. Finish your finals then, and grade them in the afternoon.

Your records still have to be in by 5 o'clock. Now you know that going in, so do what you need to do to get your grades done."

Oh my God, big furor: The union guys were all coming around saying, "You can't turn those grades in. You gotta turn 'em in Monday." "Why?" I said to the union guy. "My grades are done. I use a computer-scored final exam. I have everything else all done by that time. All I have to do is run the cards through the thing after the exam. I have it done before the kids are off the school bus."

But the union guy said, "Man, I don't care, you can't turn them in. Because, by God, if you turn those grades in by 5 that last day, we'll never get the old system we had back in the contract, we'll never get those two half-days and that full records day."

Merton paused for a moment. Then he sat back in his chair and said, "That's another one of those things about teaching that is nothing more than a sweet memory now. The union hassles and all that kind of stuff. . . ."

In effect, this former teacher had to deal with two organizations: the school system and the teacher's union. Each made demands on him. Each attempted to limit his autonomy. Combined, they made for a situation in which Merton felt constrained at every turn.[1]

The Role of Autonomy in Recovery from Burnout

The professionals who recovered from early career burnout, like those who never succumbed to it, managed to avoid demoralizing bureaucratic obstacles and organizational politics. In most cases, they had to change jobs, but eventually they found work settings in which they had a high degree of autonomy.

Mark Connor, for instance, described his first job as "more of a dictatorship," and he said that he "felt powerless." When he quit and took a job as a psychologist in another school system, the situation changed dramatically. "In my new district," Mark noted, "we always had input. The director always made the final decision, but we gave him input, and many times he modified his decisions. So, I felt that we had some power, and we still do have power in this district." But not only did Mark have more "input," he also had a great deal of autonomy in his own job. "What's nice is the school district allows me to do basically what I want to do."

Overload is a frequent complaint of professionals who work in organizational settings—too much work to do and not enough time in which to do it. Mark discovered that greater autonomy helped to reduce the work pressure that had been such a problem in his first job: "See, I pick and choose now. If I'm feeling like I'm overloaded, I don't have to see anyone. When I do see students, I can see them on a short-term basis, and I may see them for only half an hour, or 20 minutes. . . . So I don't feel pressured at all now."[2]

High school teacher Eugenia Barton, another subject who recovered from early career burnout, also talked about how important professional autonomy was. In discussing what she liked most about teaching, she said, "I like the independence. We can mumble and complain about principals and superintendents and all sorts of boards of education. But when you close that door to your room, you really are independent. I've never once had a principal ask me even the content of a class I taught. It's a very independent situation. And I like that."

An increase in professional autonomy was also decisive for public health nurse Angela McPherson. As a nursing supervisor, she found it difficult to work through her subordinates rather than do the nursing work herself. Supervision, while it increased her formal authority, actually seemed to reduce her professional autonomy. She was more dependent on others than she had been when she was a staff nurse. Fortunately, Angela didn't remain in her first supervisory position too long. After just three years, she took a central office staff job that gave her much more autonomy. She spent most of her time working alone on special projects. Then, when she finally went out on her own and became a health care planning consultant, Angela's professional autonomy increased still further.

In fact, all of the professionals who recovered from early career burnout found themselves in work settings where they enjoyed a high degree of autonomy within a few years after beginning their careers. And this autonomy seemed to be a critical factor in their recovery.

A Supportive Work Setting

Even seasoned professionals need a certain amount of support along with autonomy. They need to feel that the organization for which they work values and appreciates their contribution. They need both tangible and emotional support to sustain a high level of commitment and caring. The professionals who recovered from early career burnout didn't have that support initially, but they found it before they became so burned out that they left the field.

Trust and Confidence of the Boss

A professional's superiors are especially important in determining how supportive the work setting feels. The issue of trust seems to be especially critical. Some professionals enjoyed particularly high levels of trust and confidence from their superiors. Others were not so lucky. Those who lacked their boss's support usually did not lose their jobs, but they suffered a great deal.

Nursing administrator Rebecca Simpson was a professional who didn't have the trust and respect of her boss, and she described how disruptive it had been for her. Rebecca had worked her way up to a high level position in a large public health agency, but then something happened that soured the relationship between Rebecca and her supervisor, the director of nursing. This is how Rebecca described the impact this situation had on her:

> I think ... part of the effect it had on me was losing some initiative and creativity. I would try to solve a problem, and I would come up with new, maybe innovative or creative solutions, and then they weren't well received. And I really felt like I did lose a lot of creativity and initiative after a while, and I started not feeling very good about myself, which I think, probably sometimes came across in my work.... I would have liked to have avoided the whole mess because that was not good for me, as far as my confidence goes, and self-image, and everything.

Public health nurse Jessica Andrews, in contrast, had a particularly good relationship with her boss, and this was an important source of support for her during the first decade of her career. Jessica was one of the few professionals who avoided early career burnout and sustained her dedication into the next decade. During all that time, she worked for a person who seemed to have a great deal of respect for her ability and who communicated that respect in a variety of ways.

Jessica had "grown up" in the public health agency where she worked, and she was commonly regarded as the nursing director's protégé. Jessica noted that they were "very much alike in terms of style." She also mentioned that, at one point, her boss took her out to lunch and said to her, "You are the person I am most comfortable with." After telling me this, Jessica smiled and added, "My boss thinks I'm wonderful. And that is a wonderful support system to have."

Having the boss's trust could translate into political support. Jessica described another incident that conveyed how important it was to have her boss's backing. She had "locked horns" with the local sheriff over the way in which nurses were treated at the jail. Without hesitation, her boss supported her. "I got to my boss immediately and said, 'This is what happened, and if you want to reprimand me, go right ahead, but he deserves one back. He was out of bounds.' And I was supported. In fact, my boss went in to talk to the sheriff and got him to agree he was wrong to do that. And he has not done it since."

Many factors affect the quality of the relationship between professionals and their superiors. From the superior's point of view, it depends primarily on the subordinate's performance. The subordinate, on the other hand, is likely to attribute any problems to the boss's unrealistic expectations or prejudices. To a third party, the problem often seems to be a poor fit between the two—the "chemistry" is just not right.[3]

External factors are also important. As I noted in chapter 2, public support for the human services has always been ambivalent at best, and support has deteriorated even further during the last 15 years. This dwindling support has meant that administrators themselves have experienced considerable stress. Their stress has been as great, if not greater, than the stress of their subordinates. Stressed-out administrators often find it difficult to trust and support their subordinates.

On the other hand, administrators do differ in the way they treat their staffs. Even in a stressful environment where the costs of failure are high, some administrators are more willing than others to trust their subordinates to behave responsibly.[4] Professionals who work under these kinds of people will enjoy more support and confidence and thus will be less likely to burn out. Stress levels may be high, but the trusting relationship between boss and professional will enable them to work together effectively to cope with whatever problems confront them.[5]

The Importance of Recognition and Feedback

Many administrators assume that veteran professionals no longer need positive feedback and recognition to remain motivated. But meaningful signs of praise and recognition did seem to be important for these professionals, even after more than a decade of practice. The professionals seemed to become even more dedicated and caring in their work when they received special recognition for their efforts.

A notable example was high school teacher Victoria Goble. She received special recognition for two of the special curriculum projects that she had initiated. The first recognition came when she was awarded grants for the projects. She then received even more recognition when her curriculum work was identified as exemplary by the state office of education. As she put it, that kind of recognition was "a real high," and the satisfaction associated with it was "simply tremendous." It was rare for the professionals in my study to receive this kind of formal recognition for their efforts.[6]

Active Interest of the Boss

It's easy to see how stressful a critical and demanding boss can be for a professional, and how valuable it is to have a boss who has trust in one's abilities. But administrative support often involves more than just confidence that the professional can do the job. Professionals also want their bosses to take an active interest in their work.

Special education teacher Carol Potter, who had made a good recovery from burnout, had some positive things to say about her current principal's active interest in her work: "He is very, very interested in learning more about special education. He's at all the meetings, he is excellent dealing with the parents . . . dealings with parents can be real sticky, very emotional, and he's very supportive and good dealing with them. I feel he's real helpful. I feel like I've learned a lot, working with him."

Professionals thus want a boss who is able and willing to remove barriers that they encounter. They want a supervisor who is skillful enough to offer technical support and who provides a model from whom they can learn.

There is another important way in which administrators provided support to some of the professionals. Organizations can become dysfunctional for various reasons, and when they do, those who work in them experience high levels of stress. When administrators act to prevent and alleviate organizational dysfunction, they provide support in another important way.

Mark Connor's boss, for instance, brought in outside consultants to help make the work setting a healthy and supportive one. This is how Mark described it: "When I started working here, I discovered that they had meetings with outside consultants periodically to improve staff relationships, improve communication skills, and to work things out with each other. They met with us each month. Our supervisor would attend also."

Mark's boss recognized that communication problems and conflict could make the work environment difficult, and so he took steps to prevent these problems from getting out of hand. In doing so, he was helping to ensure that the work setting remained a supportive one.

In order for administrators to support their staffs, they must be effective advocates with *their* superiors. Mark's director seems to have been strong in this dimension of administrative leadership as well. I had commented on how unusual it was for a school district to pay for outside consultants to come in and work on issues such as staff communication. I wondered whether this reflected on the director's ability to secure political support within the system. Mark readily agreed that it did: "He was very strong politically. He knew when to put his cards in and when not to put his cards in. He was very savvy, *very* savvy. . . . He knew what he was doing."

Mark's experience shows how humanistic attitudes on the part of administrators aren't always enough to provide professionals with the kind of support that nurtures caring and commitment.

Administrators must also be effective advocates within the system to secure support for their humanistic policies and programs.

Work and Family Issues: The Need for Flexibility

With increased pressures created by dual career families, professionals need support and flexibility in dealing with conflicts between work demands and family responsibilities. The professionals who resisted burnout or made the best recovery from it were more fortunate than others in finding this type of administrative support. High school teacher Victoria Goble, for instance, enjoyed an unusual degree of understanding and support for her special needs as a working parent.

When Victoria became pregnant after teaching for three years, she resigned, planning to stay at home with her child for the next several years. But her child was born severely handicapped, and after caring for him for 14 months, Victoria felt that, for the child's sake as well as hers, she had to return to work—but only on a part-time basis. The administration at her old school allowed her to do so, even though they had not promised her any kind of job when she resigned. For the next five years she increased or decreased her part-time involvement, depending on the health status of her child. The administration continued to be responsive to her needs. This kind of flexibility and sensitivity to the needs of a working parent represented an important form of administrative support.

Organizational Support for Continued Learning

Knowledgeable supervisors are an important source of learning and professional development, but ultimately there is a limit to how much one can learn from this source. The professionals who stood out as most dedicated and satisfied after more than a decade of practice had also benefited from more formal training that occurred after their careers had begun.

Sarason (1988) has observed that "human service settings ... justify their existence by what they do for 'others,' not what these settings do for the development of their own staffs. Because the conditions for their own development are minimal or absent, the quality of their services is mammothly diluted" (p. 376). In other words, there is a link between professional development and professional caring. Professionals who are encouraged to grow and learn are more likely to be caring and committed.

The most committed and satisfied professionals in my study were strongly encouraged to receive additional training by the organizations for which they worked. This was another important form of administrative support.

Clinical social worker Diane Peterson worked in an agency that provided unusually strong support for continued learning. This agency specialized in treating recovering alcoholics. Diane had taken a course in alcoholism in graduate school, but she hadn't had much experience working with alcoholics during her clinical training. Her boss recognized this when she was hired: he told her that they didn't expect her to know what she needed in order to start working with clients. They would help her to learn it.

During the first two months, Diane saw no clients on her own. She spent all of her time observing more experienced staff people during their counseling sessions, attending seminars and workshops offered around the state, visiting other alcohol treatment programs, and reading. As she felt more knowledgeable and confident, her responsibilities increased.

Even when Diane became more skilled, the training opportunities continued: "The first few years, there were a lot of opportunities for training. On the average of one week a month, we could receive our salary and go some place or another for training." In addition to the frequent training workshops and seminars off-site, Diane and her colleagues were able to meet once a week to go over cases with a psychiatrist or psychologist hired by the agency.

Given this strong support for continuing professional education, it's not surprising that Diane was one of the few professionals who maintained her enthusiasm and dedication throughout the first year of her career. And she still was unusually committed over a decade later.[7]

Stimulating and Congenial Colleagues

Professionals develop unique perspectives on their work—perspectives that are *only* shared by professional colleagues. It's difficult for those not part of the profession to understand what "it's really like." Thus, a professional's colleagues are particularly important in determining the quality of life at work. The professionals who were most successful in sustaining their commitment and dedication had worked with particularly stimulating and supportive colleagues.

Clinical social worker Diane Peterson was fortunate to find strong collegial support in her very first job, and this factor helped her to avoid early career burnout and to sustain her enthusiasm for the next decade: "People said that in the field of addiction, one can burn out in two years. But that agency, I think for many of us, became a home. The counseling staff was just incredibly supportive of each other. . . . If someone said, 'Gee, I'm working too many nights. Would somebody else do the lecture for me on Thursday?' we had three volunteers out of four staff. I felt that in many ways that was my family. I got more support from them than I did from my sister or from my parents." Diane apparently wasn't the only person on the staff who felt this way; when she finally left after working there for 10 years, she had less seniority than any other staff person.

Reform lawyer Jean Chalmers also enjoyed an unusually supportive social climate in the agency where she worked. In the initial study, she described everyone as "very friendly" and "like a family," frequently getting together outside of work. There was a spirit of cooperative support. People took the time to help each other frequently. Not only did this collaborative atmosphere make life more pleasant, it also enabled Jean to learn from more experienced practitioners.

Colleagues were not only a source of emotional support, they also provided technical guidance. Professionals need guidance throughout their careers to help them learn, grow, and function more effectively. Those who received coaching and mentoring during the first decade of their careers were more successful in sustaining—or regaining—the high levels of caring and commitment that they had from the beginning. Colleagues were an important source of this mentoring for some of the professionals.

Guidance from colleagues was especially important during the first year or two of the career. The professionals who avoided early career burnout received helpful advice, information, and feedback from older colleagues. High school teacher Victoria Goble was one of the few professionals who did not show signs of burnout during the first year of her career, and one factor that helped her to make a positive adjustment was the unusually high degree of help she received from a colleague. Her first teaching job was in the same school where she had done her student teaching, and she had had a particularly positive relationship with a skillful and inspired "critic teacher." Victoria's former critic teacher continued to give her invaluable guidance during the first year of teaching as Victoria honed her teaching skills.

Guidance from competent colleagues was important for more experienced professionals as well. In fact, whenever the professionals made a major role transition, there was a need for guidance. Special education teacher Carol Potter provided a good example. Carol had been a resource teacher for several years, and then she was abruptly transferred to a job working in a self-contained classroom. It was an unwanted change for which she was totally unprepared. The experience ultimately proved to be a positive one, primarily because Carol was able to find a supportive colleague who became her coach and mentor: "I got a lot of support from one of the staff members who'd become a real good friend of mine. . . . She gave me a lot of ideas for organizing the classroom, and that set me up in terms of having tangible things and ideas of how to deal with certain behavior problems."

When I asked Carol if she had ever had a mentor, she referred to this colleague who helped her during that difficult year. "I don't think that she would even have any idea that I would mention her as a mentor, but she certainly is, for me. And I think probably for a lot of other people, because she just has had a lot of experience and is very good at what she does." Coaching and guidance from a knowledgeable colleague thus proved to be invaluable for Carol Potter, one of the professionals who was able to recover from early career burnout and achieve unusually high levels of commitment and caring in her work.[8]

Thus for the professionals who recovered from early career burnout, support from their colleagues seemed to be another important factor. Colleagues were a source of validation and encouragement. They were also a source of more tangible aid. There was a feeling of giving and getting. The professionals felt they were not just part of a "team"—an over-used word in the work place today. There was a genuine sense of community.[9]

The Special Situation of Minority Professionals

For professionals from minority groups, finding supportive work settings can be especially problematic. Jesse Michaels was an

African-American attorney who became more aware of the dynamics involved, when, after working in white-dominated settings for several years, he took a job in a company run by a black man. In our interview, I asked Jesse if race had been a problem at other places where he had worked. He answered,

> It wasn't a problem, but ... I guess I'd been the first and only for so long that I'd gotten used to it at that point. It wasn't a problem for me. But the fact that the chairman of the board was black sort of was a plus in my eyes. There's something different about that. It's like, well, you can go to the high school and be a student there, or you can go and be a student *and* be really a part of the school, be involved in the social affairs and be a leader in school politics and be an integral part of the environment there. And that's how I felt with the chairman of the board being black. I really felt that it would be a different environment for me. As it turned out, it has been. How much of that is due to the fact that he's black, I don't know. But I can tell you this. At the other company where I worked I'd get on an elevator, and people would not even bother to look at me. Knowing there were no blacks in power there, they would assume that I couldn't be anyone important, obviously. But here, the chairman is black, and ... in the elevator they look at me to make sure I'm not the chairman, I guess!
>
> Jesse chuckled and then continued, "So that does make a difference. It does change perspective quite a bit."

Jesse's current work setting also felt more supportive because there were more blacks in professional positions. "At this point, where I am now, there certainly are more black males in professional positions whom I interact with on a daily and weekly basis than I did at my previous job."

For female professionals, too, the gender composition of the work place could make a difference in perceived support. Attorney Jean Chalmers worked in an office where three of the five lawyers were women. Jean felt that because of this favorable male/female ratio, there was none of the hostility or condescension toward women that one might find in male-dominated work settings. Back

Table 11.1—Dimensions of Autonomy and Support

1. Autonomy—Freedom from

- Red tape—the civil service system—"Things take a long time to change."
- The need to document actions in order to cover oneself.
- Lack of status—"We were just go-fers."
- Politics—conflicts over turf or between different groups within the system.
- Nonprofessionals who question one's professional judgment.
- Role conflicts—being caught between concerns of different groups.
- Labor-management conflicts.

2. Administrative support

- Concern about the professional's needs.
- Resources necessary to do the job well.
- Sensitivity and flexibility around work-family issues.
- Professional receives special recognition.
- Sensitivity in giving negative feedback.
- Boss has trust and confidence in the professional and clearly communicates it.
- Boss takes an active interest in the professional's work.
- Boss advocates on professional's behalf and is effective in this role.
- Boss clearly communicates expectations.
- Boss matches the job assignments to the professional's ability level.
- Boss is emotionally stable—calm, good sense of humor.
- Boss asks professional for input—opinions, ideas.
- Boss is knowledgeable and provides technical assistance when needed.
- Boss is available when needed.
- Boss acts to prevent and, when necessary, deal with organizational pathology and dysfunction.
- Boss is open and honest.
- Encouragement and support for additional training.

3. Stimulating and congenial colleagues

- Emotional support
- Intellectual stimulation
- Mentoring

in the mid-seventies when Jean began her career, such a situation for women lawyers was rare. It was another way in which Jean's work situation was supportive.

Conclusion: Autonomy *and* Support

In recovering from burnout, the work setting was as important as the content of the work. The professionals who made the best recovery didn't necessarily begin their careers in supportive work settings, but within the first two or three years they had moved into work settings that provided them with a blend of autonomy and support. *Autonomy and support* sum up well the kind of situation that is most conducive to positive career adjustment in professionals.[10]

In studying the comments of these professionals, however, it's clear that autonomy and support refer to a number of more specific facets of the work environment. Table 11.1 summarizes the aspects that the professionals mentioned—aspects that combined to provide autonomy and support.

The many different factors we've considered also seem to be related to the theme of professional self-efficacy. In order to feel efficacious in their work, even seasoned veterans sometimes need help; they need technical assistance and tangible resources; they need their bosses' trust and confidence; and they also need sufficient autonomy to be able to use their knowledge and skills effectively. When professionals are able to work in settings where there is a high degree of both autonomy and support, they feel more efficacious. It is in such settings that one finds professional commitment and compassion.

12

Antidotes to Burnout
What the Individual Brings to the Work

In the previous chapter, I discussed aspects of the work setting that helped a few professionals recover from early career burnout. But what about the individuals themselves? Did they bring certain personal qualities to their careers that helped them to cope and recover? And what experiences earlier in their lives helped them to develop these qualities?

Challenging Experiences Prior to Entering the Profession

The professionals who made particularly good recoveries from burnout—or who resisted it from the beginning—seemed to have greater resilience. When they encountered stress and disappointment, they assumed a more active stance. Rather than give up or give in, they sought ways of overcoming their difficulties. When they did all they could to make the situation better, and still found it unrewarding, they changed jobs.

Traditional psychological theory would seek explanations in the early childhoods of these individuals. The foundation of character is formed during the first few years of life, so it seems reasonable to assume that this resilience was developed at the same time. While there may be some truth to this explanation, I wanted to see if there were other sources of individual coping effectiveness. I believed that later experiences might also contribute to a professional's ability to deal with stress and frustration.

In studying the lives of these professionals, I found that I didn't need to go all the way back to early childhood to find a way in which some professionals developed greater personal resilience. I discovered that the professionals who made the best recovery had had special kinds of experiences during their early adult years. They did not go directly into their fields. They had worked in other fields before returning to school for their professional training, or they had taken time off to raise two or more children before completing their training. And they had been successful in meeting the challenges posed by these "pre-career" experiences.

Mark Connor, for instance, had taught in an inner-city school for three years before returning to graduate school for a degree in psychology. He vividly described the challenges that he faced as a teacher: "I was trying to figure out, 'How am I going to beat this draft thing?' And I knew teaching was one route. So I went into teaching and ended up teaching elementary. In Detroit. With no experience in elementary, and no courses. I didn't have any courses at all. Well, my first year I was thinking, 'Maybe I should join the service.' It was so hard. I was thinking, 'Maybe I'll go to Vietnam. This is like Vietnam!' It was real hard my first year. My second and third year were great because I coped, finally, and learned how to handle the kids. I learned what to do. I learned how to teach."

Carol Potter also had been involved in challenging work experiences before entering teaching. She had traveled all over the country for a period of five years, living in different regions and working a variety of jobs before returning to school to obtain her teaching credentials. In Carol's case, her previous work experience was challenging in the amount of novelty, diversity, and change with which she had to cope: "I had done a lot of other things before going into teaching. I worked in a bank, and from that I went to work at the Renaissance Fair—I had done that in California. And I also had worked in Oklahoma in an alcoholism center. I was an administrative assistant there. So I'd done some business kinds of things. . . . I guess I was feeling my oats, and sort of traveling around, doing different things. . . . I was just kind of exploring."

Carol had also worked as an aide in a special education classroom before returning to school for her teaching credential. This experience gave her a good idea of what teaching would actually be like, and it helped her to crystallize her career choice.

The other three professionals who made good recoveries from burnout had also been involved in challenging occupations before entering their present professions. Angela McPherson had worked as a public health nurse for several years before returning to school to earn a master's and enter nursing administration. And Eugenia Barton and Jennifer Talmadge had successfully raised several children—also a challenging work experience.

Challenging experiences seemed to help professionals recover from burnout in several ways. The first has to do with goals and expectations: challenging experiences in the "real world" helped future professionals develop more realistic expectations. Poverty lawyer Jean Chalmers, for instance—one of the few professionals who didn't burn out during the first year of practice—came to her work with more realistic expectations and more modest goals because of her previous work experiences. After graduating from college, Jean worked in VISTA, the domestic version of the Peace Corps. She spent a year working with the poor in an inner-city neighborhood, and it was here that her interest in law as a career began to form. When Jean completed her stint in VISTA, she went to law school, and while there she worked in the school's "urban law clinic." This noncredit program gave students experience in handling real cases and working with low-income clients.

Working in VISTA and at the urban law clinic helped Jean to develop more realistic expectations about what her clients would be like when she became a poverty lawyer. She knew well what their limitations were, that it was unrealistic to expect them to be virtuous or appreciative just because they were victims of poverty and injustice. She had fewer illusions than did the other poverty lawyers. Jean's previous experiences also helped her to begin her work with a more realistic time perspective. She realized that change in the legal system usually occurs through compromise—and at a slow pace.

Margaret Williams, another poverty lawyer with an activist bent, brought a very different set of experiences and expectations to the job. Margaret had gone right from a prestigious college to a prestigious law school. She was committed to serving the poor, but she had never had any contact with them before her first week at legal aid. When she suddenly found herself working in a neighborhood legal aid office in the middle of the inner city, she suffered a bad case of "reality shock." She was not prepared for the difficulties she encountered in working with the poor.

The professionals who had already worked in a variety of roles also benefited because they had explored other options. This was how teacher Carol Potter thought about it: "I've often thought that it's really, for me, been a real advantage that I didn't go directly into teaching, because I think had I done that, I would have needed to have gone out and done some other things.... You were asking would I want to think about a field outside of education. And I think at this point, no, because I've tried some other things, and I just think that this is where I want to stay." Carol already knew about alternatives to teaching. Unlike many of her colleagues, who wondered whether they might be happier working in the business world, Carol had already done so. This previous experience had convinced her that she would be happier in teaching than in business.

But perhaps the most important benefit conferred by challenging work experiences prior to becoming a helping professional was that they enhanced the person's feelings of self-efficacy. This self-efficacy was a valuable resource that helped the individual better cope with the trials and tribulations encountered during the first year of professional work. For instance, Mark Connor had successfully overcome the stresses associated with being a white teacher in a predominantly black, inner-city school; there were few subsequent professional challenges that would equal that one. He had demonstrated to himself that he could go into an extremely difficult situation, and not only survive, but excel. A professional like Eugenia Barton, who had raised three children, had also successfully handled numerous crises and problems. Her many "small victories" as a parent left her with a more secure feeling about her abilities to cope with difficulties she encountered in her professional role.

Because they had had positive work experiences earlier, the more successful professionals were less likely to doubt themselves when they experienced burnout early in their careers. They had the confidence necessary to persevere in the face of adversity—or to make potentially risky job changes. Thus, for a number of reasons, challenging work experience prior to entering a profession seemed to help new professionals ultimately make a more positive adjustment and to remain in public service.[1]

Developing Career Insight Early in the Career

The professionals who made better recoveries were also more realistic about their strengths, weaknesses, and preferences. They had developed a clear and accurate idea of what they liked to do best and what they could do best, and they used this insight to make better career decisions.

As I noted in chapter 7, virtually all of the professionals developed greater career insight over time, but the professionals who made the best recovery developed it sooner. Within the first two or three years of their careers, they had formed a much clearer and more accurate sense of what they most liked to do, what they did best, and what it all meant in terms of the ideal work situation.

Jennifer Talmadge was one of those professionals who quickly came to identify what kind of work she most liked to do. It took her only one year working as a school social worker: "I took a full-time job with the school system and started discovering what I really liked about what I was doing. I enjoyed working with groups at that time and particularly enjoyed working with the girls' groups. . . . I just found that was pretty much fun."

In the follow-up interview, Jennifer expressed how important she thought it was for professionals to find what they liked best to do, and then do it: "I think you should find what is important to you and where you can then make your best contribution. . . . Once you find that you have a specific bent toward something, you probably should do it. I think there are a lot of people in this field who only go into a certain area because it's a money-making area. For instance, they might go into gerontology because there's money for gerontology. And they don't even like to work with old people."

Even though Jennifer discovered her "true calling" early in her career, she periodically tested it out. After she had been practicing for about eight years, for instance, she began to wonder whether it would be rewarding to change careers and go into sales. So she decided to try it on a very limited basis: "There was a newspaper that was selling around town that I liked, and I thought, 'I'm going to try to get ads for this newspaper.' And I did. I actually did that on my spare time. I went around to all the different stores and approached them. And what I realized was, I hated it. But it was kind of fun trying it."

Jennifer developed considerable career insight early in her career. She recognized what she most liked doing, and she changed jobs in order to do it. She continued to explore other possibilities, just to make sure that the choice she had made still made sense. Jennifer's career insight helped her recover from early career burnout.

Greater Organizational Negotiation Skill

The more successful professionals also had "organizational negotiation skill." They had learned effective ways to approach organizational conflicts and "hassles." They were able to view such "systems" problems in a more sophisticated, analytical way. They were adept at avoiding or resolving stressful interpersonal conflicts, overcoming bureaucratic constraints, and securing support for innovative and meaningful new projects. Greater organizational negotiation skill helped professionals remain committed and satisfied in their work.[2]

Some Examples of Organizational Negotiation Skill

Teacher Victoria Goble provided a particularly good example of how organizational negotiation skill can help professionals feel more positive about their work. Victoria had become concerned about how little her school system did for the less able, non–college-bound student. She eventually initiated several efforts to improve curriculum offerings and teaching strategies for this group, including a $150,000 program designed to introduce less able students to computers. She found her work on developing these new programs to be an especially rewarding part of her job.

Although Victoria was fortunate to have a supportive administration, it was clear that her success also depended on her initiative and skill in dealing with interpersonal and organizational dynamics. In fact, she did encounter considerable resistance along the way, but she learned how to overcome much of it.

An excerpt from the interview was revealing: "I've been involved in so many projects that require change on the part of a large group of people. And one of the things that's happened is I've taken a much harder look at change and why people change. And I think I have a much broader awareness of the kinds of things that make change more comfortable for people, the kinds of things that make change uncomfortable, the kinds of reasons that people are willing to make changes for, the kinds of things you can do to support people while they're making changes." By reflecting on why some people resisted her change efforts, Victoria gradually learned skills that helped her to succeed in reforming the curriculum.

But it was not just "skill" that enabled Victoria to overcome resistance to change. Equally important was her confidence in her own ability to bring about such changes—her "organizational self-efficacy." "I've pretty much taken the point of view that when changes need to be made, they need to be made, and you need to find ways to make that change happen. And it may take a little longer than you anticipated, but if it needs to happen, it needs to happen, and you keep working and finding ways to make it happen until it does."

Implicit in what Victoria said is the belief that change is possible and that she can "make it happen" if she "keeps working at it." This belief is what I mean by organizational self-efficacy, which both contributes to the development of organizational negotiation skill and also increases as one acquires greater organizational negotiation skill. Victoria was not immune from frustration and discouragement, but she was able to persist because her organizational negotiation skill enabled her to succeed in making many of the changes she wanted.

A second example also involved a professional working in the public schools, but as a psychologist rather than as a teacher. Most school psychologists are required to do a great deal of testing and report writing in their jobs. That was true, as we've seen, for Mark Connor during the first few years of his career. He preferred counseling students and their families, but the testing and report writing allowed little time for this. When Mark changed jobs, the situation improved, but what really enriched his job was the counselor internship program that he created in the district. One reason that Mark was able to develop the new program was that he worked in a supportive setting, but Mark's organizational negotiation skill was also important in establishing the new program.

Mark began to formulate the plan for the new program when the school board eliminated the elementary school counselors due to budgetary pressures. It was an unpopular decision, but the board saw no alternative. Mark, however, did see an alternative. He proposed that the school district allow him to establish an arrangement in which students from graduate counseling programs in local colleges would work in the elementary schools. They would be supervised by Mark and would receive academic credit. The only cost to the district would be to hire another psychologist part-time in order to allow Mark the additional time needed to run the program. Using considerable organizational negotiation skill, Mark shepherded the proposal through all of the appropriate channels, eventually securing the support of the school board.

At the end of the first year, Mark sagely decided to evaluate the program. He sent out a survey to parents, teachers, students, and principals. The results were extremely positive, and the board approved the program for another year, agreed to pay the interns a stipend, and gave Mark more release time.

Mark wanted to expand the program even further, but the board refused to allocate more funding for it. So Mark, using his organizational negotiation skill, developed a strategy for increasing political support for more funding: "The board wants to expand the intern counseling program, but it would take more of my time. And they're not willing to pay for that yet. So this year we're rotating schools—we pulled the counselor interns out of three schools, and we'll put them in three new schools next year. And basically I told the principals at the old schools, 'If you want a program in your schools, you're going to have to fund it out of Title I money.'"

Mark's strategy showed considerable savvy. By moving his interns to three new schools after the first year of the program, there would be three more principals who could see the benefits of it. In this way, he developed a strong constituency for maintaining and expanding the program—a good example of organizational negotiation skill.

Given the positive response to the counselors, it seemed likely that Mark might just come up with the money. But even if he lost this particular battle, he had already created an unusually positive work environment for himself because of the assertive and skillful way in which he "worked the system." Mark was fortunate to work in a system that was supportive of innovation, but change would not have occurred without his initiative and skill.

Components of Organizational Negotiation Skill

The examples suggest that there are several components that make up organizational negotiation skill. First, there is the ability to avoid and resolve conflicts. Conflicts with coworkers and supervisors represent a major source of stress and burnout in the human services. How well one is able to anticipate and deal with these - conflicts represents an important part of organizational negotiation skill.

Second, there is the ability to generate organizational support for one's initiatives. Another major source of stress and burnout is the frustration associated with bureaucratic constraints, lack of resources, and lack of official sanction. We saw how Mark Connor overcame these obstacles. Both Mark and Victoria Goble seemed to be able to identify potential sources of resistance and to devise ways of reducing or neutralizing that resistance. In doing so, they were able to gain support for new initiatives that addressed the needs of clients while making their own jobs more varied and stimulating.

But there is a third component of organizational skill: it involves a *way of thinking* rather than a particular set of techniques. This way of thinking was suggested by Victoria Goble when she referred to how she had "taken a much harder look at change and why people change." Rebecca Simpson also seemed to capture the essence of this way of thinking. She described a course she had taken in "complex organizations," which suggested to her the value of being "aware of the dynamics . . . not getting caught up in them, but having fun with them." This last component of organizational negotiation skill is a way of thinking about organizational barriers and conflicts that encourages a certain degree of analytical detachment and thoughtful reflection—a problem-solving attitude toward organizational difficulties.

Much of professional training involves teaching this problem-solving attitude—whether it be teaching a lesson, working with a troubled client, or developing a strong case to bring into court. Unfortunately, helping professionals are not usually taught how to adopt this same attitude toward organizational problems. But in one way or another, the most successful professionals did learn this way of thinking.[3]

Actively Pursuing Professional Development

In chapter 10 I noted that the more successful professionals worked in settings that encouraged staff to continue learning and growing, but this was only half the picture. For the professionals to benefit from such support, they needed to seek out learning experiences and to enter them with an open, active curiosity. Four of the five most successful professionals had that quality. They didn't see themselves as "finished products" just because they had completed formal training and received a credential. They recognized the need for life-long learning, not only to keep up with current developments in their fields, but also to maintain enthusiasm and commitment to the work. This curiosity and love of learning was another important personal quality that contributed to recovery from early career burnout.[4]

Most of the professionals had attended workshops or seminars, but what distinguished the most dedicated and satisfied professionals from the others was the extent of their involvement. The professionals who resisted or recovered from burnout usually had participated in more extensive, sustained learning experiences— training programs that involved weekly meetings stretching over one or two years, for instance, or part-time post-graduate study that involved a comparable commitment.

Mark Connor had participated in more than one of these intensive post-graduate training programs. He described some of these experiences:

> I took a two-month program with two Gestalt therapists here, and they're excellent. I got training for four weeks, eight hours a day, during one summer. It's an advanced program. It's very good. I was very pleased with the training. For the morning part there would be a lecture, with some didactic information. The afternoon would be doing therapy. And in between we would have triads, and work with each other doing therapy, and they would observe us.
>
> And that's how the other training program was structured—lecture, triads, some of them videotaped, and then doing your own therapy.... That was a one-year program, and I felt I learned a lot from that one also.

In addition to participation in more formal training experiences, the most successful professionals actively sought out other, less formal opportunities to learn. Many of the most committed professionals, for instance, had had mentors during the first years of their careers. The least committed professionals hadn't had mentors. The work setting, to some extent, influences whether a professional will find a mentor, but even more important is the individual's desire for mentoring. The professionals who recognized the need for a mentor, and who actively sought one out, were able to find mentors—outside the job if not in it.[5]

The most successful professionals pursued professional development in other ways as well. Carol Potter, for instance, visited other programs to learn from colleagues when she was reassigned to a self-contained classroom: "I prepped myself a lot in terms of going and talking to others. I went to some of the other programs. We have a specialized school here where they send kids from different counties who have learning disabilities. So I tried to get as much background as possible by going there to observe and talk to the staff."

Carol's interest in visiting other programs to prepare for a new assignment wasn't an isolated occurrence. It exemplified a more general openness and interest in learning. Like the other professionals who successfully recovered from burnout, Carol was continually looking for opportunities to learn and grow on the job. And she was resourceful in finding these opportunities, both within the job and outside the work setting.

Formal training programs, mentors, and other learning experiences helped alleviate burnout in two different ways. First, they provided the professionals with specific tools that helped them to be more effective in the job. Nurse Angela McPherson, for instance, learned how to set up a successful consulting business by attending a particularly good workshop on that topic.

But these learning experiences had another positive effect. They provided intellectual stimulation. Even if the professionals couldn't immediately use everything they learned, those who had a love for knowledge came away from these experiences with a renewed sense of enthusiasm for their work. Nurse Rebecca Simpson put it well when she said, "I was not getting a whole lot of satisfaction from my job at that point. I wasn't getting the stimulation and what-not that I needed. So going back to school really helped me. . . . It helped to provide some different professional stimulation and contact with other nurses. And it helped me get back into theory and reading. It helped me to get a little bit different perspective."

Professionals are supposed to be open to learning about new advances in their fields. Professionalism means, among other things, having a strong commitment to learning; however, the professionals in my study differed in this characteristic. Some were more eager to continue learning than were others. The ones who continually sought out stimulating and useful learning experiences were more likely to recover from early career burnout and to avoid it later in their careers. Intellectual curiosity was an antidote to professional burnout.

Striking a Balance Between Work, Family, and Leisure

One of the criteria I used for successful recovery from burnout was "commitment," but a sense of personal commitment to one's career is different from a total involvement in work to the exclusion of everything else in life. The most successful professionals sustained a strong commitment to their work by modulating their involvement in work, by striking a balance between work and other parts of their lives. The most successful professionals considered family commitments and leisure pursuits to be at least as important as their careers. They didn't simply work to live, as the burned out professionals did, but neither did they just live to work.

In chapter 6 I noted that most of the professionals were interested in bringing about more balance between work, leisure, and family as they approached mid-life. However, not all the professionals were equally committed to this goal, and some were more successful than others in actually achieving it. The professionals who made the best recovery from burnout, along with those who had managed to resist it from the beginning, tended to be the most serious about achieving a balance between work and nonwork aspects of their lives. For them, balance was more than a "pipe dream."

Mental health professional Jennifer Talmadge exemplified this more balanced approach to work. She was one of the most enthusiastic, committed, and satisfied professionals at the time of the follow-up. She thoroughly enjoyed her work and was continually thinking of new ideas and projects, yet she made an effort to limit the amount of time she actually spent on her work, recognizing the need to set aside time for herself.

"I decided recently that I really needed to take time off, that's what I need to do. I don't need more work. So I started taking Mondays off, and I loved it. And then I took Fridays off, too." Jennifer went on to say that she worked ten or more hours on the days that she did work, but she had made a commitment to keep her work involvement limited to those three days a week.

Special education teacher Carol Potter also described how she had made a conscious decision to limit her involvement in her work. In her case, a primary motive was family considerations. She was the mother of two young children, and she felt it was important for them, and for herself, to commit a major part of her time and energy to their care.

An example of this commitment to balance work and family was Carol's decision to quit a part-time teaching job after the birth of her first child. In addition to her regular job during the day, she had been teaching a college class at night. She found the college teaching particularly stimulating, but she realized that she needed to conserve her energies for her family. "Once I had Anna, I continued teaching at the college for one more semester, but it was too much—I mean a regular job, plus trying to do that, and then have a baby . . . it was crazy."

The professionals who recovered were not only different in their attitudes about balance; they actually worked fewer hours. In fact, most worked less than what is normally considered to be "full time." Two were teachers and one was a school psychologist who finished work by three o'clock every day and had summers off. They also had more vacation time during the year than is typical. Another was clinical social worker Jennifer Talmadge who had limited her private practice schedule to just three days a week. The four professionals who were rated as most unhappy and disenchanted—two lawyers, a nurse, and a clinical social worker—were employed in 12-month, 40-hour-per-week positions, and they usually worked even more hours than that.

For the professionals who experienced the most frustration and disillusionment, work involvement actually tended to fluctuate from one extreme to the other. At certain times, their jobs would become the only significant commitment and source of gratification in their lives. Then, when they became stressed out and discouraged, they would withdraw to the point that work was simply a small part of life—and a relatively meaningless one as well.

Lawyer Shana Phillips was an example of the professional who fluctuated between excessive work involvement and almost complete withdrawal. Early in her career, she worked six and a half days a week and had virtually no life outside of work. She finally reached the breaking point, took a leave, and spent several weeks on a commune in the southwest. When she returned, she quit her job and took another that was easier but not particularly meaningful. Almost all of her psychic energy was invested in learning and practicing yoga, something she did several hours each week.

When I met with her 10 years later, I had the uncanny feeling of *déjà vu* as she described what her life had been like during the past two years. She had gradually become more involved in her work again, and eventually she was totally absorbed in it to the exclusion of everything else. Once again she was "working way too many hours," felt that she was under "a lot of stress," and described it as "a treadmill." So Shana did precisely what she had done before—she quit work, went off to the southwest (this time to visit a friend rather than a commune), and returned with the plan of changing jobs and limiting her involvement in work in the future. She hadn't worked in almost two years when I met with her.

I hope that Shana will have more success in the future in keeping her work involvement within tolerable limits, but the fact that the cycle had repeated itself more than once makes the prognosis cloudy. In describing herself as a "workaholic," Shana seems to have doubts herself about how successful she will be in maintaining a healthy balance in her life.

Shana represents a rather extreme example, but many of the other professionals who found it difficult to recover from early career burnout shared her tendency to swing back and forth between an excessive preoccupation with work and almost total apathy and disengagement.

Need for Achievement: More Realistic Goals and Expectations

Feelings about achievement were also important. The professionals who were least likely to recover from burnout tended to set extremely high goals for themselves. They were more perfectionistic and never seemed to feel that they had done enough. The professionals who recovered from burnout, or avoided it altogether, also set high goals, but their goals were more realistic—or became more realistic over time. They were also less compulsive about trying to achieve these goals.

Psychologist Mark Connor, for example, talked in our interview about how his expectations for his clients had become more realistic over time. "I don't expect the patients to change for me. I expect them to change for themselves if they want to change. I also accept the fact that they may not change, and that's part of therapy—for them to know and accept who they are and where they're at. . . . Some people are just not ready to change or really don't have the motivation to change. And they need to be aware of that. And once they're aware of that, then it might be a lot easier for them to accept who they are."

Mark still worked hard to help his patients, but he recognized the ultimate limits of his own contribution. He didn't expect as much from his patients and, more importantly, he didn't expect as much from himself. Yet he hadn't swung to the opposite extreme, which is what happens when professionals burn out. He still believed that patients *can* change, and he began with that belief every time he met a new patient. He also recognized that even if a patient isn't ready to change *now*, therapy may help the patient to become ready for change at some point in the future. He hadn't given up on his patients or himself, but he had taken a lot of the pressure off.

Eugenia Barton had come to adopt an attitude similar to Mark's. She said that when she first began teaching, an older colleague said that one couldn't expect much from the kids because it was a rural community. "I never quite forgot that," Eugenia said. "I don't think I've ever come to that. There are as many capable kids here as anyplace else. I haven't started patting them on their heads and saying, 'Poor little country kids, this is all you can do.' But I also have learned that they can't all do the same thing, and none of them can do some of the things I tried to make them do when I was younger."

Eugenia and Mark also had modest expectations for career advancement. Mark said that as long as his present job as a school psychologist remained intrinsically satisfying, he had no desire to move into a position of greater status and responsibility. Eugenia said the same about her career: "In teaching, there isn't a great deal of opportunity for advancement, unless you want to go into administration, and that's of no interest to me whatsoever. There's no other place I want to go."

Career changer Gloria Bennett expressed a contrasting view. She had been dissatisfied with many of her jobs in nursing during her career, and she had finally decided to leave the field and become a lawyer. When I asked her how she felt about career advancement, she answered, "I think it's important. It really is. There's always that element for me, of pushing to another limit. I think that's important for me."

Even though Gloria had been successful in her career, it hadn't been enough. She had become the assistant director of nursing in one of the most prestigious teaching hospitals in the country, yet she had decided to leave nursing and go into law, partly because of the greater prestige associated with law, and partly because she thrived on the challenge.

Near the end of the interview, Gloria became more introspective and reflective. She began to express some regrets about how important achievement and success had been to her. She talked about how "driven" she had been during much of her career, how work had always been her central life interest, how she had sacrificed everything for career advancement and success: "I have a tendency towards intenseness, and that can be very uncomfortable.... Even though there are incredible highs with being this driven, there are also a lot of lows...."

Conclusion: The Limits of "Personal Virtue"

In this chapter I've highlighted some of the individual values and outlooks that helped professionals to recover from, or to avoid, burnout. The danger in discussing individual characteristics, however, is that we tend to overemphasize their importance. People often do have the means to make their lives better or worse; and highly educated, middle-class professionals in our society are particularly able to do so. But what they think, how they feel, and what they do are strongly shaped by the social contexts in which they live. Recognizing that certain individual characteristics help professionals avoid burnout shouldn't distract us from the powerful factors in the work environment that also affect professional burnout.

The experience of clinical social worker-turned-real estate agent Karla Adams suggests how complex is the interaction between individual and social variables. Karla's experience also suggests the limits of an individual factor such as "previous challenging work experience." Karla was one of the oldest of the "new professionals," and she had worked previously in the field of social work. After working as a case worker in adoptions for many years with just a bachelor's degree, she decided to go to graduate school to earn a master's degree in social work. When she completed her graduate work and took a job as a *professional* social worker, Karla had more experience than most.

As a master's-level clinical social worker, however, Karla worked in a particularly frustrating, unstimulating setting—a large state institution for mentally retarded persons. When she was at the institution, her time was taken up with meetings and paperwork. She found her colleagues and supervisors to be unstimulating, uncommitted, and preoccupied with making things run smoothly. The bureaucratic obstacles and political infighting were depressing. There were some positive aspects to the job, but in general her experience was discouraging.

When I interviewed Karla again 12 years later, I learned that she had become increasingly discouraged in her first job. After a year or so, she changed jobs, transferring to another state institution for mentally retarded persons. This second setting was newer and seemed to value innovation to a greater extent, but Karla soon encountered many of the same frustrations. She eventually concluded that social work was just not right for her, and she went into real estate.

Based on her previous work experiences, Karla should have been one of the professionals to overcome early career burnout. She had several of the individual characteristics associated with successful recovery, but unlike the professionals who did recover, Karla didn't find a more rewarding and supportive work environment when she changed jobs. Her second job in social work wasn't significantly better than the first.

Thus, in Karla's case, the failure to move into a more favorable work setting early in the career offset the positive impact of previous experience and maturity. Karla's experience shows that the work environment exerts a strong effect on professional commitment. Individual factors are important, but the work setting's influence can't be ignored. Ultimately it is the dynamic interaction between individual and setting that determines how a professional will change during the first part of the career.

13

Some Implications
for Policy and Practice

When I completed the initial study, the professionals were at the end of their first year of professional practice in public service settings. Most were burned out or well on their way to becoming burned out. Initially I had set out to study the stresses associated with making the transition from student to professional. I ended up conducting one of the first published studies of professional burnout, but one year doesn't make a career.

It would be inaccurate to say that I had *no* idea what I would find when I set out a decade later to do a follow-up study. I actually had many different, even conflicting ideas. Some of them were offered by interested friends and colleagues, and some were ideas of my own. What I ultimately discovered was more complex, and therefore more interesting, than anything that I had expected.

Most of the professionals were no longer burned out when I found them 12 years after their careers had begun. A few had made particularly good recoveries from early career burnout, but none of the professionals was as committed as they once had been, and the nature of their caring and commitment had changed.

The professionals were no longer burned out: Some of their aspirations for work had become less ambitious ("adjustment downward"). Their work situations had improved in certain important ways. They had found more autonomy, higher status, greater financial rewards, and more opportunity to work with grateful and cooperative clients. Their work was more interesting and, most of the time, not overly taxing. They felt, for the most part, competent and efficacious.

The most interesting stories were those of professionals who had been among the most burned out at the end of the first year but who had recovered—so much, in fact, that a decade later they were among the most satisfied, dedicated, and caring. One reason their stories were interesting was that the outcome was unexpected. Another equally important reason is that in recovering from early career burnout, these individuals help us to more clearly identify ways in which all professionals can be helped to achieve greater levels of caring and commitment in their work.

There are many practical lessons that come out of this study, but seven are particularly important.

1. Planning for Better Work Environments

The work environment has a significant impact on professionals' caring and commitment, and there are many ways supervisors and administrators can make the work environment more stimulating and supportive, particularly by emphasizing prevention.

For instance, in designing new human service programs, planners should pay more attention to the likely impact on the caregivers. The way we go about designing the physical environment provides a good model. In any major new land development, for instance, we now require an "environmental impact" study. The designers then use the results of the study to modify the plans to minimize adverse effects on the environment.

Administrators could use the same approach with new human service programs. When a program has been designed, but before it becomes operational, someone could conduct a study to assess the likely impact on important aspects of the providers' work environment, such as challenge and stimulation, nonprofessional duties, types of clients to be seen, variety and change, and allowances for individual differences. The study should pay particular attention to the degree of organizational autonomy and support for service providers. Based on this assessment, the planners would alter the program design to make the new program a more positive work setting.

These impact studies need not be expensive or time-consuming. One approach would be to submit the proposed program design to an expert on professional stress and burnout. Such a strategy would be similar to what is done now when plans for a new development are reviewed by an environmental engineer. The expert would not necessarily approve or reject the program; rather, he or she could merely indicate ways in which the proposed design might have adverse effects on staff. The expert could also provide suggestions for enhancing the quality of the work environment.

An alternative approach would be to have administration and staff address work environment issues together during the first few months the program is operational. These kinds of concerns tend to be neglected as staff address many of the pressing "housekeeping issues" that confront new programs (Sarason, 1972). If the program implementers are committed to making the program as supportive as possible for the staff, they can set aside time for this purpose.

Administrators and supervisors could also improve the work environment in existing programs. Many human service programs already engage in periodic morale surveys in which staff perceptions of the work environment are assessed. These surveys point to specific sources of dissatisfaction and stress. The most effective way to use these surveys is to share the results with the staff and then allow them to generate solutions to the problems that are identified. Hunicutt and MacMillan (1983) described a project in which they introduced such an approach in several different community mental health programs. Evaluation data revealed that staff burnout could be reduced by conducting a careful study of the work environment and then using the results to plan modest changes.

2. Providing Opportunities to Develop Special Interests

Many of the professionals in my study made their work more rewarding by developing special interests on the job. Professional burnout could be further reduced if administrators did more to encourage such enterprises.

Goldenberg (1971) described an example of how this was done in one program—a residential program for disadvantaged youth in the community. Each staff member was expected to design a special program for the residents and their families. The staff could develop any kind of program they wished. In fact, the more interesting it was for them personally, the better. One staff member set up a carpentry shop in the basement and offered lessons to the youth. (Community members and other staff people could also receive lessons.) Another staff member offered karate lessons. Still others developed various kinds of educational, recreational, and cultural programs. Ultimately the programs were as rewarding for the staff people who developed them as they were for those who participated.

Some professionals will need little more than explicit permission to develop a special interest on the job. Others will need more support, direction, and coaching. Administrators can facilitate the process by discussing it with their staffs and formally sanctioning it. Models like the ones I presented in chapter 9 can be especially helpful in this regard. I also provided in that chapter some specific guidelines on how to get started. Cultivating a special interest should become part of every professional's job description.

3. Making It Easier to Work with Difficult Clients

The professionals generally became more caring and compassionate toward clients over time, but their frustration and intolerance toward the more difficult clients didn't abate. In fact, they often adopted practices that adversely affected the more difficult clients. There were, however, the exceptions.

Professionals—even experienced ones—need sensitive supervision and training to help them deal with their psychological reactions to difficult clients. Simple exhortation will not work. Professionals need opportunities to share their feelings about these clients in a supportive atmosphere. Maslach (1982) has shown how small support groups in which professionals are able to discuss their feelings can help to mitigate burnout. After professionals have had an opportunity to "vent," they should be helped to develop the perspectives that make it easier to cope with difficult clients and their problems.

Colarelli and Siegal (1966) provided a particularly good example of how program administrators and supervisors can help human service employees develop a realistic but positive perspective toward their work. The authors described an innovative treatment program that was set up in a mental hospital. The clients were chronic schizophrenics, many of whom who had been in and out of hospitals for years—a particularly difficult and frustrating population with which to work. After the first year of the project, the staff and directors sat down together and developed a framework that helped each staff member to set realistic goals for the patients and to see small but meaningful signs of progress. An evaluation of the program showed that these employees were significantly more satisfied with their work than were those on other wards of the hospital. The authors believed that one factor contributing to this greater satisfaction and fulfillment was the guiding framework that helped staff set realistic goals and monitor incremental progress.

Expectations are critical. Professionals often expect too much of themselves and their clients. These expectations are fueled by administrative demands to cover a certain amount of material in a semester, or to discharge a certain number of patients from the hospital each month. But there also is a cultural element. Many professionals internalize the expectation that they are supposed to bring about dramatic changes in clients—in spite of the many obstacles and limited resources with which they must work.

How can training programs address these unrealistic expectations in ways that do not lead to the opposite problem? There is always the danger that when professionals give up unrealistically high aspirations, they will fall into a kind of passive fatalism. Expectations can become self-fulfilling prophecies; therefore, we do not want to encourage professionals to adopt goals for their clients that are too low.

Kramer (1974) has shown one way of helping practitioners to develop more realistic expectations for practice. She began with the observation that nurses are often taught a mode of practice that is realistic only in ideal work settings—settings that rarely exist in the real world. She developed a course for student nurses in which the class learned about specific incidents that nurses typically face—incidents in which bureaucratic demands and constraints prevent a nurse from practicing in the ideal way. After the students discussed these situations and tried to come up with their own solutions, they learned about some approaches that creative and effective practitioners had used. Kramer carefully evaluated the course and found that when the students became practicing nurses, they experienced less role strain and maintained their initial idealism to a greater extent than did a matched control group. She subsequently developed a similar course for neophyte nurses who were already practicing. The course helped reduce stress and disillusion-ment for this group as well.

What is most important about Kramer's work is that it shows how training experiences can be structured in a way that encourages professionals to adopt meaningful but realistic expectations. But formal courses, seminars, or workshops represent only one strategy. Less formal approaches could involve coaching from supervisors and experienced colleagues.

Expectations represent only part of the problem. Professionals must now deal with situations that they never were trained to handle. Teachers, for instance, are being asked to work with severely handicapped children who previously had been placed in special classes. Psychotherapists must work with more disturbed clients who often present a complicated combination of problems, such as drug abuse *and* schizophrenia *and* mental retardation. Human service programs need to devote more time and resources to professional development to help professionals become more effec-tive in these situations. In thinking about professional develop-ment, we should rely less on formal training experiences. Seminars and workshops can be helpful, but professionals should also have more time for consultation with colleagues and supervisors. Pro-fessionals often learn most from informal discussions with those who have experienced similar problems and who have developed helpful strategies for dealing with them.

4. Increasing Organizational Negotiation Skill

Another important area for training is organizational negotia-tion skill. As I noted in Chapter 2, greater emphasis in the human services tends to be placed on efficiency and accountability than on compassionate, responsive care, but this does not mean that profes-sionals are penalized for being responsive, compassionate, or even creative. The most successful professionals are those who can dis-cover ways to be both efficient and kind.

The professionals in my study who were most successful in meeting both administrative demands and client needs knew how to "work the system." They were savvy about the ways organi-zations work, the ways people respond to change, and the most effective strategies for bringing about change. They used all of this knowledge to negotiate new arrangements that met the twin needs of efficiency and compassion.

The most successful professionals usually didn't learn these skills in school. In fact training programs usually teach a model of practice that is overly simplistic, because it assumes that there is only one relevant audience or stakeholder in a helping relationship: the client. In reality, professionals working in human service organizations must balance demands from several stakeholders: family members, supervisors, higher-level administrators, and coworkers. The professionals' success with a particular client—and in the workplace more generally—depends on how effective they are in mediating and negotiating among these often conflicting interests.

The few professionals in my study who learned organizational negotiation skills in a more formal way usually did so later in their careers, in post-graduate and continuing education programs. This is probably where these skills are best taught. Students in preservice training programs tend to be too preoccupied with learning the technical aspects of their work. The best time to begin training in organizational negotiation skill seems to be after professionals have been working for two or three years, when they have developed some confidence in the technical aspects of the job and are ready to think about broadening their focus.

But a survey of the offerings in continuing education programs for professionals reveals a glaring neglect in this critical area. In mental health, nursing, education, and other fields, most of the courses and seminars that are offered focus on technical skill development. For instance, I see circulars for teachers describing workshops on cooperative education. I see advertisements directed to therapists offering seminars on treating victims of incest. But I never see any programs for teachers or therapists that teach them how to negotiate more effectively within complex organizations.

One way to make such training useful is to organize it around "planned change projects." Participants would begin by identifying a problem within their work setting that they wish to address. The trainer would help them to define the problem in such a way that it could be solved—one of the most important skills to learn. Then, the professionals would learn a variety of strategies and techniques that could be used in addressing the problem. They would conclude the first phase of training by formulating an action plan.

Then they would go back to their work settings and attempt to implement their plans. After a few months, there would be another training session in which the professionals would report on their successes and setbacks and receive help in overcoming any problems they encountered.

At the conclusion of the program, many of the participants would have succeeded in making significant changes in their work settings, and all would have learned new perspectives and techniques for negotiating in complex organizations. But whatever form it takes, training in organizational negotiation skill should become a major component of continuing education programs.

5. Relying More on the Quality of Previous Work Experiences in Selection for Professional Training

The most successful professionals were individuals who had worked successfully in challenging situations in the past. They seemed to have matured in those situations and learned valuable coping skills. Some professional training programs already give preference to older, more mature applicants in the selection process. This practice seems to be a wise one. But an applicant's age is less important than what the applicant has done in the past. What seems to be most critical is that the individual has successfully mastered a challenging job.

"Job" should be interpreted broadly. Parenthood, for instance, qualifies as a challenging job: individuals who have successfully raised one or more children have a reservoir of strength and commitment that can help them to master the demands of becoming a professional. Hobbies could also qualify as challenging "jobs" if they involved enough challenge.

Application forms for professional training programs should explicitly ask candidates to describe any previous work experiences that they have had. The selection committee should read those descriptions and then rate them in terms of how challenging the work experiences were and how well the individual seems to have mastered the challenges. Academic excellence must continue to be a primary criterion for admission; but when the candidates are similar in grades and test scores, preference should be given to those who have been involved in challenging work experiences in the past and who have done particularly well in those situations. Academic criteria are important, but the quality of one's previous work experiences may ultimately be more important in predicting whether one will become a committed and caring professional.

6. Providing More Career Counseling and Professional Development

Most of the professionals gained "career insight" during the first 12 years of their careers. They learned what they liked to do best and what they were good at doing, and they gradually felt more comfortable making career decisions based on that insight. The most successful professionals developed career insight earlier in their careers, which gave them a distinct advantage over those who didn't develop it—or did so much later.

Career counseling is one way of helping professionals develop career insight earlier in their careers. Career counseling is a burgeoning profession in its own right.[1] Career counselors help individuals develop greater career insight and make constructive career decisions. Such counseling has been readily available to college students for many years. Given the importance of career insight for positive professional functioning, career counseling should also be made more readily available to practicing professionals, especially after they have completed the first two or three years of practice.

In addition to helping professionals evaluate their careers, career counselors could encourage them to take their own development more seriously and to seek out interesting learning experiences. The most successful professionals in my study had an unquenchable thirst for learning. Career counseling could be used to promote greater interest in professional development. Career counselors could also help professionals evaluate the wide variety of continuing education offerings and decide which ones would be most useful, given their goals, interests, and needs. Career counselors could also help the professionals tap into informal vehicles for professional development within their own work settings. For example, a career counselor might encourage a teacher to ask colleagues for permission to observe in their classrooms.

Career counselors could also help professionals strike more of a balance between work, family, and leisure pursuits. The professionals in my study usually saw the virtue of striking such a balance, and they tried hard to do so, but many encountered difficulty. Career counselors could help professionals gain insight into the factors that prevent them from achieving more balance in their lives. Counseling could also help them to make changes that would remove some of those obstacles.

Career counseling can be especially effective when it occurs on a regular basis. Just as one visits a dentist every 6 to 12 months for a dental check-up, professionals should visit a career counselor every few years for a "career check-up." If everything is fine and the career seems to be on track, the visit can be a short one. If the session reveals some uncertainty and concern, then a few more sessions can be scheduled to address the problems.

Career counseling could be offered directly by the human service organizations and schools that employ professionals, but a more realistic and effective strategy might be to provide professional employees with vouchers they could use to purchase career counseling from a list of approved providers. Someone not affiliated with the employing organization will have more objectivity and credibility than a counselor who is also an employee.

Although counseling is usually provided on a one-to-one basis, group counseling is an interesting alternative. Large corporations have been offering "career development" programs to their employees in this way for some time. Employees who go through these programs typically attend a few group sessions at which facilitators help them to assess their current interests and abilities and to make career plans. Group sessions are more economical, and there is some advantage to being able to talk with other professionals who are grappling with the same issues. But there is also a place for individual counseling.

Whether done on an individual or group basis, career counseling is relatively inexpensive. Much can be accomplished in just a few sessions.

7. Giving Professionals a Greater Role in the Planning of Change

The professionals in my study became more resistant over time to change imposed by outsiders. Simultaneously, they became more willing to experiment on their own. Those who wish to introduce change into a profession need to take this finding into account in planning their change strategy. In education, for instance, reformers should give teachers more opportunities to experiment on their own—and to learn from each other's experiments—rather than give them curricula developed by others or indoctrinate them in the latest teaching methods. Outsiders from universities, government, and other settings have a role to play in promoting change, but they should work more as collaborators with practitioners than as outside experts who attempt to sell to or instruct them.

A good example of how change might be introduced to professionals involves reform in math and science teaching. One approach is for an outsider, usually a mathematics or science professor from a university, to come into a school district and show the teachers a "better" way of teaching math or science. Frequently the outsider brings with him or her a fully-developed curriculum that spells out in great detail each step that the teacher is to go through in teaching the subject. This approach usually meets with great resistance on the part of some teachers, and the intended changes in classroom practices rarely occur.[2]

A better approach would be to bring the outside experts together with the teachers who are to adopt the new methods. The experts and teachers would begin by discussing the problems that teachers face in trying to make math or science interesting for students. The experts, during the course of these discussions (and they would be discussions, not lectures!), would present their ideas concerning how best to teach the subject. The teachers would have an opportunity to critically discuss these ideas in light of their own experiences. Eventually, the discussions would move into planning: given what is known about children, their needs and interests, and the realities of the classroom, what is the best way of teaching mathematics or science?

The teachers would be the ones who would ultimately decide what changes to make, but the experts would have considerable influence over the process because of their knowledge and status. This kind of collaborative process would give the professionals a greater sense of ownership, and thus they would be more open to change and experimentation. In addition, the unique perspective and knowledge of practitioners would be included in the planning process, which would lead to more realistic innovations.

One objection to this proposal is that it is too time-consuming. But it may not require much more time than the traditional approach to reform in which outsiders try to get reluctant professionals to adopt innovations that the professionals do not like. And even if a more collaborative approach does require more time, it may be worth it if the results are more positive. A more "economical" approach that ultimately ends in failure or minimal change is no bargain.

These seven recommendations, if implemented, would go a long way toward reducing the incidence of professional burnout in the human services, but there is one other area that deserves attention. It is something that even the most satisfied professionals failed to find in their work: a sense of meaning and transcendence. In fact, not only was it missing—the professionals had given up the quest for meaning so completely that they didn't even refer to it—it wasn't even articulated as a problem. But the lack of meaning in work *was* a problem because the *need* for meaning hadn't disappeared. The professionals were simply no longer conscious of it.

14

What's Missing?
The Quest for Meaning

"He who has a *why* to live for can bear with almost any *how.*"
—Nietzsche

What they don't talk about may be as important as what they do talk about.

In this book I've described what the public service professionals said about the first 12 years of their careers. I've noted the changes that have occurred in their perspectives, and I've identified some of the factors that contributed to recovery from early career burnout. All of this has been based on what the professionals explicitly remarked upon. I have told the story in their own words.

But that is only part of the story. Something important was left out because the professionals could only reveal it in what they didn't talk about. (Perhaps the professionals didn't talk about it because it is such a basic part of the cultural and historical milieu in which we live.)

The missing factor in these interviews is the quest for meaning—or rather, the gradual abandonment of the quest by almost all of the professionals I studied. When they began their careers, they were looking for work that would be meaningful. They entered a public service profession because they wished to serve. But they not only wished to serve; they also wished to make the world a better place, to "repair the world." That mission was what gave their lives meaning.

The professionals in my study also wanted a decent standard of living and economic security, but in the late sixties and early seventies, "relevance" was of primary importance for those who chose to become teachers, public health nurses, poverty lawyers, and mental health professionals. A *relevant* occupation was one in which a person could contribute to the improvement of the human condition—and do so in a meaningful way.

When the professionals finished their training and became practitioners, they found that several of the rewards they had expected were elusive. Many subsequently left public service. Some left their profession altogether. Many, however, remained; and they were able to gradually carve out a comfortable niche for themselves. They found much of the autonomy, the collegiality, and the security they had hoped for. They found interesting work—work that was challenging and that gave them a sense of accomplishment—but even the most satisfied professionals ultimately failed to find *all* the rewards they initially sought. There was one reward in particular that remained beyond their grasp. Few of them could recover—or discover—that sense of purpose, that feeling of transcendence, which fueled their efforts in the beginning.

When I interviewed the professionals again 12 years after they began their careers, they didn't talk much about meaning, purpose, or transcendence. It just didn't seem to be a significant aspect of their work. Their failure to talk about meaning in work could have reflected a lack of concern about this issue. But more likely the professionals had just learned to give up any hopes of achieving meaning in their work. This lack of attention to such an important issue is one of the most important findings of this study.

A Visit to an Unusual Program

I first became aware of the helping professionals' unrequited quest for meaning not from these interviews, but through a visit I made to an unusual human service program—a residential program for severely mentally retarded people. It was a program where there should have been a high incidence of burnout—but there was almost none. At that time I was working at the Illinois Institute for Developmental Disabilities, and as part of my job I had visited many of these programs. In general they were dismal places, but this setting was different. It was bright and clean. The atmosphere exuded a warmth that I had never felt in such facilities before. The residents seemed to be well cared for, and the staff people with whom I talked were unusually lively, enthusiastic, and content with their work. They found it meaningful and rewarding in every possible way.

Then I learned about the working conditions of the staff. Their pay was minuscule. They worked seven days a week. They had little autonomy. Everyone—even highly trained professionals—was expected to share in the most menial tasks, such as cleaning the floors. In short, all of the working conditions that are associated with high levels of burnout were present, yet almost no one burned out.

Turnover among the staff was extremely low. Almost no one ever left. I did interview one who did, and I discovered that she hadn't left because she became burned out; rather, she left over philosophical differences.

What accounted for this seeming anomaly—a setting in which all the ingredients for burnout were present, but where burnout was virtually unheard of? I eventually discovered that what kept the staff committed, caring, and content in this setting was something that is absent in almost every other human service setting—a shared commitment to a set of moral beliefs.

This unusual facility was run by a religious order—a group of nuns (or "sisters" as they preferred to be called) who had joined the order to lead a religious life and serve others. This unusual human service program, therefore, wasn't just a human service program—it was a religious community.

One explanation for the high degree of caring and devotion that I saw is that these were unusually committed people. Not many individuals choose to renounce all worldly pleasures and ties to join a religious order. Those who do must surely be unusually dedicated, and the ones who sustain that commitment through the novitiate stage and take orders as nuns are an even more select group. The staff avoided burnout in part because they began with an unusual degree of devotion to service.

But they weren't just unusual people. They also worked in an unusual setting—a religious community that constantly reinforced its members' commitment. It was a setting in which everyone shared a deep and abiding commitment to the same ideology, where all members came together several times a day to reaffirm their faith in, and commitment to, that ideology. It was also a setting in which status distinctions between the members of the community were minimal and where individuals had to make significant sacrifices and investments just to join the community. The setting, in other words, was designed to maximize commitment.[1]

The Link Between Professional Burnout and the Quest for Meaning

This religiously oriented human service program reveals a great deal about the link between meaning and professional burnout. It is a link that few people have recognized or appreciated,[2] although the importance of meaning for human motivation has long been recognized.

The Existentialists taught that the search for meaning was a central drive of modern people. Camus (1955, pp. 3–4), for instance, wrote that "the question of life's meaning is the most urgent of questions." Frankl (1962) founded a whole school of psychotherapy on the "will to meaning," which, he argued, is the primary motivational force in human beings. He contrasted this view with that of Freud, who saw the "will to pleasure" as primary, and Adler, who gave primacy to the "will to power." Frankl believed that people only become preoccupied with the quest for pleasure or power when the will to meaning is thwarted. "What man (sic) actually needs," wrote Frankl (1962, p. 107), "is not a tensionless state but rather the striving and struggling for some goal worthy of him."[3]

Even before the Existentialists, Marx and Durkheim wrote not only about the importance of meaning in human affairs, but also about how meaning was absent in modern life. Durkheim wrote about "anomie," a planlessness in living, and Marx wrote about "alienation"—the loss of meaning in work.

Most writers on professional burnout have identified "stress," not lack of meaning or alienation, as the root cause. Burnout, according to this view, occurs when the individual is unable to overcome or escape from chronic work-related stress. Eventually, the individual becomes emotionally exhausted and burns out.

But the religiously oriented human service program that I studied suggests that stress, by itself, doesn't cause burnout. As Pines

(1993, p. 38) put it, "Stress does not necessarily cause burnout. People are able to flourish in stressful and demanding jobs if they feel that their work is significant." For the nuns I met, work was highly significant. Thus, all of the job characteristics that are normally associated with stress and burnout—lack of autonomy, menial and boring work, heavy workloads, and lack of visible progress in most clients—had little effect on them.

Frankl (1962) had recognized this insight much earlier. He wrote, "Suffering ceases to be suffering in some way at the moment it finds a meaning such as the meaning of a sacrifice" (p. 115). One can substitute "stress" for "suffering" and see how Frankl's statement applies to the problem of burnout. Burnout is a response to stress, but the root cause isn't stress (or suffering). It's the lack of meaning for the suffering, the loss of moral purpose. Burnout wasn't a problem for the nuns because the stresses they experienced at work were perceived as meaningful sacrifices. There was a moral purpose or meaning to their stress or suffering, and so it ceased to even feel like stress.

Thus burnout is not a "disease of overcommitment," as some have proposed (Freudenberger & Richelson, 1980). Those who succumb to burnout may be overinvolved in their work, but they aren't overcommitted—at least not in the sense of moral commitment. For those prone to burnout, commitment to their work is egoistic. Their self-esteem is strongly affected by how well they perform. This is different from the kind of moral commitment shared by the nuns. Their commitment was to a set of ideas, and to a group devoted to those ideas. Their commitment was based on a belief in something greater than themselves. It was transcendent.

Burnout is often synonymous with emotional exhaustion.[4] But one doesn't become emotionally exhausted when one engages in activities that are meaningful. As Marks (1979, p. 31) put it, "Our energy tends to become fully available for anything to which we are highly committed, and we often feel more energetic for having done it. We tend to find little energy for anything to which we are *not* highly committed, and doing these things leaves us feeling 'spent,' drained, and exhausted."

But how can meaning be a problem for people who devote their lives to helping others—and who often succeed? This was true for the professionals I studied. They spent their days helping others in significant ways through teaching, psychotherapy, nursing, and legal aid. And while they found their work to be satisfying and rewarding in many ways, no one described it as "significant" or "meaningful." So what does make work meaningful?

Pines (1993) argues that human service professionals experience work as meaningful when they are able to help people, when they are able to have a significant impact on their lives, but many professionals who help people still find that their work lacks meaning. There must be something else, and the nuns I visited suggested what it is: a moral framework for the work. The nuns working in the program for mentally retarded individuals didn't help people any more than did the professionals in my study, but they experienced their work as far more meaningful because it was linked to larger, more transcendent goals. In doing the work, they connected not only with their clients, but also with a set of ideals—and a community of people who shared those ideals. Helping professionals are less likely to burn out when they are committed to a transcendent set of moral beliefs, and when they work in a community based on those beliefs. Under those conditions, the professional's work is meaningful, and burnout is less likely to occur.

It was those conditions—those social arrangements—that made the religiously oriented human service program so unusual. It was those social conditions, not just their positive effects, that made this program such an anomaly. The typical residential program for mentally retarded persons isn't operated by a religious order, and the typical professional working in the field of mental retardation isn't a member of a religious order. The real significance of this religiously based program is that it is so rare. In fact, it's an anachronism.

But religion isn't the only basis for meaning in life. Frankl (1962) identified three sources of meaning: a cause to which one commits oneself, the love of another person, and belief in God. People, in other words, can find meaning in activities done for the sake of a cause, for the sake of a loved one, or for the sake of a higher being. The nuns who resisted burnout found meaning in their belief in, and commitment to, the service of God. The ultimate source of their commitment was religious.

Pines (1993) observed that religion is a particularly good source of meaning. She also pointed out that for most people in modern, secular society, religion is no longer a viable source of meaning.

People now tend to rely more on work for meaning in their lives. But work—and love—have become, like religion, increasingly problematic as sources of meaning.[5]

The Elusiveness of Meaning in Modern Life

Why has meaning become so problematic? Why is it that programs like the one I visited—and the kind of commitment and caring that they encourage—are so rare? They weren't always so unusual. Only a hundred years ago there were many more programs in the human services that were operated by religious orders or that had a strong religious orientation. One can still see traces of this, for instance, in all of the hospitals that have religious names. Their links to religious institutions, in most cases, are much weaker today than they were in earlier times, but the names reveal that there were strong linkages in the past.

Religious communities—and the kind of devotion to service that they engender—are rare today because something fundamental has changed in our society. We no longer live in a society that encourages the development of such communities. In fact, we now live in a society that strongly discourages religious commitment, and the same forces that discourage religious commitment also undermine the kind of dedication and caring that we would like our human service professionals to have.

Those social forces affect all of us, not just human service professionals. One of the oldest is capitalism, which Marx saw as the root cause of alienation, but Marx believed alienation was primarily a problem for industrial workers. Up to the present time professionals have been seen as the group least likely to suffer from work alienation. Sarason (1977) questioned this assumption, arguing that for many professionals work had become devoid of fulfillment and meaning. More recently Sarason (1985) noted how professional caring and commitment tend to be diluted in capitalist societies, because such societies stimulate and reinforce the desire for individual material gain. Success is often equated with conspicuous consumption. Striving for upward social mobility is an accepted goal.[6]

But the erosion of meaning and moral commitment has quickened in recent decades as new social forces have emerged, forces unimagined by Marx. Merser (1986) has identified many of these forces. First was the mobility and loosening of ties to close families, supportive communities, and religions. The growth in suburbs after the Second World War was a manifestation of this mobility, and it greatly accelerated it.

There has also been a dramatic increase in the number of individuals who receive education and in the growing education gap between parents and children. Another important social force that undermined religion and moral commitment was the human potential movement: "Fulfillment . . . became, for the first time in America's history, a middle class obsession" (Merser, 1986, p. 75).

Yet another influence was the civil rights movement of the sixties, which gave way to the anti–Vietnam War movement and numerous other movements of social protest. All of these protest movements reflected—and galvanized—a general loss of faith in all established social institutions.

These protest movements spawned a host of new social institutions, such as communes, alternative schools, alternative businesses, and the like, which supported the new ethos of liberation, fulfillment, and social justice, but these new institutions lacked the moral authority of the old. They rapidly lost their appeal and, in most cases, faded away.

Public service professionals have been affected by this *zeitgeist* as much as anyone else, making it difficult for them to sustain a sense of moral commitment to their work. Within the professions there have been additional forces that make meaning and commitment more problematic.

By the early nineteenth century, the professions (with the exception of the clergy) had shed their commitment to a moral-religious paradigm and replaced it with the scientific-technical paradigm. Their work was based on research, scholarship, and rational analysis. Such a basis for practice encourages a critical, detached attitude toward the world, an attitude that weakens a professional's ability to form a strong commitment to an ideology or a group. Professionalism also emphasizes individualism and autonomy, which further undermines moral authority. The professions, under the influence of the scientific-technical paradigm, are preoccupied with competence and control, which further dilutes moral commitment and compassion.[7]

It isn't surprising, therefore, that the professionals in my study found it difficult to talk about their work as meaningful or morally significant. Some of the professionals were able to recover from burnout by changing jobs, cultivating special interests, and maintaining a balance between work and nonwork parts of their lives. They were able to find work that was interesting and challenging; they were able to find work settings that provided both autonomy and support; but meaning and moral commitment were far more difficult to achieve. In our society, it's still possible for professionals to find interesting, satisfying work. Finding work that is meaningful, however, achieving transcendence through work—such outcomes are so rare that the professionals didn't even bother to mention them. I wonder how often the professionals—or any of us—even notice their absence.

Conclusion: Transforming Human Service Programs Into Moral Communities

The way things are isn't necessarily the way things have to be. Even in a society where a sense of moral transcendence has become fleeting, it's possible to infuse a particular institution with greater moral relevance, and the human services are an area where such a transformation could begin.

We should begin to view human service programs—such as schools, poverty programs, mental health clinics, and even hospitals—as moral communities, not "service delivery systems." There needs to be a radical change in the way we regard these settings. We also need to learn more about the social arrangements that foster strong commitment in moral communities. Sociologists like Kanter (1972) have made a good start in this direction. What is now needed is applied research that translates these findings into arrangements that are suitable for modern human service programs. How can we translate, for instance, what Kanter discovered about nineteenth-century communes into organizational arrangements for public schools? How can schools, in other words, be transformed into moral communities in which teachers, administrators, parents, and students share a commitment to learning? The same questions can be posed for mental health clinics, visiting nurse agencies, and other kinds of programs. And they should be.

Appendix

Research Methods

In this section I set forth a more detailed description of the research methods used in both the original and the follow-up studies. Some of the information was presented in the first chapter, but I've included it again here to make this description more coherent and complete.

Research Participants

The original panel consisted of six lawyers, seven high school teachers, six public health nurses, and seven mental health professionals. All had just completed their professional training and were in their first year of full-time professional practice. The participants were recruited from lists of graduates obtained from local training programs. From these lists I chose individuals who were employed in public agencies and who lived in the immediate vicinity. Only two individuals (a high school teacher and a lawyer) refused to participate when approached.

Participants had been working for an average of 3.5 months when first interviewed. Demographically there were 24 whites and two blacks, nine males and 17 females. Their mean age was 27.8 years, with a range of 22 to 38 years. Fifteen were single or divorced and 11 were married.

By design all worked in publicly funded agencies rather than industry or private practice. Two of the mental health professionals worked in outpatient settings, one worked in a local alcoholism program, three worked in a suburban public school system, and one worked in a state institution for mentally retarded persons. All of the teachers worked in public school systems. Three worked in a middle- to upper-middle-class suburban school district located in a university community, two taught in primarily blue-collar suburban districts, and two taught in a smaller, rural district.

The lawyers' work settings were also diverse. Two worked in neighborhood legal aid offices, one in a city public defender's office, one in a state appellate defender's office, one in a small reform law center, and one in a university-based foreign student center. The nurses all came from either a public health department serving a large suburban county or a visiting nurses association serving a large urban county.

The participants were also diverse in the degrees they held. Four of the public health nurses had MPH degrees, while two had bachelor's degrees in nursing. Six of the mental health professionals had master's degrees in social work; one had a master's in psychology. The lawyers all had JD's; and the teachers all had bachelor's degrees in education.

The participants in the original study also had diverse roles. Five of the mental health professionals were primarily in therapist or counselor roles, one was a social worker developing and monitoring community residential placements, and one was a school psychologist in a psycho-diagnostician role. The teachers taught in a variety of fields: two in math, two in business, one in science, one in foreign languages, and one in art history. Five of the six lawyers were involved in litigation—two on the criminal side and three on the civil side. The sixth lawyer advised foreign students on immigration law. Among the nurses, three were in staff nursing positions providing direct service to individuals in the community, and three were in supervisory positions.

All of the original participants were located for the follow-up study. One of them, a white, female lawyer, was deceased; however, her spouse was interviewed to obtain some data concerning her life and career between the time of the original study and her death in 1985. Another participant, a black, male lawyer, could not be included in the study because he had contracted multiple sclerosis and was unable to remember anything about his life before he had to stop working.

Procedures

Interviews. Data from both the original and follow-up studies came primarily from interviews.

In the original study, I conducted the interviews along with three graduate students in psychology. Before conducting the interviews, I trained the graduate students. Training consisted of readings and lectures on the interview methodology to be used, followed by listening to and discussing tapes of interviews that I had conducted in the past. Finally, the students did pilot interviews that were tape-recorded and then reviewed by me. I provided corrective feedback as needed.

In the initial study, we interviewed each person at least twice. Most were interviewed three or four times. Some were interviewed even more often. After the first set of interviews, there was at least one follow-up interview that occurred about five months later. In most cases there was more than one interview in the beginning because we believed that more than one interview was necessary to develop the kind of rapport and comfort that is conducive to inquiry. In conducting the interviews, my students and I attempted to maintain informality while covering a number of general topic areas. The participants were encouraged to tell us what their work experiences were like in their own words.

The topics that we tried to touch on during the interviews included expectations the person had before beginning work, lifestyle changes that had occurred when the person began working, the nature of supervision, relations with students or clients and also with coworkers, how their new careers had impinged on their personal lives, sources of stress or dissatisfaction, changes in attitudes and values, and the structure of their work days. We also asked the participants to talk about what their training had been like. Each interview lasted at least an hour; some took as long as two hours.

In the follow-up study, I conducted all of the interviews. The geographic dispersal of the sample after 12 years made it impractical to conduct multiple interviews; thus, only one interview was conducted, lasting from 90 minutes to three hours. (A grant from the National Institute of Mental Health enabled me to go wherever the subjects were and to interview them in person.) I used the same kind of unstructured interviewing method for the follow-up study as I had for the original one.

The interviews followed the model for "biographical interviewing," as described by Levinson (1978). A biographical interview combines aspects of a research interview and a clinical interview. According to Levinson (1978, p. 15), "It is like a structured research interview in that certain topics must be covered, and the main purpose is research. As in a clinical interview, the interviewer is sensitive to the feelings expressed and follows the threads of meaning as they lead through diverse topics."

Biographical interviewing was chosen as the primary data collection method for several reasons. First, it is well suited to an exploratory study where the goal is discovery rather than verification (Cronbach, 1975). Second, the biographical approach is also appropriate for providing detailed accounts of the long-term process of development in people or to demonstrate the effects of timing and sequencing of events in a person's life (Howe, 1982). Third, biographical interviewing is a particularly effective method for gaining access to some of the important beliefs and assumptions that guide people's behavior—but are often concealed from others, or even from the respondents themselves (Frese, 1982; Lortie, 1975; Sarason, 1977).

Most important, however, I preferred biographical interviews because I was primarily interested in learning how these professionals felt about their experiences and saw their worlds—the "phenomenology" of professional work. I was afraid that if we tried to guess what the important changes were and relied on structured instruments for measuring those changes, we might lose some of the most important aspects of the experience. Too often, structured research methods get in the way of a penetrating exploration of how people truly think and feel about their lives. It was important that the subjects be able to tell their own stories in a relaxed and supportive setting that encouraged candor.

In conducting the interviews, the interviewers attempted to maintain informality while covering a standard set of questions. The questions used in the follow-up interviews, as well as spontaneous probes used by the interviewers, were guided in part by two theoretical frameworks. The first was a conceptual model for career research developed by Sonnenfeld and Kotter (1982). Their model includes the three basic areas of a person's "life space" that can change over time: work experiences, nonwork experiences (e.g., family), and individual personality characteristics. These three areas are interdependent: aspects of each influence the other two. Further, qualities of the work and nonwork situations, as well as the person, change over time, with experiences or perspectives at an earlier point in the life cycle exerting influence on later development.

The interviews were also guided by theory and research on psychological stress, coping, and adaptation. More specifically, it was assumed that changes in work-related attitudes and behaviors occur as the result of a dynamic process of adaptation in which the individual attempts to balance both internal and external demands, constraints, and supports.

In addition to these theoretical frameworks, a specific *a priori* focus of the follow-up study was on commitment and caring in human service professionals. I was particularly interested in learning more about what happens to a professional's commitment to work and concern for service recipients over time.

Based on these considerations, the questions used in the follow-up interviews covered the following general areas: 1) work history (jobs held; changes in responsibilities, work settings, or occupations; reasons for making changes; nature of each job or work situation; reactions to each work situation); 2) nonwork history (major commitments, such as marriage, divorce, parenthood; significant illness; leisure pursuits; how commitments and interests have changed over time; ways in which work and nonwork lives have affected each other; and changes in life satisfaction); 3) current attitudes (work motivation, job involvement, career goals, occupational satisfaction); and 4) plans for the future.

Data analysis. The interviews were analyzed qualitatively following the grounded theory approach, initially developed by Glaser and Strauss (1967) and subsequently refined and elaborated by Miles and Huberman (1984).

Using this procedure, I identified dozens of themes pertaining to the basic questions addressed in the study. I then rated each subject on these themes. For instance, one theme was that "status and recognition became more important over time." If I thought that the interviews with a particular subject were consistent with this theme, I rated the subject as positive on that theme.

Two graduate students who didn't know about the goals of the study then rated the subjects on each of the themes I initially had identified. Only themes that were verified independently in this way were retained as valid. This procedure yielded a much smaller number of themes that seemed to be well supported by the data. These are the themes that are discussed in the book.

The interview transcripts were also used to rate the subjects on various dimensions that had been identified *a priori*. For instance, five different graduate students rated each subject on how caring and compassionate he or she seemed to be at the time of the interviews. The raters rated both the initial interviews and the follow-up interviews. They didn't know the goals of the study or when the interviews had taken place.

Questionnaires. I also used questionnaires in the follow-up study. After completing the interviews, the professionals filled out a lengthy questionnaire about their work, their careers, and their attitudes toward life. I also asked them to identify one person who knew them especially well and to have this confidant complete a questionnaire. Data from these questionnaires is used in various parts of the book to corroborate findings from the theme analysis or to provide additional insights.

Notes

Chapter 1

1. The proportion of professionals in the population has leveled off recently and now remains at about 13 percent.
2. These figures come from *The World Almanac and Book of Facts* for 1993, p. 145.
3. A few writers have argued that human service professionals can be *too* committed and caring (Savicki & Cooley, 1983). They assert that effective performance requires that professionals maintain some emotional distance from clients. However, research suggests that idealistic professionals are usually more effective than those who lack idealism (Frank, 1973; Lortie, 1975; Motowidlo, 1984). Idealism and compassion usually contribute to greater professional effectiveness, not less. When helping professionals become less caring and compassionate, the quality of care declines.
4. It's not clear, of course, whether there's a strong relationship between a professional's professed attitudes, as revealed by a questionnaire, and the professional's actual behavior toward clients. Measured changes in "cynicism" or other interpersonal values may not be associated with actual change in behavior (Bloom, 1979). A physician who scores high in "cynicism" may be just as warm and caring with patients as one who scores lower, and compassionate behavior may vary depending on the social context. Sarason (1985) has argued that qualities like professional caring and compassion are not essences in individuals. They refer to relationships between people in particular situations. For instance, how compassionate a surgeon is toward members of a patient's family in a hospital intensive care unit may have more to do with the nature of intensive care units and the social backgrounds of the family members. Whether the surgeon took a course on compassion in medical school may have little influence on his or her behavior at that point.

5. We began the study with seven new professionals in each group—a total of 28, but one of the public health nurses, I soon learned, wasn't really a nurse; she was a "public health aide" with no formal training in nursing. I subsequently decided to drop her from the study. I also decided to drop one of the lawyers because she wasn't in a service-delivery position; she spent all of her time doing legal research for a federally funded project. Thus, even though we initially interviewed 28 professionals, only 26 completed the initial study.

6. Details on the research methods can be found in the Appendix.

7. Ten years seemed to be a good time span for a follow-up study, but by the time I had secured funding for the research and located the original subjects, 12 years had passed.

8. The term "client" will be used generically in this book to refer to the recipients of service. For nurses, the "clients" are their patients; for teachers, the clients are their students.

9. All names used in the book are pseudonyms. In some cases I have also made slight changes in nonsignificant identifying characteristics, such as places where the professionals worked or went to school, in order to protect their privacy.

Chapter 2

1. Sarason, Sarason, and Cowden (1975) studied college students who were planning to enter one of the professions. They found that students chose to enter a profession, rather than pursue a career in business, in large part because they believed they would enjoy more autonomy as a professional.

2. Sarason (1977) described well the plight of the public service professional when he wrote, "Enhanced social status is a weak base for continued satisfaction when daily reality confirms that you are not in control over your destiny, that decisions affecting your work and life are made elsewhere, often by people and forces unknown and unknowable to you. The creeping sense of impotence, strange to professionalism however defined, has made professional work more problematic than ever."

3. Other students of human service organizations have observed the same pattern. Mechanic (1976, 1989) for instance noted how medical bureaucracies give low priority to empathy for patients and rarely reward staff for humaneness.

4. Fromm (1976) is one of the most astute critics of our consumption-oriented, materialistic culture and its pernicious effects on the quality of life.

5. Sarason (1977, 1979) has pointed out that the problem of limited resources in the human services is exacerbated by the way in which the resources are utilized. He has shown how we could provide much better education and mental health care by utilizing untapped community resources in more creative ways.

6. Sarason, Zitnay, and Grossman (1971) pointed out that professionalization contained within it the seeds of public disillusionment and discontent. When a caring or helping function becomes professionalized, the profession takes over complete responsibility for meeting that need, but frequently the profession lacks the resources to do so. The public then becomes disillusioned.

Chapter 4

1. Of the 10 professionals still working in public service, four were teachers, two were in mental health, two were in nursing, and two were in law. Of the remaining subjects, seven were in the same field but no longer working in a public service capacity, six were in a different field or planning to switch to a different field when they returned to full-time employment, and two were at home full-time caring for their children but planning to return to their original field in the future.

   Of the 10 stayers, six were still in direct service roles, two were in direct service roles but had added some supervisory and administrative responsibilities, and two had been promoted to higher-level administrative positions. For the leavers, five were in direct service roles though no longer employed in a public service setting, one was a graduate student also working part-time in an administrative position, one had become a private consultant, one was at home full-time but planning to become a museum curator when she returned to work, another had become a real estate agent, two were full-time graduate students, and two worked as attorneys in the legal departments of large organizations. In addition to the 13 who definitely left public service, there were the two who were at home full-time with young children; they were planning to return to their public service jobs when their children were older, but since these plans might change, I didn't designate them as stayers or leavers.

   There did not seem to be a gender difference in whether the professional left or stayed in public service. Three of the eight males (38 percent) were still working in public service at follow-up while seven of 17 women (41 percent) were still in public service.

Chapter 5

1. Attitudes toward clients were assessed in several ways. First, the interview transcripts were read by three graduate students who rated them in terms of "how sympathetic toward clients" the professional seemed to be. Second, the professionals were asked to identify a person who knew them well, and this confidant was asked to rate the professional on the same dimension. Third, the professionals completed the "depersonalization" subscale of the Maslach Burnout Inventory (Maslach & Jackson, 1986). These three different data sources were combined to yield an overall rating of attitudes toward clients.

2. Other studies of how professional attitudes change over time have emerged with similar findings concerning increases in professional compassion over time. Mizrahi (1986), for instance, found that physicians had become more trusting and tolerant toward patients five years after completing their residencies. Blackburn and Fox (1983) also found that physicians became more concerned about the welfare of others during the years immediately following the completion of formal training.

3. Other studies have documented how professionals react negatively to clients who are unmotivated, resistant, or unappreciative. Mizrahi (1986), for instance, found that house staff in a hospital were especially irritated by patients who were abusive to themselves (e.g., drunks) or toward others (manipulators, complainers, and demanders). The physicians also had little tolerance for patients who were suspicious, disrespectful, hostile, or ungrateful. Five years after they had completed their training, when the physicians generally viewed patients more positively, they still resented patients who were more demanding and less appreciative. They identified such patients as a major source of stress in their work. Teachers also identified difficult students as a major source of stress. In fact, they often ranked "student discipline" or "behavior problems in the classroom" as the number one source of stress in their jobs (Kyriacou, 1980).

4. The perception of an inequitable social exchange may explain why the house staff studied by Mizrahi (1986) became especially irritated with patients who couldn't be dealt with and disposed of quickly, and why the most debilitated patients caused the most anger. What distinguished these patients as a group was that caring for them was more costly—they took more time and effort, and the "return" on the time was not particularly great.

5. One study found that classroom teachers who felt more efficacious tended to be more positive in their attitudes toward students. They criticized students less and praised them more (Gibson & Dembo, 1984). Other research has found that people who attribute the cause of their successes to their own ability, rather than to effort or luck, are more likely to help another person (Ickes & Kidd, 1976).

6. Mizrahi (1986) has suggested several other possible reasons why professionals become more compassionate toward most clients as they become more experienced. First, the physicians he studied had shifted to a more middle-class patient population, so it was easier for them to identify with their patients. Second, they were now in private practice and were paid directly by their patients, so they had a strong incentive to treat the patients with respect and compassion. A third possible reason was maturation. Other researchers have found that as young adults age and mature, they become warmer and more nurturant (Haan, 1989; Maas, 1989). These findings fit the developmental theory of Erik Erikson (1968), who proposed that as adults approach middle age they become more concerned about others.

Chapter 6

1. Flexibility has been relatively neglected in research on professionals and their careers. Other variables, such as work satisfaction and organizational commitment, have received more attention. But Hall (1976) has argued that "adaptability"—the capacity to acquire new skills and knowledge—should be included as an outcome in career development research.
2. Bray, et al. (1974) found that managers in one of the world's largest bureaucracies—AT&T—became more rigid during the first eight years of their careers. Goal flexibility and tolerance of uncertainty also decreased during this period.
3. It should be remembered that this finding, like others, is based on the professionals' own perceptions and beliefs. It's possible that they weren't as flexible and willing to experiment as they believed they were. The research method was designed to minimize defensiveness, but we can't know for sure how much the professionals distorted in order to present a more positive picture of themselves.
4. This finding confirms Schein's (1971) prediction that innovativeness is lowest at the beginning of a career and during major role transitions. Once professionals become more settled and confident, they're more willing to innovate. This finding is also consistent with a more general principle that rigidity, conformity, and resistance to change increase as stress and anxiety increase (Nicholson, 1984).

Chapter 7

1. By "commitment" or "dedication," I mean something similar to what Blau (1985) terms "job involvement," which has four components. A person is high in job involvement when he or she: 1) actively participates in the job; 2) holds it as a central life interest; 3) sees performance in the job as central to self-esteem; and 4) views performance as consistent with the self-concept.
2. Stelling (1982) has pointed out that high job involvement isn't necessarily positive. A professional who is totally absorbed in his or her work might have less patience for difficult clients. While there's some truth to this admonition, it would seem that *ideally* a helping professional would be both highly dedicated as well as patient and compassionate. Research suggests that while this condition may be rare, there are professionals who are able to be both committed and caring (Cherniss & Krantz, 1982).
3. Professionals, of course, aren't unique in this respect: feeling competent is important to most workers. The connection between competence at work and self-esteem is culturally conditioned. As Maccoby (1988, p. 72) pointed out, "In the United States, our self-esteem depends all too much on repeated success."

4. Arthur and Kram (1989, p. 295) concur that the major concern for many workers early in the career is competence; and, while this gives way to other concerns as the individual moves beyond the early career stage, "previous needs are neither forgotten nor altogether neglected. . . ."

5. Kanter (1989, p. 511) noted that "upward mobility" in the professions is based largely on "the reputation for greater skill." Maccoby (1988) also commented on how important "external recognition" is for professionals. Gowler and Legge (1989) have argued that career success for all workers depends on one's reputation, and that reputation is based primarily on perceived expertise and achievement. The difference between professionals and other types of workers, according to Kanter, is that professionals' reputations are determined by the perceptions of peers, while the perceptions of supervisors are more important for nonprofessionals.

6. Kanter (1989) noted that a professional's reputation is based largely on the type of work that one does. Professionals gain prestige by taking on "ever more demanding or challenging or important or rewarding assignments that involve greater exercise of the skills that define the professional's stock-in-trade" (p. 511).

7. Margaret's views about the link between money and status are widely shared. Maccoby (1988) noted that "payment and promotion are the highest forms of recognition" (p. 121).

8. These professionals weren't alone in placing greater importance on making money. Various studies during the eighties documented a shift in young Americans' concern with financial success. In 1988, for instance, the annual UCLA-American Council on Education survey of freshman attitudes found that students were more interested in "being very well-off financially" than any of their counterparts in the past 20 years (*New Brunswick Home News*, 1988). The same trend occurred in older workers. Between the early seventies and the mid-eighties, earning a high income increased in importance while "interesting and meaningful work" declined in importance, as measured by surveys conducted by the National Opinion Research Center (Stark, 1988). Making money had become more important.

9. This expectation—that the professionals would be less interested in intrinsic rewards as they matured—was also based on previous research. Rhodes (1983), for instance, reviewed all the research on the relationship between age and "growth need" strength, and found that there was an inverse correlation. In other words, as people get older, their desire for challenging, meaningful, self-actualizing work diminishes. The relationship is weak, however, and it is based on cross-sectional studies. Rhodes also believed it might not apply for more educated workers. Alderfer and Guzzo (1979), however, found the same pattern in a study of more educated workers. They looked at management students and experienced managers, and they found that growth needs did decline over time, except for an increase during the

midlife transition. Again, however, this finding was based on a cross-sectional research design.

10. A study of how physicians' values change over time came up with similar findings. Blackburn and Fox (1983) found that the value most related to intrinsic motivation, which they called "academic," dropped during the first part of the career, but it rose during the next decade. Once physicians succeed in establishing their practices, they are able to devote their attention to some of the intrinsic rewards of practice—the intellectual stimulation, the satisfaction of learning new techniques, the opportunities to experiment with new methods.

11. Many other researchers have found that people become more concerned with family and other nonwork interests once they become established in their careers (Bailyn, 1977; Bartolome & Evans, 1979; Bray et al., 1974; Hall, 1986; Tamir, 1989). Suran and Sheridan (1985), for instance, have suggested that there are four stages of professional development. During the third stage, which usually occurs between the ages of 30 and 50, finding a balance between one's career and personal life is a particularly important concern. Most of the professionals in my study were in this stage of their careers.

12. The role of children in encouraging professionals to spend less time on their careers was vividly demonstrated in a news story about Andrew Stein, former New York mayoral candidate and City Council President (Roberts, 1993). Stein had just decided to retire from politics at the age of 48. He had been in politics since the age of 22. In explaining his decision, Stein said, "My boys, Ben and Jake, are 7 and 5. In another four years, they'll be 12 and 19. You say to yourself, do you want to miss all that?" He then went on to say, "The joys of public service have always been tempered with the reality of the Little League games, the school plays and the chess tournaments I was missing. There's more to life than politics. . . ." Stein was a public service professional who is exactly the same age as the average age of my sample. He expressed the feelings of an entire cohort.

13. Professionals apparently do pay a price for reducing their psychological investment in work. Bailyn (1977) has documented the costs involved in striking more of a balance between work and family. In her studies of engineers, she identified a group she called "accommodators." These were individuals who shifted their focus away from work and invested more of their energies into family and leisure pursuits. She found that accommodators, compared to other engineers, rated themselves lower in ability to "think creatively" and to "identify and solve problems." They were also less likely to feel that they had the ability to continue to learn new things. Furthermore, accommodators who were dissatisfied with their jobs were less likely to quit than were dissatisfied nonaccommodators. In other words, they had become more passive at work and felt less personal accomplishment or self-efficacy. On the other hand, accommodators did

have a more positive family life. Their spouses were more satisfied and less conflicted, and the accommodators were more satisfied with family life.

14. For instance, Fiske and Chiriboga (1990) found that work was more often a major source of stress for men, while family and health concerns were more often major sources of stress for women, even when the women also worked. Roberts and Newton (1987) found that attachments and relationships were more important to the women they studied while achievement and autonomy were more important to the men. This finding is consistent with current theories of female development (Gallos, 1989). Other studies have found that women are less concerned about upward mobility than are men and more concerned about balancing work and family responsibilities (Gallos, 1989; Perun & Bielby, 1981).

15. The attorneys might be an exception. Historically the legal profession has been dominated by males, and discrimination against women has been well documented. On the other hand, the women attorneys in my study were working in new public service agencies when they began their careers. If one thinks of "poverty law" as a distinct field, women probably had come closer to parity in that field during the period covered by this study.

16. Other researchers have also suggested that various external factors affect the relative importance of work and nonwork domains for men and women. For instance, Fiske and Chiriboga (1990) found that some men began to feel that achievement was less important as they approached middle age, while the importance of achievement for women during this period didn't change. Other researchers have found that the relative importance of work vs. non-work concerns for women depends on when women have children (Neugarten, 1968; Rubin, 1979). In a particularly revealing study, Roberts and Newton (1989) found that for women who emphasized career in their twenties, marriage, family, and friends became more important in their thirties. Conversely, for the women who focused on marriage and children in their twenties, the career became more of a priority as they moved through their thirties.

Chapter 8

1. Many other studies have found that people generally become more satisfied as they move from early adulthood into the middle years. For instance, Fiske and Chiriboga (1990) found that adults became more positive in their views over time and that job satisfaction and self-efficacy increased between the ages of 21 and 35. They also found that young adults reported more stress than did older adults. Looking more specifically at job satisfaction, Rhodes (1983) reviewed more than 60 studies showing a positive correlation between age and satisfaction

with work—in other words, as people get older, they become more satisfied with their work.

2. This statement may seem to contradict what I wrote in the previous chapter about the increase in desire for both intrinsic and extrinsic rewards, but there really is no contradiction. Doing work that's interesting, for instance, became more important to the professionals, but the amount of stimulation they needed to be satisfied diminished.

3. Raelin (1985), in discussing why older workers seem to be more satisfied with their jobs, also mentioned these first two reasons as possible explanations. He called one the "aging effect" (older workers adjust their expectations and aspirations downward as they age), and he called the other the "career progression effect" (older workers have worked their way into better jobs). Raelin noted another possible explanation, which he called the "cohort effect": people who grew up in the thirties had more modest expectations for work and life than those who grew up in the sixties. Tamir (1989) offered yet another explanation: people reach their cognitive peak in middle age; therefore, they are happier with their work and life because they are better able to handle the challenges that they must face.

4. London (1985) coined the term, "career insight," and he defined it in much the same way: an accurate assessment of one's skills, interests, and potential for various work roles. He also argued that career insight enhances success and satisfaction.

5. Schein (1978) has also observed that people, over time, usually become more aware of their needs, talents, values, and desires for work as the result of varied work experiences.

6. Hall (1986) has noted that many people at "mid-career" begin to experience a perceived constriction in career opportunities. That was certainly true for many of the professionals in my study.

Chapter 9

1. No standard questionnaire measure of burnout was available at the time of the original study. Thus, two graduate students in clinical psychology read the original transcripts and rated them on five different dimensions that seemed to be related to the three subscales of the Maslach Burnout Inventory (Maslach & Jackson, 1986). The raters also evaluated the follow-up transcripts using the same dimensions. The subjects had completed the MBI at the time of follow-up, so the follow-up ratings could be correlated with the follow-up MBI scores to assess whether any would be good substitute measures of burnout. The dimension that was most highly correlated with burnout was worded as follows: "How satisfied is the subject with his/her occupation (not necessarily the present job)?" The correlations between the MBI and this rating scale were particularly high for one of the raters ($r = -.74$ for Emotional Exhaustion and $r = -.72$ for Depersonalization),

and the inter-rater reliabilities were also high (r = .76 on the follow-up data and r = .74 on the original data). The 12 subjects who were rated as highest in early career burnout as measured by this dimension were identified as the ones most burned out at the end of the first year. Recovery from burnout was assessed in terms of relative burnout at the time of the follow-up, as measured by the MBI. A subject was considered to have recovered if he or she scored in the low range on the Emotional Exhaustion and Depersonalization subscales and in the low or medium range on the Personal Accomplishment subscale, based on the norms suggested by the authors of the MBI. Five of the 12 professionals who were originally in the high burnout group met this criterion of recovery.

2. There were also two professionals who never burned out. They avoided early career burnout because they worked in unusually supportive and stimulating settings, and they had been able to continue working in settings that enabled them to sustain their initial commitment. I refer to some of the experiences of these professionals as well as the ones who recovered from burnout in subsequent chapters.

3. Two other professionals in the study, also public health nurses, were "new administrators" when we first studied them.

Chapter 10

1. In order to identify conditions that might facilitate recovery from early career burnout, I analyzed the interviews of all subjects following the grounded theory approach, as initially developed by Glaser and Strauss (1967) and subsequently refined and elaborated by Miles and Huberman (1984). This analysis was verified by two graduate students before the five "good recovery" subjects had been identified. More than two dozen factors that could contribute to recovery from burnout were identified. Once the five good recovery subjects had been singled out, I examined their data in terms of these possible contributors to recovery. Some of these contributors seemed to be particularly salient. These are the topics that I consider in this and subsequent chapters.

2. These changes occurred no more than three years after burnout developed. Professionals who remain in unfavorable work situations for longer periods of time may not respond so readily to a change in work environments. At some point, burnout may become so entrenched that job change is no longer effective in helping a person to recover.

3. There has been little research on the relationship between professionals' attitudes and the nature of their work, but there is reason to believe that professionals are more likely to be committed and caring when they find their work fulfilling. Maslow, for instance, suggested that when people feel enriched and fulfilled, they're more likely to develop a sense of social obligation out of gratitude (Maas, 1989).

Maas (1989) argued that satisfying, meaningful work experiences are an important contextual support for socially responsible behavior. Mortimer and Lorence (1979), in their longitudinal study of values and how they change over time, found that people who ended up in jobs that were high in challenge and opportunity for innovative thinking became more people-oriented in their values over time. Job satisfaction by itself, however, isn't necessarily associated with greater altruism. Khoury and Khoury (1982), for instance, found no relation between job satisfaction and altruism in a sample of police. Their negative findings could be related to the variables they were measuring—job satisfaction isn't the same as having work that is intrinsically interesting and meaningful. The negative results could also be due to the occupational group they studied—police. Many studies of burnout have found a relationship between fulfilling work and commitment and caring in a variety of professions (see, for instance, Maslach, 1982, and Pines and Aronson, 1988, for reviews).

4. Pines and Aronson (1988), in their book on career burnout, have emphasized the importance of significance—or lack of it—in the burnout process.

5. In his work on optimal experience, or "flow," Csikszentmihalyi (1990) has found that clear goals and immediate feedback are important ingredients. People in general are more likely to find an activity fulfilling if it has these qualities.

6. Csikszentmihalyi (1990) has suggested that the optimal experience is one where there is a close match between a person's skills and the demands of the activity. Too much challenge, therefore, can be as detrimental as too little. When the professionals in my study talked about work that was positively challenging, it probably was just challenging enough, given their skill levels.

7. Lipp (1980) described how many of the psychiatrists he studied became bored and restless when most of their time was spent dispensing medication. It made them feel that their "clinical skill" was going to waste, and their self-respect suffered, so they tried to become more involved in psychotherapy—a skill that was more central to their professional identity.

8. The characteristics that make work "meaningful," which I've noted in this chapter, have been recognized as important by other researchers. Hackman and Oldham (1976), for instance, argued that all workers will be more motivated, productive, and satisfied if their work is high in significance, meaning, responsibility, and knowledge of results. Sarata (1972) found that these qualities were associated with job satisfaction in those working in the field of mental retardation. And Kanter (1989) has suggested that it's important to professionals that they "take on ever-more demanding, challenging, important, or rewarding assignments that involve greater exercise of the skills that define the professional's stock-in-trade"

(p. 511). Unfortunately, professionals often find that their work lacks these qualities. In a study of professionals working in state government, Jeffrey Kane and I found that blue-collar workers actually reported higher levels of skill variety, task identity (i.e., the sense that one is able to work on a whole task from beginning to end rather than just a part of it), task significance, and knowledge of results (Cherniss & Kane, 1987).

9. Organizational psychologists have extensively studied "job involvement." Usually, however, they think of job involvement in global terms. They ask workers to rate how involved they are "in their jobs." Mark's response suggests that this approach may be missing something important. Workers like Mark might be highly involved in some parts of their jobs, but not in others. While overall job involvement may be important to assess and study, it could be equally interesting to study how levels of involvement vary across different aspects of the job.

Chapter 11

1. The psychological significance of autonomy and control has been a prominent theme in psychological research. Hundreds of studies have documented the importance of personal control for satisfaction, motivation, and health outcomes (e.g., Deci, 1980; Rodin & Langer, 1977; Seligman, 1975), but autonomy and control are particularly significant for the professional (Abrahamson, 1967; Raelin, 1985). Bledstein (1976), in a book about the "culture of professionalism," wrote, "The professional person absolutely protected his precious autonomy against all assailants, not in the name of an irrational egotism but in the name of a special grasp of the universe and a special place in it. In the service of mankind—the higher ideal—the professional resisted all corporate encroachments and regulations upon his independence, whether from government bureaucrats, university trustees, business administrators, public laymen, or even his own professional associations" (p. 62). Many studies have documented the aversive effects of restricted autonomy on professionals. Lipp (1980), for example, found that psychiatrists became especially frustrated when they felt that a patient should be treated in a certain way, but couldn't mandate it because someone else was the primary therapist. Several studies have pointed to the importance of professional autonomy for the prevention of burnout (Friedman, 1991; Jackson, Schwab, & Schuler, 1986; O'Driscoll and Schubert, 1988). Based on these findings, Burisch (1993) has argued that lack of autonomy is the root cause of professional burnout.

2. Sarason (1985) has observed how destructive time pressure is for professional caring and compassion. When professionals' work is regulated by the clock, when their time must be filled by as many

income-producing activities as possible, caring and compassion for the clients inevitably suffer. Time pressure also leaves "little time to think, reflect, raise questions, or pose issues. . . ." (p. 51).

3. There is some scientific support for this interactionist view. Graen, Novak, and Sommerkamp (1982) have shown that the same supervisor may be rated very differently by different subordinates. In fact, the subordinates who work for the same supervisor often differ more in their perceptions of that supervisor than do two subordinates working for two different supervisors. Graen et al. believe that this pattern reflects the importance of "leader-member exchange." When subordinates and supervisors give each other what each needs to achieve their goals, the relationship is positive. The quality of the relationship is influenced by a reciprocal exchange process.

4. Douglas McGregor (1960) formulated a model of leadership behavior based on differences in leaders' beliefs about followers. McGregor proposed that leaders believed in one of two theories of human nature. "Theory X," the more pessimistic one, views people as inherently lazy and selfish. They need strong, firm direction, close surveillance, and the threat of punishment to make them do what needs to be done. The other view, which McGregor called "Theory Y," sees people as inherently self-motivated and responsible. People want to do a good job, and if they work in a positive, supportive environment, they will perform at high levels with little need for prodding or encouragement. McGregor recognized that in practice many workers did not conform to the more positive view, but he explained this by noting that leadership expectations tend to be self-fulfilling prophecies. If a supervisor believes in Theory X, he or she will treat workers in ways that discourage their creativity and commitment, and the workers will begin to act just the way Theory X would predict. Conversely, leaders who believe in Theory Y will act in ways that encourage their followers to be responsible, motivated, and committed.

5. Foner (1994) has shown that even administrators working in stressful environments can be supportive and considerate toward employees. In the nursing home where she spent many months as a participant observer, she saw that the supervisors of the nursing aides varied considerably in their management styles, even though all were affected by the same structural demands. Aides who worked under supervisors who were kind and considerate were more satisfied, less stressed, and more willing to accept direction—even when those supervisors were firm and had high standards.

6. Maccoby (1988) wrote that for the professional experts, "It is important to be respected as professionals" (p. 121) and that "external recognition" is especially valued by professionals in this regard.

7. Lawler (1990), in discussing the need to change the nature of work in the post-industrial age, has noted that the most innovative companies have made worker development a top priority. Part of this emphasis

has been to link pay increases and promotions to learning. The more skills a worker acquires, the higher the pay. In other words, advancement and development have become linked for many workers, not just professionals like Diane Peterson.

8. Kram (1986), in discussing the benefits of mentoring for positive career development, noted that colleagues, friends, family members, and even subordinates can provide the same positive functions that are usually associated with an older mentor. In proposing a broader and more complex view of mentoring, Kram defined it in terms of nine functions that can be provided in any relationship. These include: sponsorship, coaching, protection, role modeling, counseling, acceptance, and confirmation.

9. Kerr (1977) has argued that for professionals, collegial relationships are a more significant source of stimulation and support than is supervision. In fact, colleagues can provide a "substitute" for supervision. There is some research that supports this view. A study of professional social workers, for example, found that their relations with coworkers were the main source of esteem, satisfaction, and meaning in their work. Few satisfactions came from relationships with administrators or clients (Pithouse, 1985). In a study of correctional personnel, Gerstein, Topp, and Correll (1987) found that burnout levels were more strongly associated with the quality of relations with coworkers than with the workers' characteristics such as age and length of employment.

10. Hall and Schneider (1973), in an extensive study of the work lives of priests, suggested that the two qualities in the work environment that were most important for positive career development were autonomy and support. They also found that it was the rare priest who had working conditions high in both these qualities. More recent studies have continued to find that organizational support, along with autonomy, is important for helping professionals. Leiter and Maslach (1988) found that poor interpersonal relations among nurses in a general hospital greatly exacerbated burnout. O'Driscoll and Schubert (1988) discovered that problematic interactions between central office administrators and sections of the agency significantly contributed to emotional exhaustion in staff working in a social service agency, while positive interactions and communication levels within sections of the agency were associated with stronger feelings of personal accomplishment. Drory and Shamir (1988) looked at a wide range of variables and found that lack of management support was the major correlate of burnout in a sample of prison guards.

Chapter 12

1. McCall, Lombardo, & Morrison (1988) reached a similar conclusion in a study of business executives. They were interested in learning about

what kinds of experiences help executives to become successful. They queried 400 executives in seven Fortune 500 corporations, and they discovered that the best teachers for rising executives had been "turning-point jobs involving financial and personal risk." When they probed more deeply to discover what about these jobs was so beneficial, they found that it was the sense of mastery that successfully meeting the challenge had provided.

2. Dalton (1989) argued that professional employees find it hard to maintain a sense of efficacy without "organizational and people skills and interests" (p. 103). He urged professionals to move beyond technical proficiency and to develop the "broad perspective necessary to get things done in a complex organizational setting" (p. 103).

3. Few professionals, unfortunately, develop good organizational negotiation skill. Shinn, Rosario, Morch, and Chestnut (1984), for instance, in a study of group therapists working in a variety of settings, found that most of them coped with stress on the job by focusing on interests outside the job or by "adopting a positive outlook." Only about 20 percent coped by trying to change the job.

4. Dalton (1989) acknowledged the importance of individual commitment to development for positive career outcomes. He wrote that an ability to form "mutually developmental relationships" is crucial for career satisfaction (p. 103).

5. In a thoughtful analysis of the mentoring process, Kram (1986) proposed that people's psychological make-up affects their willingness to enter into mentoring relationships. More specifically, any concerns that people have about authority, intimacy, self-esteem, competence, competition, or conflict will impede the development of mentoring relationships. Attitudes toward the importance of work, and whether learning is perceived as a collaborative process, are also important, according to Kram.

Chapter 13

1. For a good introduction to the field of career counseling and counseling technique, see Yost and Corbishly (1987).

2. Sarason (1982) has described in more detail the typical process used by reformers in trying to change the way mathematics is taught in public schools.

Chapter 14

1. In her fascinating book on communes, Kanter (1972) has identified a number of "commitment mechanisms" that were used in the most successful communities. These mechanisms included a clear, explicit, formal ideology, which reduced ambiguity and self-doubt, a specific program of behavioral norms that linked daily activity with

the ideology, and practices that brought members into meaningful contact with one another and that broke down social distinctions among them. The most successful communities also required members to make a heavy investment of time, energy, and money, and they often had rituals that involved self-mortification. All of these commitment mechanisms could be found in the religious community that I studied.

2. A notable exception is Pines (1993) who has argued that the root cause of professional burnout is the frustrated quest for meaning in work. "When people try to find meaning in their life through work and feel that they have failed, the result is burnout" (Pines, 1993, p. 33).

3. Frankl (1962) also questioned the main tenet of the humanistic school of therapy, represented by thinkers like Maslow and Rogers. "Self-actualization," wrote Frankl (1962, pp. 112–113), "is not a possible aim at all; for the simple reason that the more a man would strive for it, the more he would miss it. . . . Self-actualization cannot be attained if it is made an end in itself, but only as a side effect of self-transcendence."

4. The most popular and respected measure of burnout is the Maslach Burnout Inventory (Maslach & Jackson, 1986). This instrument has three scales. The item, "I feel burned out from my work," loads on the "emotional exhaustion" scale when the items are factor analyzed. Thus, in the minds of most helping professionals, burnout and emotional exhaustion are synonomous.

5. An interesting counter-trend is the growth in religious affiliation during the last two decades, and the particular attraction of fundamentalist religious groups. The powerful sense of meaning, structure, and community provided by the fundamentalist groups seem to strike a special chord for many, but, while these groups have grown in recent years, a large majority of North Americans and Western Europeans remain detached from religious institutions—even if they attend services more or less regularly.

6. Another psychologist, Erich Fromm (1976), also wrote about the psychological costs of modern capitalism—how it encourages people to value personal success more highly than social responsibility. Self-esteem and identity, in such a society, are based on what one has and what one consumes. "Greed for money, fame, and power," he wrote, "has become the dominant theme in life" (p. 19).

7. Bledstein (1976) has trenchantly analyzed the basic ideological foundations on which modern professions are based.

References

Abrahamson, M. (1967). *The professional in the organization.* Chicago: Rand McNally.

Adler, S., & Aranya, N. (1984). A comparison of the work needs, attitudes, and preferences of professional accountants at different career stages. *Journal of Vocational Behavior, 25,* 45–57.

Alderfer, C. P., & Guzzo, R. A. (1979). Life experiences and adults' enduring strength of desires in organizations. *Administrative Science Quarterly, 24,* 347–361.

Arthur, M. B., & Kramm, K. E. (1989). Reciprocity at work: The separate, yet inseparable possibilities for individual and organizational development. In M. B. Arthur, D. T. Hall, & B. S. Lawrence (Eds.), *Handbook of career theory* (pp. 292–312). New York: Cambridge University Press.

Bailyn, L. (1977). Involvement and accommodation in technical careers: An inquiry into the relation to work at mid-career. In J. Van Maanen (Ed.), *Organizational careers: Some new perspectives* (pp. 109–132). New York: Wiley.

Bartolome, F., & Evans, P. (1979, Spring). Professional lives versus private lives: Shifting patterns of managerial commitment. *Organizational Dynamics, 7*(4), 3–29.

Batson, C. D. (1991). *The altruism question.* Hillsdale, NJ: Lawrence Erlbaum.

Becker, H. S., Geer, B., Hughes, E. C., & Strauss, A. (1961). *Boys in white.* Chicago: University of Chicago Press.

Belkin, L. (1992, June 4). In lessons on empathy, doctors become patients. *New York Times,* A1, B5.

Berkowitz, L. (1970). The self, selfishness, and altruism. In J. Macaulay & L. Berkowitz (Eds.), *Altruism and helping behavior* (pp. 143–151). New York: Academic Press.

Blackburn, R. T., & Fox, T. G. (1983). Physicians' values and their career stage. *Journal of Vocational Behavior, 22,* 159–173.

Blau, G. J. (1985). The measurment and prediction of career commitment. *Journal of Occupational Psychology, 58,* 277–288.

Bledstein, B. J. (1976). *The culture of professionalism: The middle class and the development of higher education in America.* New York: Norton.

Bloom, S. W. (1979). Socialization for the physician's role: A review of some contributions of research to theory. In E. C. Shapiro & L. M. Lowenstein (Eds.), *Becoming a physician* (pp. 3–52). Cambridge, MA: Ballinger.

Brager, G., & Holloway, S. (1978). *Changing human service organizations: Politics and practice.* New York: Free Press.

Bray, D. W., Campbell, R. J., & Grant, D. L. (1974). *Formative years in business: A long-term AT&T study of managerial lives.* New York: Wiley.

Burisch, M. (1993). In search of theory: Some ruminations on the nature and etiology of burnout. In W. B. Schaufeli, C. Maslach, & T. Marek (Eds.), *Professional burnout: Recent developments in theory and research* (pp. 75–94). Washington, DC: Taylor & Francis.

Campbell, R. J., & Moses, J. L. (1986). Careers from an organizational perspective. In D. T. Hall (Ed.), *Career development in organizations* (pp. 274–309). San Francisco: Jossey-Bass.

Camus, A. (1955). *The myth of Sisyphus.* New York: Random House.

Cellis, W., III. (1992, November 4). Many teachers, required to make do with less, are giving less in return. *New York Times,* D2.

Cherniss, C. (1980). *Professional burnout in human service organizations.* New York: Praeger.

Cherniss, C., & Kane, J. S. (1987). Public sector professionals: Job characteristics, satisfaction, and aspirations for intrinsic fulfillment through work. *Human Relations, 40,* 125–136.

Cherniss, C., & Krantz, D. (1982). The ideological community as an antidote to burnout in the human services. In B. A. Farber (Ed.), *Stress and burnout in the human service professions.* New York: Pergamon.

Colarelli, N. O., & Siegal, S. M. (1966). *Ward H: An adventure in innovation.* New York: Van Nostrand.

Cronbach, L. J. (1975). Beyond the two disciplines of scientific psychology. *American Psychologist, 30,* 116–127.

Csikszentmihalyi, M. (1990). *Flow.* New York: Harper.

Dalton, G. (1989). Developmental views of careers in organizations. In M. B. Arthur, D. T. Hall, & B. S. Lawrence (Eds.), *Handbook of career theory* (pp. 89–109). New York: Cambridge University Press.

Deci, E. L. (1980). *The psychology of self-determination.* Lexington, MA: D. C. Heath.

De Fleur, M. L. (1964). Occupational roles as portrayed on television. *Public Opinion Quarterly, 38,* 57–74.

de Grazia, S. (1962). *Of time, work, and leisure.* New York: Vintage.

Dressel, P. (1984). *The service trap: From altruism to dirty work.* Springfield, IL: Charles Thomas.

Drory, A., & Shamir, B. (1988). Effects of organizational and life variables on job satisfaction and burnout. *Group and Organization Studies, 13*, 441–455.

Erikson, E. H. (1968). *Identity, youth, and crisis.* New York: W. W. Norton.

Fiske, M., & Chiriboga, D. A. (1990). *Change and continuity in adult life.* San Francisco: Jossey-Bass.

Foner, N. (1994). *The caregiving dilemma: Work in an American nursing home.* Berkeley, CA: University of California Press.

Frank, J. D. (1973). *Persuasion and healing.* Baltimore: Johns Hopkins University Press.

Frankl, V. E. (1962). *Man's search for meaning.* New York: Clarion.

Frese, M. (1982). Occupational socialization and psychological development: An underemphasized research perspective in industrial psychology. *Journal of Occupational Psychology, 55*, 209–224.

Freudenberger, H. J., & Richelson, G. (1980). *Burnout: The high cost of high achievement.* New York: Anchor Press.

Friedman, I. (1991). *High and low burnout schools: Sources of stress at the classroom and school level.* Paper presented at the Conference on Teacher Stress and Burnout, Teachers' College, Columbia University, New York, NY.

Fromm, E. (1976). *To have or to be.* New York: Harper & Row.

Gallos, J. V. (1989). Exploring women's development: Implications for career theory, practice, and research. In M. B. Arthur, D. T. Hall, & B. S. Lawrence (Eds.), *Handbook of career theory* (pp. 110–132). New York: Cambridge University Press.

Gerstein, L. H., Topp, C. G., & Correll, G. (1987). The role of the environment and person when predicting burnout among correctional personnel. *Criminal Justice and Behavior, 14*, 352–369.

Gibson, S., & Dembo, M. H. (1984). Teacher efficacy: A construct validation. *Journal of Educational Psychology, 76*, 569–582.

Glaser, E. M. & Strauss, A. (1967). *The discovery of grounded theory.* Chicago: Aldine.

Goldenberg, I. I. (1971). *Build me a mountain: Youth, poverty, and the creation of new settings.* Cambridge, MA: MIT Press.

Goleman, D. (1991, November 13). All too often, the doctor isn't listening, studies show. *New York Times*, C1, C15.

Gordon, S. (1991). *Prisoners of men's dreams: Striking out for a new feminine future.* Boston: Little, Brown, & Co.

Gould, R. J. (1978). *Transformations: Growth and change in adult life.* New York: Simon & Schuster.

Gow, K. M. (1982). *How nurses' emotions affect patient care.* New York: Springer.

Gowler, D., & Legge, K. (1989). Rhetoric in bureaucratic careers: Managing the meaning of management success. In M. B. Arthur, D. T. Hall, & B. S. Lawrence (Eds.), *Handbook of career theory* (pp. 437–453). New York: Cambridge University Press.

Graen, G. G., Novak, M. A., & Sommerkamp, P. (1982). The effects of leader-member exchange and job design on productivity and satisfaction: Testing a dual attachment model. *Organizational Behavior and Human Performance, 30,* 109–131.

Gray, R. M., Moody, P. M., & Newman, R. E. (1965). An analysis of physicians' attitudes of cynicism and humanitarianism before and after entering medical practice. *Journal of Medical Education, 40,* 760–766.

Haan, N. (1989). Personality at midlife. In S. Hunter & M. Sundel (Eds.), *Midlife myths* (pp. 145–156). Newbury Park, CA: Sage.

Hackman, J. R., & Oldham, G. F. (1976). Motivation through the design of work: Test of a theory. *Organizational Behavior and Human Performance, 16,* 250–279.

Hall, D. T. (1976). *Careers in organizations.* Pacific Palisades, CA: Goodyear.

Hall, D. T. (1986). Breaking career routines: Midcareer choice and identity development. In D. T. Hall (Ed.), *Career development in organizations* (pp. 120–159). San Francisco: Jossey-Bass.

Hall, D. T., & Mansfield, R. (1975). Relationship of age and seniority with career variables of engineers and scientists. *Journal of Applied Psychology, 60,* 201–210.

Hall, D. T., & Nougaim, K. E. (1968). An examination of Maslow's need hierarchy in an organizational setting. *Organizational Behavior and Human Performance, 3,* 12–35.

Hall, D. T., & Schneider, B. (1973). *Organizational climates and careers: The work lives of priests.* New York: Seminar Press.

Howe, M. J. (1982). Biographical evidence and the development of outstanding individuals. *American Psychologist, 37,* 1071–1081.

Hughes, J. R., & Carver, E. J. (1990). Overcoming barriers to the use of facilitative empathy in practice. In R. C. MacKay, J. R. Hughes, & E. J. Carver (Eds.), *Empathy in the helping relationship* (pp. 168–181). New York: Springer.

Hunicutt, A. W., & MacMillan, T. F. (1983). Beating burnout: Findings from a three-year study. *Journal of Mental Health Administration, 10* (2), 7–9.

Ickes, W. J., & Kidd, R. F. (1976). An attributional analysis of helping behavior. In J. H. Harvey, W. J. Ickes, & R. F. Kidd (Eds.), *New directions in attributional research* (Vol. 1, pp. 311–334). Hillsdale, NJ: Lawrence Erlbaum.

Jackson, S. E., Schwab, R. L., & Schuler, R. S. (1986). Toward an understanding of the burnout phenomenon. *Journal of Applied Psychology, 71,* 630–640.

Kanter, R. M. (1972). *Commitment and community: Communes and utopias in sociological perspective.* Cambridge, MA: Harvard University Press.

Kanter, R. M. (1989). Careers and the wealth of nations: A macro-perspective on the structure and implications of career forms. In M. B.

Arthur, D. T. Hall, & B. S. Lawrence (Eds.), *Handbook of career theory* (pp. 506–522). New York: Cambridge University Press.

Kerr, P. (1991, October 10). Tempus fugit, but you can buy it. *New York Times*, D1, D8.

Kerr, S. (1977). Substitutes for leadership: Some implications for organizational design. *Organization and Administrative Science, 8*, 135–146.

Khoury, R. M., & Khoury, D. C. (1982). Job satisfaction and work performance in police. *Psychological Reports, 51*, 282.

Korman, A. K., Wittig-Berman, U., & Lang, D. (1981). Career success and personal failure: Alienation in professionals and managers. *Academy of Management Journal, 24*, 342–360.

Kram, K. E. (1986). Mentoring in the workplace. In D. T. Hall (Ed.), *Career development in organizations* (pp. 160–201). San Francisco: Jossey-Bass.

Kramer, M. (1974). *Reality shock.* St. Louis: C. V. Mosby.

Kyriacou, C. (1980). Sources of stress among British teachers: The contribution of job factors and personality factors. In C. L. Cooper & J. Marshall (Eds.), *White collar and professional stress* (pp. 3–17). Chichester, England: Wiley.

LaMonica, E. L., Carew, D. K., Winder, A. E., Haase, A. M. B., & Blanchard, K. (1976). Empathy training as the major thrust of a staff development program. *Nursing Research, 25*, 447–451.

Lawler, E. E. (1990). Achieving competitiveness by creating new organization cultures and structures. In D. B. Fishman & C. Cherniss (Eds.), *The human side of corporate competitiveness* (pp. 69–101). Newbury Park, CA: Sage.

Leiter, M. P., & Maslach, C. (1988). The impact of interpersonal environment on burnout and organizational commitment. *Journal of Occupational Behavior, 9*, 297–308.

Levinson, D. J. (1978). *The seasons of a man's life.* New York: Knopf.

Lipp, M. R. (1980). *The bitter pill: Doctors, patients, and failed expectations.* New York: Harper & Row.

London, M. (1985). *Developing managers.* San Francisco, CA: Jossey-Bass.

Lortie, D. C. (1975). *Schoolteacher.* Chicago: University of Chicago Press.

Lynn, K. S. (1965). *The professions in America.* New York: Houghton-Mifflin.

Maas, H. S. (1989). Social responsibility in middle age: Prospects and preconditions. In S. Hunter & M. Sundel (Eds.), *Midlife myths* (pp. 253–271). Newbury Park, CA: Sage.

Maccoby, M. (1988). *Why work?* New York: Simon & Schuster.

Marks, S. (1979, Summer). Culture, human energy, and self-actualization: A sociological offering to humanistic psychology. *Journal of Humanistic Psychology, 19* (3), 27–42.

Maslach, C. (1982). *Burnout: The cost of caring.* Englewood Cliffs, NJ: Prentice-Hall.

Maslach, C., & Jackson, S. E. (1986). *Maslach Burnout Inventory: Second Edition.* Palo Alto, CA: Consulting Psychologists Press.

McCall, M. W., Jr., Lombardo, M. M., & Morrison, A. M. (1988). *The lessons of experience: How successful executives develop on the job.* Lexington, MA: Lexington Books.

McGregor, D. (1960). *The human side of enterprise.* New York: McGraw-Hill.

Mechanic, D. (1976). *The growth of bureaucratic medicine: An inquiry into the dynamics of patient behavior and the organization of medical care.* New York: Wiley.

Mechanic, D. (1989). *Painful choices: Research and essays on health care.* New Brunswick, NJ: Transaction.

Merser, C. (1986). *Grown-ups: A generation in search of adulthood.* New York: Plume.

Miles, M. B., & Huberman, A. M. (1984). *Qualitative data analysis.* Beverly Hills, CA: Sage.

Mizrahi, T. (1986). *Getting rid of patients: Contradictions in the socialization of physicians.* New Brunswick, NJ: Rutgers University Press.

Mortimer, J. T., & Lorence, J. (1979). Work experience and occupational value socialization: A longitudinal study. *American Journal of Sociology, 84,* 1361–1385.

Motowidlo, S. J. (1984). Does job satisfaction lead to consideration and personal sensitivity? *Academy of Management Journal, 27,* 910–915.

Moyers, B. (1989). Michael Josephson, ethicist. In B. Moyers, *A world of ideas* (pp. 14–27). New York: Doubleday.

Neugarten, B. L. (1968). The awareness of middle age. In B. L. Neugarten (Ed.), *Middle age and aging: A reader in social psychology* (pp. 93–98). Chicago: University of Chicago Press.

New Brunswick Home News. (1988, January 15). College freshmen oriented on careers, A5.

Nicholson, N. (1984). A theory of work role transitions. *Administrative Science Quarterly, 29,* 172–191.

O'Driscoll, M. P., & Schubert, T. (1988). Organizational climate and burnout in a New Zealand social service agency. *Work and Stress, 2,* 199–204.

Pelz, D. C., & Andrews, F. M. (1966). *Scientists in organization: Productive climates for research and development.* New York: Wiley.

Perun, P. J., & Bielby, D. D. (1981). Toward a model of female occupational behavior: A human development approach. *Psychology of Women Quarterly, 6,* 234–250.

Pines, A. (1993). Burnout: An existential perspective. In W. B. Schaufeli, C. Maslach, & T. Marek, (Eds.), *Professional burnout: Recent developments in theory and research* (pp. 33–51). Washington, DC: Taylor & Francis.

Pines, A., & Aronson, E. (1988). *Career burnout.* New York: Free Press.

Pithouse, A. (1985). Poor visibility: Case talk and collegial assessment in a social work office. *Work and Occupations, 12,* 77–89.

Prottas, J. M. (1980). *People-processing: The street-level bureaucrat in public service bureaucracies.* Lexington, MA: D. C. Heath.

Raelin, J. A. (1985). Work patterns in the professional life-cycle. *Journal of Occupational Psychology, 58,* 177–187.

Rhodes, S. R. 1983 Age-related differences in work attitudes and behavior: A review and conceptual analysis. *Psychological Bulletin, 93,* 328–367.

Rhodes, S. R., & Doering, M. (1983). An integrated model of career change. *Academy of Management Review, 8,* 631–639.

Roberts, P., & Newton, P. (1987). Levinsonian studies of women's adult development. *Psychology and Aging, 2,* 154–163.

Roberts, S. (1993, June 30). Stein pulls out of advocate race, saying his political career is over. *New York Times,* A1, B4.

Rodin, J., & Langer, E. J. (1977). Long-term effects of a control-relevant intervention with the institutionalized aged. *Journal of Personality and Social Psychology, 35,* 897–902.

Rothman, D. J. 1978 The state as parent: Social policy in the Progressive Era. In W. Gaylin, I. Glasser, S. Marcus, & D. J. Rothman (Eds.), *Doing Good: The limits of benevolence* (pp. 67–96). New York: Pantheon.

Rubin, L. B. (1979). *Woman of a certain age: The midlife search for self.* New York: Harper & Row.

Sarason, S. B. (1972). *The creation of settings and the future societies.* San Francisco: Jossey-Bass.

Sarason, S. B. (1977). *Work, aging, and social change.* New York: Free Press.

Sarason, S. B. (1985). *Caring and compassion in clinical practice.* San Francisco: Jossey-Bass.

Sarason, S. B. (1988). *The making of an American psychologist.* San Francisco: Jossey-Bass.

Sarason, S. B., Carroll, C., Maton, K., Cohen, S., & Lorentz, E. (1977). *Human services and resource networks.* San Francisco, CA: Jossey-Bass.

Sarason, S. B., & Lorentz, E. (1979). *The challenge of the human resource exchange network.* San Francisco, CA: Jossey-Bass.

Sarason, S. B., Sarason, E., & Cowden, P. (1975). Aging and the nature of work. *American Psychologist, 30,* 584–593.

Sarason, S. B., Zitnay, G., & Grossman, F. K. (1971). *The creation of a community setting.* Syracuse, NY: Syracuse University Press.

Sarata, B. P. V. (1972). *Job satisfactions of individuals working with the mentally retarded.* Doctoral dissertation, Yale University.

Savicki, V., & Cooley, E. (1987). The relationship of work environment and client contact to burnout in mental health professionals. *Journal of Counseling and Development, 65,* 249–252.

Schein, E. H. (1971). The individual, the organization, and the career: A conceptual scheme. *Journal of Applied Behavioral Science, 7,* 401–426.

Schein, E. H. (1972). *Professional education: Some new directions.* New York: McGraw-Hill.

Schein, E. H. (1978). *Career dynamics.* Reading, MA: Addison-Wesley.

Seligman, M. E. P. (1975). *Helplessness: On depression, development, and death.* San Francisco: Freeman.

Shinn, M., Rosario, M., Morch, H., & Chestnut, D. E. (1984). Coping with job stress and burnout in the human services. *Journal of Personality and Social Psychology, 46,* 864–876.

Sonnenfeld, J. & Kotter, J. P. (1982) The maturation of career theory. *Human Relations, 35,* 19–46.

Stark, E. (1988, February). For love or money? *Psychology Today,* 18.

Stelling, J. G. (1982). Review of *Professional burnout in human service organizations,* by Cary Cherniss. *Contemporary Sociology, 11,* 105–106.

Suran, B. G., & Sheridan, E. P. (1985). Management of burnout: Training psychologists in professional life span perspectives. *Professional Psychology: Research and Practice, 16,* 741–752.

Tamir, L. M. (1989). Modern myths about men at midlife: An assessment. In S. Hunter & M. Sundel (Eds.), *Midlife myths* (pp. 157–180). Newbury Park, CA: Sage.

Truax, C. B., Altmann, H., & Millis, W. A., Jr. (1974). Therapeutic relationships provided by various professionals. *Journal of Community Psychology, 2,* 33–36.

Turnbull, A. P., & Turnbull, H. R. (Eds.) (1979). *Parents speak out.* Columbus, OH: Merrill.

Van Maanen, J. (1977). Experiencing organizations: Notes on the meaning of careers and socialization. In J. Van Maanen (Ed.), *Organizational careers: Some new perspectives* (pp. 49–64). New York: Wiley.

Veysey, L. (1975). Who's a professional? Who cares? Review of *Advocacy and objectivity: A crisis in the professionalization of American Social Science, 1865–1905,* by M. O. Furner. *Reviews in American History, 3,* 419–423.

Weber, M. (1947). *The theory of social and economic organization.* New York: Free Press.

Yost, E. B., & Corbishly, M. A. (1987). *Career counseling: A psychological approach.* San Francisco: Jossey-Bass.

Index

Abrahamson, M., 208
Accommodators, 203
Accountability
    demands for, 35
Achievement, need for, 164–166
Adaptability
    see Flexibility
Adler, A., 184
Adler, S., 90
Administrative demands
    impact on professionals' expec-
    tations, 173
Administrative support, 140–145,
    148–150
Administrators
    attitudes towards employees,
    67–68
    becoming an, 67–68, 112–113
    conflicts with, in new profes-
    sionals, 20–23
Admissions criteria for professional
    training, 176
Adopting more modest goals, 37–39
Adult development
    research and theory on, 88–89
    research on creativity during,
    78–79
Advancement stage, 88

Affirmative action policies, 74
African-American professionals,
    147–148
Alderfer, C. P., 202
"Alice Harris," 14, 89–90
Alienation, 184, 187
Alienation from work
    see Commitment
Altmann, H., 5
Altruism
    decline in, 68
    loss of, in new professionals,
    42–43
Ambivalence towards helping the
    needy in American society,
    32–36
American Medical Association, 6
Andrews, F. M., 82
"Angela McPherson," 56–57, 90,
    93–94, 96, 112–114, 123,
    132–133, 139, 153, 161
"Anita Warren," 52, 54–55, 61, 102
Anomie, 184
Anti-war movement, 35
Applications to professional train-
    ing programs
    changes in, 45
Aranya, N., 90

Aronson, E., 207

Arthur, M. B., 202

Aspirations
  lowering of, and increased satis-
    faction, 98

Assassinations of popular leaders,
  35, 45

Association of American Medical
  Colleges, 6

AT&T, 88, 201

Attitudes, professional
  changes in, 37–43, 62

Attorneys
  see Lawyers

Autonomy, professional, 31, 35,
  135–139, 149, 208–210
  as cause of career change, 57
  as reason for choosing to enter a
    profession, 198
  increase in, over time, 98
  lack of, in new professionals, 20,
    21

Bailyn, L., 203

Balance between work and nonwork parts of life, 91–95, 144,
  162–164
  difficulty in achieving, 94–95
  growing importance of, over
    time, 91, 203–204

Bartolome, F., 203

Batson, C. D., 68, 70

Becker, H. S., 6

Belkin, L., 6

Berkowitz, L., 70

Bielby, D. D., 204

Blackburn, R. T., 7, 200, 203

Blanchard, K., 5

Blau, G. J., 201

Bledstein, B. J., 208, 212

Bloom, S. W., 197

Boredom, 25–26, 125–126

Boss
  see Supervisor

Brager, G., 30, 32

Bray, D. W., 88, 201, 203

Bureaucracy, 28–31
  as barrier to change, 113
  constraints and obstacles in, 73
  lack of support for compassion
    in, 198
  as contributor to burnout,
    136–138, 167

Burisch, M., 208

Burnout, 8, 10–12, 23, 37–47, 78
  as reason for leaving public ser-
    vice, 52–53
  as reason for remaining in job,
    59
  lack of meaning and significance
    in work as cause of, 184–186
  prevention, suggestions for,
    169–179

Bush, G., 74

"Calvin Miller," 19, 34, 38–41, 66,
  80, 102

Campbell, R. J., 88, 90

Camus, A., 184

Career change, 12–13, 51–52
  gender differences in, 199
  impact of cultural values on, 61
  impact of family support on,
    114, 115
  impact on satisfaction with life
    and work, 101
  motives for, 60
  see also Change in role

Career counseling, 176–178, 211

Career insight, 155, 205
  career counseling as way of
    developing, 176–178
  increases in, over time, 99–101

Carew, D. K., 5

Caring
  see Compassion
"Carol Potter," 81–82, 116–119,
    126, 142, 147, 152, 154, 161, 163
Carver, E. J., 69
Celis, W., III, 5
Challenge
  and flow, 207
  as antidote to burnout, 123–125
  as reason for career change, 54
  growing importance of, 89–91
  lack of, for new professionals,
    25–26
  see also Intellectual stimulation
Challenging pre-professional expe-
    riences
  impact on burnout, 151–153,
    210–211
Change in role
  as stimulant of creativity, 82
  as antidote to burnout, 118–119,
    126, 167
  contribution to increased career
    insight, 100
"Charlotte Noble," 73, 80, 92–93
Cherniss, C., 9, 201, 208
Chestnut, D. E., 211
Chiriboga, D. A., 70, 79, 204
Clients
  concentrating on a few, as way
    of coping, 37–38
  effect of social change on behav-
    ior of, 35–36
  negative behavior of, 23–25, 40,
    108
  professional attitudes towards,
    39–42, 63–67, 199–200
  see also Difficult clients
Clinical psychologists
  see Mental health professionals
Clinical social workers
  see Mental health professionals

Clinton, B., 51
Colarelli, N. O., 72, 172
Colleagues
  as source of support, 26–27, 91,
    145–147, 210
  impact on recovery from
    burnout, 115, 117, 118, 145, 147,
    167
  improved relations with, over
    time, 98
Collective bargaining, 35
  see also Labor-management con-
    flict
Collegiality
  lack of, for new professionals,
    26–27
Commitment, 201, 208
  changes in, 43–45, 62, 83–84
  impact of growing awareness of
    mortality on, 93
  impact of historical change on,
    94
  impact of job satisfaction on,
    206–207
  impact on professional effective-
    ness, 197
  moral vs. egoistic, in etiology of
    burnout, 185–186
  organizational mechanisms for
    increasing, 211–212
Compassion
  changes in, 60–62, 68–69
  impact of job satisfaction on,
    206–207
  impact of social context on,
    28–36
  impact on professional effective-
    ness, 197
  lack of, in professions, 4–7
Competence
  concern about, in new profes-
    sionals, 18–20, 25, 201–202

effect of limited resources on, 33
emphasis on, in the professions,
18–19, 188
see also Self-efficacy in professionals
Competition
see Success
Confidence
see Competence, Self-efficacy in
professionals
Continuing education
see Professional development
Control
see Autonomy
Cooley, E., 197
Corbishly, M. A., 211
Correll, G., 210
Counter-culture, 35
Cowden, P., 198
Cronbach, L. J., 194
Csikszentmihalyi, M., 207
Cultural values
influence on career change, 61
influence on conceptions of
career success, 61–62
impact on stress in new professionals, 28–36
see also Historical change
Cynicism
in new professionals, 41–42
in physicians, 6–7

Dalton, G., 211
Deci, E. L., 208
De Fleur, M. L., 17
de Grazia, S., 33
Dedication
see Commitment
Dembo, M. H., 200
"Diane Peterson," 145, 146, 210
Difficult clients, 63–74, 172–174,
201

as reason for career change,
57–58
as threat to professionals' sense
of efficacy, 69, 75
decline in tolerance towards, 63,
65–66, 68, 200
uneven distribution of, in professions, 73–74
see also Clients
"Douglas Furth," 27, 57–58, 61, 66,
71, 99
Drory, A., 210
Durkheim, E., 184

Education
see Teachers
Efficacy, sense of
see Competence, Self-efficacy in
professionals
Egoistic commitment
see Commitment
Emotional exhaustion
see Burnout
Empathy
see Compassion
Erikson, E. H., 200
Escalante, J., 18
"Eugenia Barton," 13–14, 41–42, 60,
63, 69, 72, 73, 79, 88, 94, 98,
107–109, 123, 126–127, 129, 132,
139, 153, 154, 165
Evans, P., 203
Expectations
cultural influences on, 173
impact on attitudes towards
clients, 65
impact on recovery from
burnout, 164–165
of public, for human services, 35
of new professionals, 17, 24
program to help professionals
develop more realistic, 173

Extrinsic rewards
  growing importance of, 205
  motivation for, 84
  professional attitudes towards,
  42–43

Family and work
  see Balance between work and
  nonwork parts of life
Family demands
  and career change, 54–55
  as career constraints, 102–104,
  108
  as reason for remaining in job, 60
Feedback
  from administrators, 142
  impact on burnout, 109, 114,
  122–123, 142
  lack of, 113
Financial rewards
  see Money
Fiske, M., 70, 79, 204,
Flexibility, 77–78, 201
  changes in, 78–79, 201
  impact of stress on, 82, 201
  see also Innovation, Resistance
  to change
"Flow," 207
Foner, N., 28, 29, 31, 33, 209
Fox, T. G., 7, 200, 203
Frank, J. D., 197
Frankl, V., 184, 185, 186, 212
Frese, M., 194
Freud, S., 184
Freudenberger, H. J., 185
Friedman, I., 208
Fromm, E., 198, 212

Gallos, J. V., 204
Gender
  impact on attitudes towards
  work, 95–96, 204

Gerstein, L. H., 210
Gibson, S., 200
Glaser, E. M., 195, 206
"Gloria Bennett," 59, 95, 96, 99,
  124, 125, 130, 137, 166
Goals
  adopting more modest, in new
  professionals, 37–39
  clear, and "flow," 207
  unrealistic, 37–39, 164–166
  see also Expectations
Goldenberg, I. I., 171
Goleman, D., 4
Gordon, S., 74
Gould, R. J., 88
Gow, K. M., 5
Gowler, D., 202
Graen, G. G., 209
Grant, D. L., 88
Gray, R. M., 6
Grossman, F. K., 199
Growth need strength
  see Intrinsic rewards
Guzzo, R. A., 202

Haan, N., 78–79, 88, 200
Haase, A. M., 5
Hackman, J. R., 207
Hall, D. T., 88, 201, 203, 205,
  210
Helping behavior
  research on, 69–70
Historical change
  impact on ambivalence towards
  helping needy, 32–34
  impact on attitudes towards
  work, 89, 90, 94
Holloway, S., 30, 32
Howe, M. J., 194
Huberman, A. M., 196
Hughes, E. C., 6, 69
Hunicutt, A. W., 171

Ickes, W. J., 200
Idealism
  as motive for entering profession, 4
  changes in, 39, 46, 61
  impact on professional effectiveness, 197
  in professionals, 13
In-service training
  see Professional development
Income
  see Money
Independence
  see Autonomy
Individual characteristics
  impact on recovery from burnout, 151–168
Individualism
  and professionals' conceptions of success, 61
  as source of frustration, 61
  belief in, and ambivalence towards helping needy, 32
Innovation, 78–79
  ways to promote, in the human services, 80
  see also Flexibility
Intellectual stimulation
  professional development as source of, 161–162
  see also Challenge
Intrinsic rewards
  growing importance of, 89–90, 202, 203, 205
Involvement in work
  see Commitment

Jackson, S. E., 199, 205, 208, 212
"Jean Chalmers," 19, 122–123, 124, 146, 148, 153
"Jennifer Talmadge," 86–87, 114–116, 124–125, 127, 130–131, 153, 155–156, 162, 163

"Jesse Michaels," 100, 101, 102, 136, 147–148
"Jessica Andrews," 60, 67–68, 86, 124–125, 130, 140–141
Job change
  and recovery from burnout, 121, 167–168
  as way of securing greater autonomy, 138–139
  contribution to increased career insight, 100
Job involvement
  see Commitment
Job satisfaction
  see Satisfaction with life and work
Josephson, M., 45
Jung, C., 94

Kane, J. S., 208
Kanter, R. M., 189, 202, 207, 211
"Karla Adams," 96, 136, 167
Kennedys, the, 45
Kerr, P., 94, 210
Khoury, D. C., 207
Khoury, R. M., 207
Kidd, R. F., 200
King, M. L., Jr., 45
Korman, A. K., 83
Kotter, J. P., 194
Kram, K. E., 202, 210, 211
Kramer, M., 18, 173
Krantz, D., 201
Kunstler, W., 44
Kushner, H., 94
Kyriacou, C., 200

Labor-management conflict
  impact on growth of bureaucracy, 31
  impact on stress and burnout, 137–138
LaMonica, E. L., 5

Lang, D., 83
Langer, E. J., 208
Law school clinics, 153
Lawler, E. E., 209
Lawyers
    effect of seniority on improved
    working conditions in, 98
    gender differences in, 204
    lack of caring and compassion
    in, 5
    see also Poverty lawyers
Layoffs
    impact on organizational
    climate and burnout, 137
Leader-member exchange theory,
    209
Leadership style of supervisor
    impact on recovery from
    burnout, 111
    see also Supervisor; Theory X
    and Theory Y management
    styles
Legal aid, 24, 25, 34
    lack of opportunity for big cases
    in, 122
    routine work in, 26
Legal aid lawyers
    see Poverty lawyers
Legge, K., 202
Leisure
    see Balance between work and
    nonwork parts of life
Leiter, M. P., 210
Levinson, D. J., 88, 194
Life satisfaction, 97–99
Lipp, M. R., 207, 208
Locus of control
    impact on willingness to help
    others, 200
Lombardo, M. M., 210–211
London, M., 205
Lorence, J., 207
Lortie, D. C., 194, 197

Lynn, K. S., 4

Maas, H. S., 70, 200, 206
Maccoby, M., 201, 202, 209
MacMillan, T. F., 171
Malcolm X, 45
Management style
    see Leadership style of super-
    visor
Mansfield, R., 90
"Margaret Williams," 24, 26, 34,
    42, 43, 47, 52, 85–86, 87–88, 96,
    122, 123–124, 153–154
"Mark Connor," 110–112, 127, 129,
    132, 133, 135, 138, 143, 152,
    154, 157–158, 159, 160, 165
Marks, S., 185
Marx, K., 184, 187
Maslach, C., 172, 199, 205, 207,
    210, 212
Maslach Burnout Inventory, 199,
    205, 212
Maslow, A., 206, 212
Materialism
    and ambivalence towards help-
    ing needy, 32–33
    in capitalist society, 187, 198
    increases in, during 1980s, 46
McCall, M. W., Jr., 210–211
McGregor, D., 209
"Me Decade," 45–47
Meaning in work and life, 181–189
    as central motive, 184
    college student attitudes
    towards, 89
    elusiveness of, 182
    lack of, as cause of burnout, 185,
    212
Meaningful work
    as antidote to burnout, 121,
    206–207
    as stimulus to professional
    growth, 125

characteristics of, 121–134, 207
pursuit of, 121
Mechanic, D. 198
Medical education, 6
training in empathy, 6
Medical residents
attitudes towards patients, 69
Mental health professionals, 18
and difficult clients, 70–71
and professional self-efficacy, 84,
86
and status, 84, 86–87
becoming less reliant on particular techniques, 79
career change in, 52, 57–58
inadequacies in training of, 71
importance of autonomy for, 208
lack of caring in, 5
psychotherapy as core function
for, 124–125, 207
Mentors
as antidote to burnout, 146, 161
colleagues as, 146, 147, 210
functions of, 210
willingness to seek out, determinants of, 211
Merser, C., 187, 188
"Merton Douglas," 25, 26, 53, 61,
103–104, 137–138
Methodology of research, 7–13,
191–196, 205–206
Miles, M. B., 195, 206
Millis, W. A., Jr., 5
Minority professionals, 147–148
Mizrahi, T., 69, 200
Money
as indicator of status, 87–88, 202
as reason for leaving public service, 52–53
as reason for not changing jobs
or careers, 60
attitudes towards, 42–43, 87–88

growing importance of, during
1980s, 202
Moody, P. M., 6
Moral commitment
effect of social change on decline
in, 189
loss of, as cause of burnout,
184–187
see also Commitment
Moral-religious paradigm vs. scien-
tific-technical paradigm, 188
Mørch, H., 211
Morrison, A. M., 210–211
Mortimer, J. T., 207
Moses, J. L., 90
Mother Teresa, 61
Motivation
decline in, in new professionals,
43–45
Motives for entering a helping
profession, 4
Motowidlo, S.J., 197
Moyers, B., 46

Needy
ambivalence towards helping
the, in American society,
32–34
Neugarten, B. L., 204
New Brunswick Home News, 202
"New narcissism," 45
New York City schools, 31
New York Times, 4
Newman, R. E., 6
Newton, P., 204
Nicholson, N., 82, 201
"Nick Fisher," 21, 22, 23, 30, 38,
79, 80, 84, 85, 91–92
Nietzsche, F., 181
Non-professional duties
as source of burnout, 124–125,
207

Nonwork involvements
see Balance between work and
nonwork parts of life
Nougaim, K. E., 88
Novak, M. A., 209
Nurse practitioner role
as career alternative for nurses,
54
Nurses
increasing specialization in,
54–55
interpersonal relations among,
and burnout, 210
lack of empathy in, 5
program to help prevent reality
shock in, 173
publishing as reward for, 61

O'Driscoll, M. P., 208, 210
Occupational change
see Career change
Oldham, G. F., 207
Openness to change, 77–82
impact of stress on, 82
ways to promote, 81
Organizational climate
encouragement of experimentation in, 116
impact of budget cuts on, 137
impact of labor-management
conflict on, 137–138
impact on recovery from
burnout, 108, 111
supportive, as antidote to
burnout, 146, 210
Organizational conflict
see Organizational politics
Organizational negotiation skill,
156–159, 211
impact on recovery from
burnout, 156
lack of, in professionals, 211

ways to increase, 174–176
Organizational politics, 174–176
as contributor to burnout,
136–137, 167
as source of resistance to
change, 136–137
impact of dwindling resources
on, 137
Organizational self-efficacy
impact on recovery from
burnout, 157
Outlook, changes in
see Attitudes, professional
Overload
see Stress; Time pressure; Work
load

Paperwork
as contributor to burnout, 167
as source of frustration, 115
Part-time work
as antidote to burnout, 163
Pelz, D. C., 82
Perfectionism
impact on recovery from
burnout, 164–166
"Perry Curtis," 24
Perun, P. J., 204
Physicians
attitude change in, 6–7
attitudes towards patients, 69
changes in values of, over time,
203
lack of caring and compassion
in, 4, 6–7
Pines, A., 184, 186, 207, 212
Pithouse, A., 210
Plateauing at midcareer, 94
Politics, organizational
see Organizational politics
Positive feedback
see Feedback

Poverty lawyers, 19, 26
  career change in, 52–54
  changes in attitudes, 42–45,
    85–86, 87
  importance of big cases for,
    122–123
Pre-professional work experiences
  impact on recovery from
    burnout, 152–154
Prestige
  see Status
Private practice as career alterna-
    tive, 53–54, 58
Professional development
  as antidote to burnout, 144–145,
    160–162
  need for more emphasis on, 173,
    209–210
  teaching organizational negotia-
    tion skill and, 175
  value of less formal experiences
    for, 174
Professional self-efficacy
  see Self-efficacy in professionals
Professional training
  effect of limited resources on, 33
  inadequacies of, 22, 71
  selection criteria for, 176
  see also Professional develop-
    ment
Professionals
  quality of work environment,
    compared to blue collar workers,
    208
  role in society, 3–4, 197
Professions
  emphasis on individualism and
    autonomy in, 188, 212
  ideological basis of the, 212
  public attitudes towards, 4–6
  reasons for choosing to enter
    the, 198

Prottas, J. M., 79
Psychiatrists
  see Mental health professionals
Psychotherapists
  see Mental health professionals
Public health nurses, 18, 23
  adoption of more modest goals
    by, 39–40
  and difficult patients, 72–73
  career change in, 52, 54–55,
    56–57, 59
  changes in attitudes, 39–40,
    64–65
  growing importance of status
    and recognition for, 86
  in public schools, 20–21, 29–30
  isolation in, 26–27

Raelin, J. A., 205, 208
Reagan, R., 45
Realistic expectations
  see Expectations
Reality shock, 18, 46, 85, 154
"Rebecca Simpson," 96, 102–103,
    140, 159, 161
Recognition
  from administrators, impact on
    burnout, 142, 209
  growing importance of, 86, 88
  impact on satisfaction, 142
Recovery from burnout
  see Burnout
Red tape
  see Bureaucracy
Reform
  professionals' attitudes towards,
    77
  usual way in which imple-
    mented, 81, 211
"Reginald Smith," 42
Relationship with boss
  see Supervisor

Reputation
    as measure of success in professions, 202
    concern about, in new professionals, 19
Research methods
    see Methodology of research
Resistance to change
    impact of stress on, 82
    in professionals, 77–82
    see also Flexibility
Resources, limited
    as cause of professionals' feelings of inadequacy, 33, 34
    inevitability of, when professionalization occurs, 199
    poor utilization of resources and, 198
Results
    see Feedback
Rewards
    see Extrinsic rewards; Intrinsic rewards; Money
Rhodes, S. R., 202, 204
Richelson, G., 185
Rigidity in professionals
    see Flexibility
Roberts, P., 204
Roberts, S., 203
Rodin, J., 208
Rogers, C., 212
Role
    change in, as antidote to burnout, 125–126
    change in, effect on career insight, 100
    conflicts over, in new professionals, 21
Rosario, M., 211
Rothman, D. J., 35
Routine
    see Boredom

Rubin, L. B., 204

Salary
    see Money
"Sarah Prentiss," 19, 20–21, 23, 27, 30–31, 34, 39–40, 64–65, 66, 72, 73, 136
Sarason, E., 198
Sarason, S. B., 4, 83, 85, 144, 171, 187, 194, 197, 198, 199, 208–209, 211
Sarata, B. P. V., 207
Satisfaction with life and work, 97–99
    changes in, 205
    relation to altruism, 207
Savicki, V., 197
Schein, E. H., 3, 77, 201, 205
Schneider, B., 210
School social workers, 21, 22
    adoption of more modest goals by, 38
    effect of bureaucratic ethos on, 30
Schools, 38
    and social control, 32
    as bureaucracies, 28
    see also Teachers
Schubert, T., 210
Schuler, R. S., 208
Schwab, R. L., 208
Schweitzer, A., 61
Scientific-technical paradigm
    effect on moral commitment, 188–189
    vs. moral-religious paradigm, 188
Self-confidence
    see Self-efficacy in professionals
Self-efficacy in professionals, 69–70
    and attitudes towards clients, 63–64
    and willingness to take risks, 79

contribution of colleagues to, 27
impact on attitudes towards
clients, 64–65, 69–70
impact on recovery from
burnout, 109
impact on satisfaction with
work, 101
importance of, 84
importance of autonomy and
support for, 150
increase in, over time, 98
see also Competence
Self-esteem
impact of competence on, 201
impact on helping behavior, 70
Seligman, M. E. P., 208
Sense of community in work setting
as antidote to burnout, 146
Shamir, B., 210
"Shana Phillips," 42–45, 47, 52–54,
96, 125, 164
Sheridan, E. P., 203
"Sherman Reynolds," 18, 101
Shinn, M., 211
Siegal, S. M., 72, 172
Social exchange
helping others as, 68
inequitable, in working with
difficult clients, 200
Social work, 71
Sommerkamp, P., 209
Sonnenfeld, J., 194
Special interests in the job, 126–133
as antidotes to burnout, 109,
111, 126
Special projects
see Special interests in the job
Specialization
increasing, in professionals, 54
effect on conflict in bureaucra-
cies, 31

Stand and Deliver, 18
Stark, E., 89, 202
Status
as reason for career change,
55–56
as tangible mark of success, 84
growing importance of, 54, 84,
85, 88
importance of, men vs. women,
96
lack of, in public service jobs, 61
money as measure of, 87, 202
Stelling, J. G., 201
Stimulation
see Challenge
Strauss, A., 6, 195, 206
Stress
minimizing, as reason for staying in public service, 60
impact on conformity and resistance to change, 82
in administrators, 141
in new roles, 82
sources of, in new professionals,
18–27
Strikes
see Labor-management conflict
Student teaching
inadequacy of, 33
Students
see Clients
Success
Western idea of, impact on professionals, 61
concern with, during 1980s, 74
status and prestige as measures
of, 84–85
see also Competence; Status
Supervisor
conflict with, 113–114
impact of stress on support
from, 141

impact on recovery from
burnout, 111, 140–144, 167, 209
lack of support from, 108, 113,
117
management style of, 209
Support
aspects of, 149
importance of, for recovery from
burnout, 108, 111, 115, 118–119,
150
importance of, for professionals,
210
need for, when put into new
role, 82, 118
see also Colleagues; Supervisor
Supportive work setting, 140–147
as antidote to burnout, 140, 146
role of supervisor, 140–144
Suran, B. G., 203

Tamir, L. M., 203, 205
Teachers, 25
adoption of more modest goals
by, 38–39
and bureaucratic constraints in
large district, 73
and difficult students, 19, 21,
40–41, 66, 69, 70–71, 72, 73
assignment of busy work by, 39
attitudes about making money,
88
autonomy of, 109, 139
career change in, 52, 55–56, 60
community-school relations,
impact on burnout, 108–109
effect of large class size on, 33
effect of seniority on working
conditions in, 98
lack of caring and compassion
in, 5
lack of preparation, 7
lack of resources for, 33

loss of idealism in, 7
professional self-efficacy of, 69,
84
public criticism of, 5
resistance to change, 80
routine and monotony in, 26
status of, 61
stress in, compared to other
groups, 107
uneven distribution of difficult
students among, 73
Theory X and Theory Y management styles, 209
Therapists
see Mental health professionals
Time perspective
unrealistic, as source of frustration, 61–62
Time pressure
effects of, on professionals,
208–209
Topp, G. C., 210
Training
see Professional training;
Professional development
Truax, C. B., 5
Turnbull, A. P., 5
Turnbull, H. R., 5

Unions
see Labor-management conflict

Van Maanen, J., 94
Veysey, L., 3
"Victoria Goble," 79, 84, 128, 129,
142, 144, 146, 156–157, 159
Visiting nurses, 54, 56
VISTA
as positive pre-professional
experience, 153

War on Poverty, 35, 77

Weber, M., 28
Welfare programs
    amount of money spent on, 4
    and social control, 32
    as bureaucracies, 28–29
Winder, A. E., 5
Wittig-Berman, U., 83
Women's Movement, 115
Work
    nature of, impact on recovery
    from burnout, 109, 111,
    113–114, 115–116, 118
Work and family
    see Balance between work and
    nonwork parts of life
Work as a central life interest
    see Balance between work and
    nonwork parts of life

Work involvement
    see Commitment
Work load
    impact of heavy, on family,
    108
    heavy, during first year of
    practice, 108, 110, 113
    role of autonomy in reducing,
    138–139
Work satisfaction
    see Satisfaction with life and
    work

Yost, E. B., 211

Zitnay, G., 199